MONTANA PORTRAIT

BY JOHN A. ALWIN

MONTANA GEOGRAPHIC SERIES

NUMBER 17

WITHDRAWN

MONTANA MAGAZINE
AMERICAN & WORLD GEOGRAPHIC PUBLISHING

This book is dedicated to
the memory of
MILTON "JIM" EDIE
Emeritus Professor of Geography
Montana State University

Library of Congress Cataloging-in-Publication Data

Alwin, John A.
    Montana portrait / by John A. Alwin.
        p. cm. -- (Montana geographic series ; no. 17)
    Includes index.
    ISBN 1-56037-008-4
    1. Montana--Geography. I. Title. II. Series.
F731.8.A49 1993
917.86--dc20   93-9396

Printed in Hong Kong.

MICHAEL JAVORKA

ABOUT THE AUTHOR

John Alwin received a B.S. in geology from Wayne State University in 1968, a geology M.S. from Washington State University in 1970 and a geography M.A. from the University of Montana in 1978. Dr. Alwin received his geography Ph.D. in 1978 from the University of Manitoba in Winnipeg.

Alwin joined the geography faculty at Montana State University in 1977. While at M.S.U. he authored Volumes 2 and 5 in the Montana Geographic Series, geographies of eastern and western Montana that this volume replaces. In 1985 he left to work full time at the geographic publishing company he started with his wife, Ann. His *Between the Mountains: A Portrait of Eastern Washington*, published by their company, won the coveted annual J.B. Jackson Prize from the Association of American Geographers as the nation's best human geography for the general public. Alwin returned to higher education in the 1988-89 academic year as visiting Associate Professor of Geography at Dartmouth College. In 1989 he moved back to his beloved greater Northwest, where he now is Associate Professor of Geography at Lewis-Clark State College in Lewiston, Idaho. He resides with his wife and two children, Ali and Robby, in Moscow, Idaho—fully embraced in an empowering place where the Northern Rockies' verdant west side meets the rolling hills of the Palouse.

CONTENTS

MICHAEL CRUMMETT

GARRY WUNDERWALD

Left: *The annual Race to the Sky sled-dog competition takes mushers along the Continental Divide from Helena to Holland Lake and back.*
Facing page: *Traditional wind-power in the Flathead Valley.*

Title page: *The Bears Paw Mountains rise from the plains of north central Montana.* JOHN REDDY

Front cover: *The Yellowstone River.*
LARRY MAYER/BILLINGS GAZETTE
Back cover, left: *Missoula seen from the Rattlesnake.* GARRY L. WUNDERWALD
Right: *Spring lambs.* MICHAEL CRUMMETT

3

PREFACE

The introduction of this native Detroiter to Montana dates back to 1969. That summer, while a graduate student at Washington State University, I attended a six-week geology field camp in the Tobacco Root Mountains. Within days I had fallen hopelessly in love with Montana. Twice since then I have been drawn back to the Big Sky—first as a geography graduate student at the University of Montana and, after a wistful residence on the eastern Canadian prairie, as a faculty member at Montana State University. During my eight-year tenure at Bozeman, learning about Montana and sharing my findings with others were both my vocation and avocation. Absent from the state since 1988, my bonds are as strong as ever, but my perspective has broadened and I now am able to view Montana in a larger context from the vantage point of my Palouse home in Moscow, Idaho.

These are times of dramatic change in Montana, change that potentially could result in a very different state. This book is for those who share a love of this place, a kinship with its landscapes, a fascination with its past and present, and a concern for its future.

JOHN REDDY

MICHAEL JAVORKA

Above: *Below the Mission Mountains, Jesuits located St. Ignatius Mission in 1854 among the Flathead people.*
Left: *A pensive young dancer at the annual North American Indian Days powwow on the Blackfeet Reservation, Browning.*

The Bull River Valley in the Cabinet Mountains.

SENSE OF PLACE

Topophilia, or love of place, is pandemic in Montana and evidently is highly contagious. For non-natives the strong attachment and deep devotion symptomatic of a full blown case of topophilia can best be described as the Paradise Syndrome. Residents sympathize with tourists who are bewitched by the Montana magic, so completely captivated by the place that they exhibit all the signs and symptoms of love sickness. In milder cases the symptoms may subside when the afflicted return to their home states, but for others this is only the beginning.

In advanced cases Paradise Syndrome almost always manifests itself in a determination to move to Montana. The urge is strong, seemingly instinctual, to leave the crime, pollution, congestion, two-hour daily commutes and other maladies of the city, and settle in the Big Sky Country—preferably in a mountain-rimmed western Montana valley where life, when viewed through the windshield of a Winnebago, seems to parallel the script of a Disney movie.

Each summer local chamber of commerce offices in Montana are flooded by requests for information about jobs and business prospects from hopeful tourists. And a surprising number of out-of-state subscriptions to such newspapers as the *Missoulian, Bozeman Daily Chronicle* and Helena's *Independent Record* bring eagerly awaited "Help Wanted" classifieds to an army of hope-to-be Montanans. A fortunate few refugees from smoggy, crime-plagued southern California, and crowded Denver, and other urban escapees are able to pick up and start again in Montana—even if that means a new arrival with a graduate degree has to begin his or her Montana career as a checkout clerk at a local Kmart.

However, the prospect of uprooting families, the limited employment opportunities and other harsh economic realities shatter the hopes of most who yearn to make Montana a permanent home. For these would-be residents, Montana cabins and condos, annual hunting trips and family vacations are enough to keep them in touch with this special place.

In a "passages"-like ascent, new arrivals with Paradise Syndrome are likely to join a majority of locals with more mature cases of topophilia. How else can one explain faculty members at the University of Montana tolerating the lowest average salaries among all state universities in the nation or underemployed professionals who forgo certain career advancement so they can continue to call the Flathead Valley or Bridger Canyon home?

Montana's population may have been on the decline in the 1980s, but that was the decade the nation discovered Rocky Mountain Montana in a big way. It almost seems as if western Montana is on line to be the next Colorado, and Bozeman (evolving symbolic capital of this magical kingdom) the next Boulder.

John Denver now has given the nation a "Montana Christmas" television special, Ted Turner and Jane Fonda are at home on their Ponderosa-sized, 130,000-acre Flying D Ranch on the north flank of the Madison Range (replete with buffalo), and megabucks national celebs from Tom Brokaw to Jeff Bridges to Jim Nabors have claimed their pieces of western Montana. It is almost as if Montana has entered a monarchical phase, with media stars the new royal families.

Gentrification, spawned by an influx of millionaires and other of the well-to-do with their sprawling hobby ranches and $200,000-plus homes (the number in this value category increased from 312 in 1980 to 1,294 in 1990), is in stark contrast to average residents and their traditional Montana lifestyles. In 1990 Montanans' personal income ranked them 39th in the nation, median home value was $56,600 and trailers were home to many thousands of resident families.

What is it about Montana that so firmly affixes natives to this place and tugs at out-of-staters with such forcefulness? Clearly, of late, it has not been high paying jobs or a robust economy. Topophilia and a powerful sense of place may provide an explanation for what has been called the Montana mystique. Three overriding aspects of Montana combine to help explain the multitude of Big Sky topophiliacs: the magnitude and

prevalence of nature, a mythic Old West aura with all its permutations, and the synergism of these two factors.

Montana as nature

This isn't "America's Dairyland," the "Land of Lincoln" or the "Famous Potato" state. As Montana license plates proudly proclaim, this is the Big Sky. Thank you, A. B. Guthrie, Jr.! The Big Sky with its eye-stretching nature below is firmly etched in the Montana mindset. Nature, in all its scenic beauty and dramatic proportions, is the Montana keystone.

In Montana, "oohs" and "ahs" generally are reserved for expressions of nature—for downy cumulus clouds against a Big Sky blue canvas, the play of colors and tonality and textures of a badlands vista, the stillness and serenity of a freshly snow-flocked mountainside forest, or a fleeting glimpse of a massive seven-point bull elk. Such architectural achievements as skyscrapers (of the 20-story Montana variety) and large hydro dams, bridges and sports arenas do not go unnoticed, but sensory highs here tend to be of the natural variety.

Montanans and mountains

As its Spanish-sounding name suggests, Montana has something to do with mountains. For some this clearly is the overriding aspect of the state, even though Rocky Mountain Montana accounts only for the state's western third. Montana's geologically young mountains look just right, the way mountains are supposed to look— grand, spectacular, overpowering and majestic. They are the "high" and the "handsome" in the title to Joseph Kinsey Howard's classic *Montana: High, Wide and Handsome*. So overwhelming and pervasive is their natural splendor that it actually is difficult to take a bad mountain landscape picture. The scenic substance is unrivaled, and the thin and dry air of this elevated country somehow sharpens pictures and intensifies natural colors. Are there any western Montana residents or tourists who haven't taken at least a few Kodachromes they feel merit publication in *National Geographic*?

Mountains not only dominate the physical scene for a majority of Montanans, they set a Montana mood and are just as central to the psyche of residents. The names of the Bridger, Whitefish, Cabinet, Pioneer and Tobacco Root ranges are second nature to residents of the region. They would no more call one of them the Rocky Mountains than a resident of Chicago would call Lake Michigan the Great Lakes. Prominent landscape features breed familiarity and help instill a sense of place. Understandably, Montanans are a mountain-conscious and mountain-addicted group.

Rocky Mountain Montana residents who dare move out of the region to less topographically endowed environments, places where mere nubbins on the face of the earth are revered as monuments, find they suffer from what might be described facetiously as a variety of agoraphobia, the abnormal fear of open spaces. The degree of stress varies with individuals, but the symptoms are much the same. These include a critical rejection of the offending flat landscape and erratic, sometimes frantic, searches to ferret out something, anything, that even suggests topographic relief.

The Beartooths, Crazies, Madison and Gallatin ranges, Bitterroots and Missions exert a strong pull, and invariably former western Montana residents suffering terminal agoraphobia arrange for trips back home as often as possible. Barring that privilege of pilgrimage, sufferers may find themselves plastering their family room wall with a full-color, eight-foot-tall mountain scene with the same obsessive compulsive behavior that drove Richard Dreyfuss's character to build a living room-sized Devil's Tower in the film, *Close Encounters of the Third Kind*.

Within western Montana, mountains and their divides provide the spatial framework for regional identities. The Montana Rockies are not a single mountain chain, but rather a surprisingly diverse region made up of more than two dozen distinct ranges separated by valleys of varying width. In the southwest, ranges rise as detached, forested islands between intermontane valleys up to 50 miles across. Farther to the northwest, closely spaced and seemingly overlapping ranges leave little room for constricted valleys.

Professor John Crowley, a mountain geographer at the University of Montana, recognizes three distinct environmental regions within Rocky Mountain Montana, which he has named the Columbia Rockies, Broad Valley Rockies and Yellowstone Rockies.

Columbia Rockies. The Columbia Rockies region is classic mountain landscape. A humid climate, luxuriant and varied natural vegetation, and narrow, forested valleys are characteristic. Mountains here show considerable variation—from the more subdued and verdant Appalachian-like Salish Mountains, to the towering, wind-swept and bare peaks of the Lewis Range. Overall, the feel within much of the region is distinctly Pacific Northwest, and it is easy to see why some geographers consider this highland realm to be part of the greater Northwest.

The eastern prong of the Columbia Rockies claims some of the most scenic mountain terrain in Montana and the West. Most Montanans would agree that Glacier National Park, the 1,600-square-mile extravaganza of mountains, is Montana at its scenic best. Park brochures and pamphlets refer to it in such phrases as the "Crown of the Continent" and "A Place Touched by Magic." Its array of lofty 8,000- to 10,000-foot, glacially sculpted peaks, 50 active glaciers, 200 alpine lakes and more than 700 miles of trails beckons more than 2 million visitors annually.

Broad Valley Rockies. The adjacent Broad Valley Rockies environmental region claims the majority of Rocky Mountain Montana and spills over into a small adjacent section of Idaho centered in the Lemhi and Lost River ranges country. Its basic topographic unity is open mountains, a distinctive and rare setting with high, detached mountain ranges separated by broad, smooth-floored valleys. Here the dry intermontane valleys may cover up to 50 percent of an area, whereas in the Columbia Rockies region they generally account for less than 20 percent.

Broad Valley ranges dramatically present themselves from flattish intermontane valleys. Higher snow-capped mountain peaks rise to 9,000 feet and more, comparable to those in the most lofty sections of the Columbia Rockies. At 11,230 feet, Crazy Peak in the Crazy Mountains is the highest in this Broad Valley region, topping Glacier's tallest by almost 800 feet. As in Glacier National Park, ice-scalloped, bare-rock crests of the higher ranges attest to the same alpine glaciation that sculpted the park's more famous peaks.

Spacious valleys within the Broad Valleys region carry the names of the major rivers that drain them—the Bitterroot, Big Hole, Madison, Gallatin and Smith. Even in their lowest sections these broad valleys generally vary between 4,000 and 7,000 feet above sea level, with large sections of only the Bitterroot and Flathead valleys dropping below 3,500 feet. Such skyward settings afford residents a chance to use the high altitude baking directions printed on the sides of cake-mix boxes. They also provide Bozeman's Montana State University, at an elevation of almost 5,000 feet, an ideal location for its innovative program for high-elevation studies.

Human habitation and economic activity clearly are concentrated in the valley areas where population densities are among the state's highest. The Broad Valley environmental region provides generous living space and one result is that Montana is the only Rocky Mountain state with the majority of its residents living within, not just next to or near, the Rockies. It also is the site of the capital city, the state's two major universities and many of its largest cities.

In contrast, fewer than 30 percent of neighboring Idaho's population is scattered through the Rocky Mountain two thirds of that state, and in Colorado fewer than 15 percent call the mountainous western 60 percent of their state home. For most residents of the other Rocky Mountain states, the Rockies are a sparsely populated neighboring area, an impractical permanent home, a place where they retreat only for recreation.

Human habitation and economic activity clearly are concentrated in the valley areas where population densities are among the state's highest.

For more than half of Montana's residents the mountains are home, a place where you cover your tomatoes in July and have not yet put away your snow shovel when your downlander neighbors already are tuning up their lawn mowers.

Distinct regional identities have evolved in the mountain-rimmed broad valleys. People here view themselves as residents of the Bitterroot, Big Hole, Madison or Flathead. The barriers imposed by ranges are striking on a state highway map, which graphically illustrates how main highways avoid cresting mountains wherever possible. Travel tends to be circuitous, paralleling rivers and following nature's paths of least resistance. But in such a mountain-studded area, crossing mountains is inevitable, and mountain passes are a grudgingly accepted fact of life. Each winter residents locate their pass-conditions phone number and renew their respect for Homestake Pass (elev. 6,375), MacDonald Pass (elev. 6,325), and Kings Hill Pass (elev. 7,393). Even innocuous sounding

M.S.U.'s Yellowstone Center for Mountain Environments

DIANE ENSIGN

Montana State University began life in 1893 as the state's agricultural college.

Globally, mountains cover about 20 percent of the earth's surface and are home to at least 500 million people. But according to one mountain geographer, these elevated tracts are critical to the life-support systems of at least half the world's population—some 2.5 billion of us. Especially critical is the role mountains play in triggering precipitation and serving as fresh water reservoirs for residents of downstream lowland areas. Downlanders from the hundreds of millions who depend on irrigated agriculture in India's Ganges River Valley, to Missoulians drawing their tap water from the mountain-fed Rattlesnake Creek, are tied to mountainous headwaters for aspects of day-to-day life.

Population pressures in the world's developing nations are forcing people to move into previously lightly populated mountain areas in search of living space. And closer to home in Montana and the western U.S., mountain addicts as well as timber and mineral interests continue to place increasing demands on highlands. Unfortunately, steep slopes, cool to cold climates and lack of biodiversity in some sections may mean that deforestation, overgrazing, soil erosion, mining activities and ill-conceived and haphazard residential and recreational developments can have amplified consequences in mountainous areas. And the negative environmental impacts can have dire results well beyond the mountainous headwaters.

As the state's land-grant institution, Montana State University has a long history of dealing with real-world problems, especially those relating to relationships between people and the natural environment. Couple that tradition with an active and diverse research faculty and a mountainous setting and it is difficult to imagine a more ideal home base for a program for high-elevation studies.

According to geographer and program director Dr. Katherine Hansen, a primary goal of the M.S.U. program is to sensitize graduate students to this often fragile mountain world and to show them the importance of a comprehensive approach to problem solving and land use management. Through cross-disciplinary courses, fieldwork and workshops, program participants learn to view mountain environments in their interconnected physical, biological, political, cultural and economic contexts. It is expected that master's students and doctoral candidates graduate with an understanding of integrated approaches to conservation and sustainable development in the mountainous world.

"passettes" the likes of Evaro Hill and Norris Hill, not identified on highway maps, garner deference.

Yellowstone Rockies. East of Ennis and south of Bozeman and Big Timber the broad valley landscape abruptly yields to the rugged northernmost extension of an expansive highland centered on Yellowstone National Park. This is Montana's Yellowstone Rockies environmental region. It includes all the Madison Range, most of the Gallatins and Beartooth Plateau, and the northern Absaroka Range. Combined, these uplands are the most mountain-dominated of the state's three Rockies environmental regions. This is rugged highland country where valleys generally are confined and steep-sided. The only major exception to narrow valley floors is the Yellowstone River's Paradise Valley south of Livingston, which is reminiscent of the wide valleys to the north and west. No section of Montana has more extensive areas above 9,000 feet, and the Beartooth Plateau is the only Montana upland where peaks exceed 12,000 feet. More than two dozen rise above the rugged 10,000-foot plateau to elevations in excess of 12,000 feet, including Granite Peak, the state's highest at 12,799.

Mere association with mountains is viewed positively in Montana. Here chambers of commerce in cities outside the Rockies, like Billings, may employ considerable cartographic license with brochure maps that "move in" mountains to the point that it appears you can reach out and touch them from downtown. In the case of Billings, the Yellowstone Rockies are 60 miles away.

Springtime blossoms on Hogback Mountain in the Big Belt Mountains near Helena.

JOHN REDDY

Grizzly & Wolf: Montana Wildlife Celebs

CONRAD ROWE

Grizzly bears *(Ursus arctos horribilis)* are high-profile residents in Montana. Almost any news about them provides the makings for front page stories in the state's newspapers and, as with perceptions of many celebrities, these tend to be love/hate affairs.

Wildlife biologists like to refer to the grizzly as an indicator species for high-quality wildlands, meaning the animal's presence in an area is testimony to the existence of truly wild habitat. *Ursus arctos*

and humans generally do not mix well, and historically it has been the bear that had to retreat when people moved into grizzly country. Today in the lower 48 states the Great Bear is relegated to just one percent of its former range and may number only about 1,000, down from an estimated 100,000 in the mid-1800s. The overwhelming majority of this remnant population is found within Montana. Without exception these last-stand refuge areas are centered in relatively remote, mountainous terrain.

A few grizzlies roam the Washington Cascades and may live in the central Idaho mountains, and perhaps 15 individuals cling precariously to existence (illegal hunting has decimated their numbers) in the Selkirk Mountains of north Idaho and northeastern Washington. All other grizzly areas have a Montana link.

The expansive and wild North Continental Divide country, extending from Glacier National Park south through the Bob Marshall complex of wilderness areas, may be home to 500 to 800 grizzlies. Outside of Alaska, this is the nation's most secure grizzly population. In recent years wildlife managers have been delighted to see grizzlies once again move out of these mountains and onto their traditional home in the adjacent plains. According to Montana grizzly expert Charles Jonkel, the bears' forays already take them up to 40 miles out into the Montana prairie, as far east as Fairfield. Since a single male grizzly may utilize 200 to 300 square miles in a season in search of food and shelter, even the vast Continental Divide country has habitat for a finite number of bears. Jonkel thinks the plains grizzlies are surplus animals in search of territory. It would not surprise him if these

prairie denizens eventually repopulate the rugged and not-too-distant Missouri Breaks.

Farther to the south, an additional 200 grizzlies may range the wildlands of the Yellowstone Ecosystem, a 28,000-square-mile wildland system centered on Yellowstone National Park and extending into national forests in three states. Park grizzly management policies, millions of tourist visits annually, oil and gas exploration and developments, hardrock mining activities, recreational complexes, livestock grazing and seasonal homes have combined to make grizzlies an especially sensitive and controversial topic in this region.

Although the U.S. Fish and Wildlife Service would like to see 70 to 90 grizzlies in northwest Montana's Cabinet-Yaak Ecosystem, this fragmented wildlands region may be home to fewer than 15 of these bears. Some wildlife specialists think the number of bears has reached a critically low level and may no longer constitute a biologically viable population. Local opposition has repeatedly stymied bear augmentation plans. As well as expressing concern for their own backcountry safety, many Lincoln and Sanders county residents are reluctant to willingly accept more grizzlies for economic reasons. With the bear a protected species, they worry that mining activities and logging, cornerstones of the regional economy, would have to take a back seat to higher priority, protective grizzly management over even more of their corner of Montana.

While grizzly numbers declined in Montana with the advance of the white settlement frontier, the Great Bear never was eliminated in the state. Gray wolves didn't fare as well. Up until about 1910, wolves still were common in Montana despite a government eradication program begun in the 1890s, and the popular perception that the only good wolf is a dead wolf. Varmint status, loss of habitat, and pressure from ranchers and big-game hunters not wanting to share their livestock or trophy elk, helped guarantee the wolf's extermination in Montana. In 1964, some residents rejoiced, others mourned, when what many thought must be the last Montana wolf was killed near Lincoln.

Much to the disgust of anti-wolf forces, the U.S. Fish and Wildlife Service listed the gray wolf as endangered in all the lower 48 states except Minnesota in 1973. Overnight the wolf and its place in Montana became the topic of discussion at wool-growers' meetings, sporting-goods stores and cafes throughout the state. Federal listing required that plans be drawn to bring the wolf back to the Northern Rockies.

Evidently wolves couldn't wait for a formal return invitation. While politicians bickered over possible recovery plans, Canadian wolves began crossing the border and frequenting sections of Glacier National Park and the adjacent North Fork drainage. In 1986 a breeding population and the makings of a Montana wolf pack were verified with the discovery of a den in Glacier. Since then the number and distribution of resident Montana wolves have expanded.

A number of factors have combined to make this natural restocking of the species in the Northern Rockies possible. An about-face in wolf management in both Alberta and British Columbia has led to increased numbers of wolves in the southern section of both Canadian provinces. This provided a spillover population that quickly moved south into Montana. Wolves have an uncanny ability to disperse over long distances and quickly recolonize former range. A 100- to 200-mile foray by a wolf across highways and even Interstates in search of a new home is not uncommon, and there even is a report of a collared wolf migrating from northern Wisconsin to Alberta and the Canadian Rockies!

Suitable habitat stocked with near-record numbers of ungulates, the species' primary quarry, and protected status have allowed Montana wolf recovery to continue into the 1990s. Today, according to University of Montana wildlife biologist and wolf specialist Dr. Robert Ream, the state may have 30 to 40 wolves. Helena-based U.S. Fish and Wildlife Service biologists' estimates go as high as 60.

The guiding 1987 Wolf Recovery Plan for the Northern Rockies calls for 10 breeding pairs (packs of about100 wolves) in each of three suitable recovery areas before the wolf can be considered for delisting as an endangered species in the region. The three recovery areas are 1) Northwest Montana, 2) Central Idaho/adjacent Montana Bitterroot Range, and 3) the Greater Yellowstone Ecosystem. In the early 1990s wolf packs were confirmed in the first recovery area and individuals have been documented in the Central Idaho section, but the presence of wolves in the Yellowstone region is doubtful. According to Dr. Ream, there is evidence that a pack had moved into the Pioneer Mountains west of Dillon by the winter of 1991-1992, and it is possible that wolves could continue their southerly and easterly migration and naturally repopulate the Greater Yellowstone. At this time political wrangling against human-directed reintroduction of wolves in Yellowstone National Park would perhaps be more shrill and achieve higher decibel levels only if discussion centered around the release of werewolves out behind Old Faithful Inn.

ALAN & SANDY CAREY

Not surprisingly the overwhelming majority of Yellowstone visitors would like to see the wolf, this missing link in the park's ecosystem, returned. Recent surveys of Montanans show the same predilection toward the state's wolf population. Education programs that include bringing young wolves to area grade schools evidently are having an impact on public perceptions. After generations of myths and misconceptions, Montanans appear eager to restore this preeminent predator to at least some of its former haunts.

Above: *The Absaroka Mountains soar to 11,000 feet above the Yellowstone River.*
Right: *Bull elk.*

Montanans and wildlands

Mountains alone do not explain Montanans' strong sense of place linkage—even metro Los Angeles has 10,000-foot peaks rising above its skyline. It is unlikely, however, that many Montanans hiking in the Angeles National Forest north of L.A. would feel comfortable with its polluted air and water, dearth of wildlife and abundance of litter, crowds, trampled landscapes and worn trails. For Montanans nature means wildness and residents have a special interest and pride in the natural state of much of their outdoors. Stories about grizzly bears and updates on the whereabouts of radio collared wolves merit front page coverage in area newspapers.

Clearly there is a connection between Montana's mountainous areas and wildlands. Since the onslaught of European-Americans, Montana's open plains and western valleys have lured settlers while the mountains have resisted large-scale settlement. In the highlands, transportation was difficult and expensive and the land was too steep, infertile and cold for productive agriculture. Commercial mineral deposits in the Rockies tend to be concentrated in small and scattered locales and, although timber was present, harvesting the more accessible stands on lowest slopes first made better economic sense.

The 1860s gold rushes that ushered in large-scale white settlement in Montana came relatively late in American history. That historical fact and the power of mountains to repel or, at least, discourage wholesale human occupancy meant that large tracts of inaccessible terrain were left in an essentially natural state. As our nation slowly awoke to the value of the non-con-quest of nature and began to appreciate the importance of conservation and stewardship of the land, large sections of Rocky Mountain Montana fortunately remained as remnants from a pre-frontier West. The

BILL CUNNINGHAM

mountainous western third of the state survived as one of the few large areas in the lower 48 states where the total acreage of natural landscapes exceeded that of humanized landscapes.

Wilderness as touchstone. By mid-20th century a cadre of forward-looking Montanans began efforts to ensure that wildlands would remain a part of the Montana scene. That group emerged in 1958 as the pioneering Montana Wilderness Association (MWA). They acquired a critical preservation tool with passage of the landmark 1964 Wilderness Act, which provided a mechanism for extending protection to federal wildlands. With 37 percent of the state's area controlled by the federal government, most in Rocky Mountain national forests, millions of wildlands acres seemed ideally suited for inclusion in the nation's nascent wilderness system. The drive shifted into

In the Bob Marshall Wilderness Area, Flathead National Forest.

WILDERNESS AREAS

JOHN REDDY

Beargrass blooms in the mountains of Glacier National Park.

If you've walked the streets of midtown Manhattan or strolled along Chicago's State Street with their noise, congestion, foul air and almost totally people-built landscapes, then you've experienced one extreme in this country's environmental continuum. Wilderness areas are at the opposite end of this spectrum.

Wilderness is difficult to define with precision. An area dominated by wild nature might suffice for some, but for others this isn't even a beginning. Henry David Thoreau, John Muir and Aldo Leopold may have awakened Americans to the value of wilderness, but it was the 1967 publication of Roderick Nash's *Wilderness and the American Mind,* now in its third edition, that legitimized and launched modern wilderness studies. Today college and university courses on wilderness are common. The topic is approached from perspectives as diverse as history, philosophy, literature, psychology, sociology, geography and leisure studies, and published material is so abundant that it is difficult for researchers to keep up-to-date even in a single discipline.

The most easily defined wilderness is that established by law, which is the topic herein. As early as the 1920s, the U. S. Forest Service began managing sections of forest land as "primitive" and in the next decade adopted both "wilderness" and "wild" designations for some areas. These were strictly administratively based. It was not until 1964 that Congress passed the globally precedent-setting Wilderness Act (Public Law 88-577). The Act established a National Wilderness Preservation System, defined wilderness for the purposes of this Act, outlined the procedure for wilderness designation of appropriate federally-owned lands and stipulated acceptable uses.

The rationale for the Act is clearly stated in the enabling legislation. "In order to assure that an increasing population, accompanied by expanding settlement and growing mechanization, does not occupy and modify all areas within the United States and its possessions, leaving no lands designated for preservation and protection in their natural condition, it is hereby declared to be the policy of the Congress to secure for the American people of present and future generations the benefits of an enduring resource of wilderness." To be considered suitable for possible designation as a wilderness area and for addition to the National Wilderness Preservation System, an area of undeveloped federal land had to meet specific requirements. Of prime importance was the existence of a primeval character, a place where the imprints of humans' activities are substantially unnoticeable, without permanent improvements or human habitation and where forces of wild nature prevail. Additionally, the area should have outstanding opportunities for solitude or primitive and unconfined recreation and be at least 5,000 acres in area or of sufficient size to assure wilderness integrity. Unreasonably strict interpretation of standards by the Forest Service and Bureau of Land Management led to the 1974 passage of the Eastern Wilderness Act (P. L. 93-622) and the Endangered American Wilderness Act (P. L. 95-220), which provided clarification of qualifying criteria.

Since the primary purpose of designated areas is the preservation of wilderness character, most inconsistent uses are forbidden. The Act prohibits "temporary roads, motor vehicle use, motorized equipment or motor boats, landing of aircraft, mechanical transport and structures and installations." Hunting, fishing and other types of nonmotorized recreation are permitted, as are certain nonconforming, preexisting uses including aircraft and grazing of livestock.

Within wilderness the president may authorize a wide range of developments including construction of reservoirs, power projects and transmission lines "upon his determination that such use or uses in the specific area will better serve the interests of the United States and the people…" To the consternation of many wilderness advocates, the Act also allowed for staking mining claims within national forest wilderness areas through January 1, 1984, and the mining of hard-rock minerals from valid claims existing prior to the same deadline date.

Many state residents have first-hand experience with the wilderness designation process, which requires public hearings in the area of the proposed wilderness. Residents can hardly call themselves Montanans unless they have chosen sides on at least one wilderness bill and presented an oral statement or, at the least, submitted a written opinion for the record. Participation in the predictably heated "dialogue" at a wilderness hearing in Kalispell, Bozeman or Helena is almost a rite of passage for Montanans.

high gear as the MWA was joined by a sometimes vociferous array of state and national organizations devoted to the preservation and protection of federal lands.

The pitched battle for wilderness designation and protection continues, with proponents pitted against those arguing for motorized recreation, timber, mining and energy development. While opponents resist "locking up" areas with official wilderness designation, advocates talk about ecosystems and bioregions, environmental quality, endangered and indicator species, biodiversity, ancient forests and the spiritual value of solitude. Wildlands supporters, who increasingly view Montana wilderness in its national and even international context, see wilderness as a necessary touchstone with our shared past. In a crowded and more humanized world, they consider wilderness a tangible link with that past and a benchmark against which to gauge future environmental change.

By the early 1990s predictably hardfought battles had resulted in 16 designated Montana wilderness areas, all but two in the state's mountainous western third. In all, just under 3.5 million acres have official wilderness status, ranking Montana third in the lower 48 states, behind California and Idaho.

The Bob Marshall, Cabinet, Absaroka-Beartooth, Scapegoat and other U.S. Forest Service administered wildernesses are clearly highlighted on the official state highway map and in mental maps of many Montanans. Less well known are the three U.S. Fish and Wildlife administered wilderness areas within the UL Bend, Medicine Lake and Red Rock Lakes national wildlife refuges.

Hitching up the horse trailer, packing up the gear and heading off for a ten-day elk hunt in the celebrated Bob Marshall Wilderness is a hunter's nirvana. At 1,009,356 acres, the "Bob" is the nation's second-largest and most famous wilderness area. A quick check of the ads on the back pages of such hunter's magazines as *Outdoor Life* and *Field and Stream* provides ample evidence of this area's international reputation as a big-game hunters' utopia. The Bob Marshall and its two adjacent wildernesses (the Great Bear and Scapegoat) form a 100-mile-long, contiguous wilderness of more than 1.5 million acres straddling the Continental Divide—2,400 square miles unviolated by a single mile of road.

Even for many state residents who never have set foot in this wilderness complex or any of Montana's other designated wildernesses, the mere fact that these areas are there is a source of considerable solace. For others regular visits to wilderness are a sacred pilgrimage, necessary for spiritual well-being—a kind of modern-day vision quest. Clearly, wilderness now is an essential element in a Montana cosmology.

Mega-view era. In this mega-view era of satellite-based ecosystem mapping, protection efforts for the roadless, wild Northern Rockies have entered a new era. Official designation of specific wilderness areas still is a goal for many in the environmental community, but now there is a growing awareness of the need for a less piecemeal, bioregion approach to protection. To date, Missoula-based Alliance for the Wild Rockies' proposed Northern Rockies Ecosystem Protection Act is the most ambitious of this new think-big generation of wildland planning.

They see the world-class wildlands of northwestern Wyoming, western Montana, central and northern Idaho and the adjacent corners of Oregon and Washington as one large and interconnected bioregion with five major ecosystems. Although scattered within five states and administratively divided among 26 national forests, more than two dozen wilderness areas, three national parks, plus everything from national wildlife refuges and national recreation areas to Bureau of Land Management holdings, these nationally high-interest public lands are nonetheless a biologically unified region.

Hitching up the horse trailer, packing up the gear and heading off for a ten-day elk hunt in the celebrated Bob Marshall Wilderness is a hunter's nirvana.

Through Congressional passage of their Northern Rockies Ecosystem Protection Act, the Alliance hopes to extend wilderness status to an additional 13.5 million roadless acres in the five-state area. If enacted, the legislation also would designate 1.7 million acres for national park and preserve study areas and 500,000 acres for wildland restoration, and add hundreds of miles to the nation's Wild and Scenic Rivers system. A key feature would include critical connecting corridors linking the major ecosystems. Far from an economic death knell to the state's wood/forest products industry, the Act, even if passed in its proposed form, still would leave the vast majority of Montana's almost 17 million acres of national forest open to logging.

Montanans' interest in wilderness is part of a larger concern for environmental integrity. The quality-of-life revolution that swept this country in the 1960s has perma-

"The Helmet" in the Beaverhead National Forest section of the Lee Metcalf Wilderness, which was named for Montana's pioneering environmentalist U.S. senator.

nently changed the state. Pulled to western Montana by the promise of a life in an "ecotopian" environment and pushed out by seemingly insurmountable environmental, economic and social problems back home, countless refugees have made western Montana home in the last quarter century. Many arrived prepared to make their own environmental "last stand" here in Montana—determined not to let happen here what happened back home. Once newcomers got beyond their initial impulse to build a wall around the state, they linked up with locals who shared their concern for more realistic efforts at preserving and protecting the natural environment. Western Montana quickly evolved into the undisputed center of the state's influential environmentalist community.

Outdoor recreation 52 weeks a year

Montanans are an outdoor recreation-oriented people. It's not that they don't enjoy bowling, billiards or bridge, but they would have to be incarcerated not to partake of the state's varied and quality outdoor recreational opportunities. Skiing some of the best powder in the West only a half-hour from home; trying that new fly in a crystal clear, Blue Ribbon trout stream; a leisurely Sunday-afternoon drive through the vivid fall colors of Glacier; calling up rancher friends in Garfield County to see if they will put you and your hunting buddy up the opening weekend of turkey season; a cross-country skiing holiday at the Izaak Walton Inn; heading into the Bob with a string of horses; or just launching your 17-footer into Bighorn Lake—how much more could outdoor-oriented Montanans want?

Cross-country skiing is one way to enjoy the Glacier National Park area in winter.

GARRY WUNDERWALD

Above: Man and beast working the 1100-foot level of the Rarus Mine in Butte. N.A. Forsyth photo
Above right: John and Henry Haaven, blacksmiths on the homestead frontier. Henry Syverud photo
Right: The 1914 harvest for this homestead was a good one—even including watermelon. Alta Deem photo

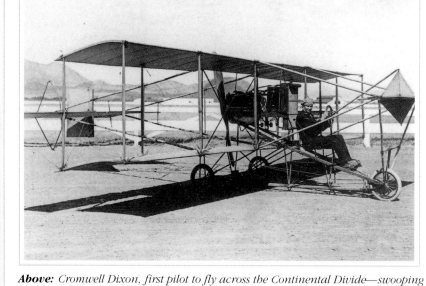

Above: Cromwell Dixon, first pilot to fly across the Continental Divide—swooping over MacDonald Pass in 1911—posed at the Montana State Fair that same year. N.A. Forsyth photo
Top row, center and right: Chief Plenty Coups of the Crow (1848-1932); Bull's Head, a Gros Ventre, on the Fort Belknap Reservation. W.H. Jackson photo.

For what to others is only a dream or, at best, a too-short Montana vacation, is available to residents 52 weeks a year.

Recent surveys provide statistical proof of Montanans' penchant for outdoor recreation. According to a University of Montana study, 77 percent of adults participate in day hiking (with each person participating a total of about 30 days per year), 56 percent fish, 52 percent camp, 42 percent partake of lake or river swimming, 39 percent bicycle, and 38 percent hunt.

Outdoor recreationists in the state are a bit of a spoiled lot, conditioned to quality and uncrowded recreational experiences. Montana skiers don't wait for an hour in lift lines at Bridger Bowl or Big Sky, don't have to plan a year ahead for a permit to visit the Selway Bitterroot Wilderness (as is the case in some more crowded parts of the nation), and feel imposed upon if they aren't alone when they cast their Royal Wulf fly into a riffle on the Blue Ribbon lower Big Hole.

Montana as Old West

Billy Crystal did it in *City Slickers* and so can you. Round 'em up and head 'em out as part of a spring Montana cattle drive from outside Townsend to summer pasture in the high country. For $1,000 (1992 price) you can join one of two Broadwater County Outfitters Association six-day drives of 600 head. Jack Palance won't be there, but there will be a sprinkling of real cowboys, chuckwagon food and sleeping under the stars. No previous riding experience required.

The Old West, the mythic West, that rough-hewn place of promise, elbow room, optimism and frontier opportunity for self-betterment, and indefatigable individualism best symbolized by the cowboy, is alive and well in Montana.

Cattle still outnumber people by three to one here. Riding the range, branding and pulling calves are occupational prerequisites for many in Montana. Each spring on the campuses of Miles Community College, Eastern Montana College and even Montana State University, class attendance drops noticeably when calving season begins and duties home on the ranch beckon. And those livestock market reports on morning TV news programs aren't just fillers. Notoriety and name recognition provided by his radio livestock market show didn't hurt Montana's junior U.S. Senator Conrad Burns at election time.

So pervasive is the cowboy complex that it has become a dominant component of local popular culture. Stockman's Bars and Cowboy Cafes seem more numerous than mini-marts, and a spin through the radio dial will turn up much more Tammy than Tchaikovsky, more Willie than Wagner. On a per capita basis, Montanans probably wear more cowboy boots and outsize belt buckles than residents of any other state with the possible exception of Wyoming. People don't look twice in Montana if young intendeds sport cowboy hats in their engagement pictures in the local paper, or if a candidate for city office poses for campaign posters wearing a Stetson.

Consistent with the traditional notion of the Old West, Montanans seem to have more time for the old-fashioned neighborliness that long since has disappeared in rapid-paced and less trusting parts of the nation. Visitors to Montana frequently comment on the informality and friendliness of its citizens, even toward outlanders. Two strangers passing on a sidewalk are as likely as not to acknowledge each other with a smile and a "Howdy." Each late summer and early fall virtually every daily paper in the state prints letters to the editor from grateful tourists back home in Minneapolis or Dallas or Seattle thanking individuals, and sometimes entire communities, for help beyond the call of duty extended in the midst of some crisis during their Montana vacations.

When Montanans hear reference to "breeding" they are more inclined to think in terms of black white-face cattle.

In the popularized Old West tradition of egalitarianism, titles by themselves don't seem to mean much to most Montanans. Even "Mr." and "Mrs." usually are abandoned and most direct people-to-people contacts are on a first-name basis. In some sections of the nation a family name and what one's parents did have a profound bearing on political, economic and social acceptance and success. Here there is an obvious disdain for such blue-blooded taxonomy. When Montanans hear reference to "breeding" they are more inclined to think in terms of black white-face cattle.

Informality means there isn't much of a market for original Yves St. Laurent or Christian Dior evening gowns in Butte or Broadus, Plentywood or Philipsburg. It's not that Montanans don't dress up. Some businessmen, for example, wear three-piece suits to work every day. But chances are in most settings they wouldn't stand out if they didn't. Even when well-turned out, a Montanan isn't bedecked in the latest Paris or even New York fashion. Tastes here seem to run a little behind many other

Wagon train buffs and visitors long have enjoyed the slow way to travel, as here in Eastern Montana.

GARRY WUNDERWALD

parts of the country. Certainly other Montanans have sensed that they aren't quite up to date when they step off a plane at Denver's Stapleton International or Seattle's SeaTac and feel as if they have just passed through some sort of fashion time warp.

Just like the Mongols who conquered China and were themselves modified by the predominant Chinese culture, new arrivals are acculturated by the potent Montana Old West–cowboy complex. This was brought home to me while a visiting professor at Dartmouth College in Hanover, New Hampshire for the 1988-89 academic year. After living in Montana for more than a dozen years, eight as a geography professor at Montana State University, I hadn't purchased a pickup truck with a gun rack, but I had unconsciously adopted the Montana-ism of commonly greeting passing strangers on the street or campus with a "Howdy." After several weeks of strange looks, I finally realized what I was doing wasn't done. To make matters worse I one day found myself in class telling the mostly Eastern sons and daughters of Fortune 500 CEO's and U.S. Senators to "mosey on back" to a table and pick up their pair of topographic maps.

In a recent article in *Western Historical Quarterly,* Dr. Michael Malone, noted Western historian and President of Montana State University, suggested that one of the four fundamental western regional bonds is the recency and residual aura of the frontier. That clearly is the case in Montana. In some sections of eastern Montana the open range didn't yield to the drylanders' fences and plows until the 1910s and even later. And in the 1990s it still is pos-sible to find Montanans who remember growing up on the settlement frontier. Coming west in an immigrant railroad car, the first winter in a dugout, breaking virgin prairie and infrequent trips to town with horse and wagon are stories you still can hear first-hand from Montana seniors.

In much of Montana the landscape legacies of the Old West are legion and help heighten people's sense of identity and continuity with these earlier times. Century-old log cabins, original homesteaders' dwellings, ghost towns and other artifacts, from rustic and weather-checked cattle chutes to fully functional downtown masonry buildings with 1880s and 1890s dates carved into decorative cornices, all are visual reminders of Montana's not very distant past.

Montana as wide open spaces

Montana is distance and space, a place built on a western scale.

At more than 147,000 square miles, the state is larger than the overwhelming majority of the world's nations, including the United Kingdom, Germany and Japan. All but five of Montana's 56 counties are larger than Rhode Island and several exceed Connecticut in area. Automobile travellers crossing the state for the first time via Interstate 90 and 94 invariably are struck by its sprawling girth and the requisite second day to traverse the Big Sky. The 652 east-west highway miles from the Montana–North Dakota line to the Idaho border high atop Lookout Pass is about the same distance as from Portland, Maine, to Richmond, Virginia, or Detroit, Michigan, to New York City.

To residents, great distances are an un-avoidable fact of life. Montanans routinely make evening and one-day trips that might cause family members to contemplate involuntary commitment if undertaken in eastern states. Small-town residents think nothing of driving 80 miles one-way to see the latest Hollywood movie in a larger community, returning home the same night. And a 500-mile "Sunday drive" to check out the fall color in Glacier National Park or a late spring excursion to Yellowstone to spot wildlife—before the tourist onslaught—are comparable to a round-trip between New York City and Washington, D.C.

Despite generous spatial dimensions, the 1990census enumerated a diminutive population of just 799,065. That's fewer people than live in metropolitan Birmingham, Alabama, or metro Honolulu, Hawaii. But the Montana populace is distinctly non-metropolitan. Fewer than a quarter of residents live in metropolitan areas, ranking the state 48th in the nation. Size-wise, even the state's two metropolises are small by national standards. The 113,419 people with a Billings address cause the city to rank the city 247th in size, and metropolitan Great Falls, with a population of 77,691, checks in nationally at 276th. Despite metro status, both communities retain a manageable scale. Residents can drive almost anywhere within each city in 15 minutes or less. Even in Billings, for workers making the heavy commute between the Heights and downtown via Exposition or Main Street, the day is still far in the future when tuning to a local traffic-copter report will become a drive-time requisite.

Not only is Montana non-metropolitan,

Montana Frontier Counties

Shading indicates 1990 population density of fewer than 2 people per square mile

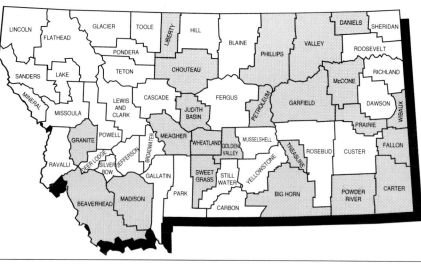

1980-1990 Montana County Census Change

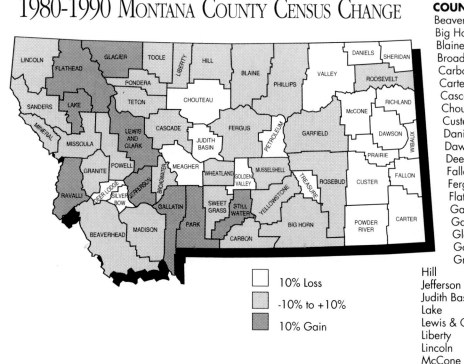

□ 10% Loss
▨ -10% to +10%
▩ 10% Gain

COUNTY	1980-90	COUNTY	1980-90
Beaverhead	1.6%	Madison	9.9%
Big Horn	2.2	Meagher	-15.6%
Blaine	-3.9%	Mineral	-9.8%
Broadwater	1.6%	Missoula	3.5%
Carbon	-0.2%	Musselshell	-7.3%
Carter	-16.5%	Park	13.2%
Cascade	-3.7%	Petroleum	-20.8%
Chouteau	-10.5%	Phillips	-3.8%
Custer	-10.8%	Pondera	-4.4%
Daniels	-20.1%	Powder River	-17.1%
Dawson	-19.5%	Powell	-4.9%
Deer Lodge	-17.9%	Prairie	-24.7%
Fallon	-17.5%	Ravalli	11.2%
Fergus	-7.6%	Richland	-12.5%
Flathead	14.0%	Roosevelt	5.1%
Gallatin	17.7%	Rosebud	6.1%
Garfield	-4.0%	Sanders	-0.1%
Glacier	14.0%	Sheridan	-12.6%
Golden Valley	-11.1%	Silver Bow	-10.9%
Granite	-5.6%	Stillwater	16.8%
Hill	-1.8%	Sweet Grass	-1.9%
Jefferson	12.9%	Teton	-3.4%
Judith Basin	-13.8%	Toole	-9.2%
Lake	10.4%	Treasure	-10.9%
Lewis & Clark	10.4%	Valley	-19.6%
Liberty	-1.5%	Wheatland	-4.8%
Lincoln	-1.5%	Wibaux	-19.3%
McCone	-15.8%	Yellowstone	5.0%

it is barely an urban society. According to the U.S. Bureau of the Census, 52.5 percent of Montanans were urban residents in 1990 and 47.5 percent were classified as rural. Nationally, just over 75 percent of Americans live in communities of at least 2,000 and therefore are considered urban. While the national society has grown increasingly more urban, Montana's rural areas and its Big Timbers (pop. 1,557), Troys (pop. 953) and Jordans (pop. 494) continue to be home to about half the state's residents.

In true western tradition, Montana still is small-town America, a place where the elevation of a community in feet above sea level usually exceeds its population. This holds true even for many mid-size towns including Hamilton (pop. 2,723 and elev. 3,524 feet) and Dillon (pop. 3,991 and elev. 5,406 feet). Towns with populations of 10,000 or less, mere burgs in many parts of the nation, are high-order urban centers in Montana. Havre (pop. 10,201), Miles City (pop. 8,461) and Lewistown (pop. 6,051) command extensive trade hinterlands and merit bold print on state highway maps.

Consistent with the popularized image of the Old West, Montanans are overwhelmingly of European ancestry. But within that similarity is a fascinating mix of people. Today's place-to-place variation is testament to the state's rich settlement history: Butte's amalgam of Irish, Finns and Slovacs; Norwegians and French in the far northeast corner; Dutch west of Bozeman and others add to Montana's ethnic mosaic.

Native Americans, the Indians of Old West days, account for about 6 percent of the population and are the largest ethnic minority group. Contrary to misconceptions of some out-of-staters, Native Americans are not required to live within the state's seven Indian reservations.

In rural parts of the state there undoubtedly are adults who never have met a Black, Hispanic or Asian. These three groups are present at significantly less than their national representation. Combined, they account for just over 2 percent of the population.

If all Montanans were spread evenly throughout their spacious state, there would be a mere 5.5 people per square mile, ranking the state 48th in population density. In Connecticut the figure would be a cramped 960 people per square mile and in New Jersey an eye-popping 1,024. Tiny Deer Lodge County (Montana's second smallest) would barely exceed New Jersey's population density even if it were home to *all* Montanans!

Big Sky residents, of course, are not spread evenly over their state. Humanity tends to be strung out along major irrigated river valleys and transportation corridors in Great Plains Montana and to cluster in the broad valleys in the mountainous west. The state's four most populous counties (Yellowstone, Cascade, Missoula and Flathead) account for only 9 percent of the state's area, but are home to 41 percent of residents. Large unpopulated and sparsely settled expanses between population clusters and necklace-like strings of settlement tend to accentuate Montana's overriding sense of distance and space.

Judging from the 1990 census returns, Montana is not about to lose its abundant elbow room. State population evidently peaked in 1985 at an estimated 825,000 and then declined to the 1990 census count of 799,065. While population in the 13 American Far West states grew by more than 22 percent during the eighties, Montana managed only a 1.6 percent gain. This was not enough growth relative to the rest of the country to keep its two seats in the U.S. House of Representatives, and Montana joined North and South Dakota, Alaska and Wyoming as a single-congressional–district state.

Consistent with the popularized image of the Old West, Montanans are overwhelmingly of European ancestry.

Montana's composite, slow-growth demographics mask stunning regional differences. Like most of agricultural Great Plains America, almost all eastern Montana counties and many of the region's hamlets and towns lost population in the eighties. Double-digit percentage drops in population were commonplace. Among counties, the most dramatic drops were experienced by Prairie (-24.7 percent), Petroleum (-20.8 percent) and Daniels (-20.1 percent). Depopulation was even more gut-wrenching in some communities, with such towns as Judith Gap, Flaxville, Richey and Fairview losing more than a third of their residents. Even Eastern Montana "metropoles" Glasgow and Glendive gave up almost 20 percent of their population.

The thinning of population over large swaths of the rural West has not gone unnoticed by geographers and historians, some of whom now are writing about a new, 20th century American frontier.

One hundred years ago legendary historian Frederick Jackson Turner agreed with the census director who declared America's settlement frontier closed. In 1890, the director had defined "frontier" as an area with fewer than two people per square mile. After studying census returns for that year,

One of Montana's statehood centennial events in 1989 was this horse-drawn cavalcade from Bannack, the first of three territorial capitals, to Helena, the last territorial (and sole state) capital.

Turner was quick to theorize on the demise of the frontier. He saw that there was no longer a north-south line separating fully settled areas on the east from sparsely settled areas with the requisite fewer than two people per square mile to the west.

In Montana's 23 counties with population densities of fewer than 2 people per square mile, Turner's 100-year-old epitaph for the frontier seems premature. Covering more than 40 percent of the state's area, and concentrated in Great Plains Montana, these frontier counties face special economic and social challenges associated with a sparse and thinning settlement fabric. With so much of its area in frontier counties, it is no wonder a 1991 *Newsweek* article considered Montana part of America's "Outback" and that the state was part of the "Empty Quarter" in Joel Garreau's popular *The Nine Nations of North America*.

Professor Frank J. Popper, chairman of the Urban Studies Department at Rutgers University, and his geographer wife Deborah E. Popper have proposed that a consortium of private institutions and the federal government buy up scores of rapidly depopulating Great Plains counties and return them to their natural state. The heavily government subsidized ranchers and farmers would be moved off marginal land the Poppers feel never should have been converted to agriculture and, in their place, the world's largest game preserve—the Buffalo Commons—would take form. The Poppers' proposal includes nine Eastern Montana counties. Needless to say their proposal is more than controversial among many of the ranchers and farmers who would be required to step aside in this "let's put them out of their misery" propos-

al. Many wonder what a Harvard educated professor in New Brunswick, *New Jersey,* really knows about farm and ranch life on the Great Plains. More than one rancher in Blaine, Garfield, Carter and other included counties probably thinks it might save the U.S. government more welfare dollars and be more ecologically imperative to level all communities in New Jersey and return the state to a natural condition.

While depopulation dominated Great Plains Montana, most Rocky Mountain counties were experiencing at least modest growth. Wilderness counties, those that contain or are adjacent to counties with federally designated wilderness areas, grew most rapidly. Each of Montana's ten fastest growing counties in the eighties was a wilderness county—Gallatin (+17.7 percent), Stillwater (+16.8 percent), Flathead (+14 percent), Glacier (+14 percent) and Park (+13.2 percent) led the way.

In today's El Dorados, high levels of amenities and desirable quality-of-life factors, not the placer gold deposits of 120 years ago, are a powerful draw for migrants. In their study of migration to wilderness counties in the West, University of Idaho geographers Gundars Rudzitis and Harley E. Johansen found that physical and social factors collectively ranked higher than employment opportunities in decisions to move to wilderness counties. They concluded that ready access to outdoor recreation, a slower pace of life, scenery, environmental quality and other non-economic factors probably will assure a continued influx of population into such wilderness counties.

The Old West and creation myth

Each generation looks back at the past with fresh perspectives from a new now, armed with different biases and priorities and asking a new set of questions. Even though the past cannot be altered, interpretation of that past can change, with the result being new histories. This is precisely what has been happening with the history of the American West in recent years. New western history suggests a place that was only marginally as portrayed in Zane Grey's novels and Tom Mix and John Wayne movies. Freedom and self-sufficiency, class, gender, race and the environment are central foci in this new western historiography.

Until quite recently, the Old West was seen as male turf, both written by and focused on men.

Western author Wallace Stegner recently described the Old West cowboy, the epitome of western self-sufficiency and freedom, as "an overworked, underpaid hireling, almost as homeless and dispossessed as a modern crop worker, and his fabled independence was and is chiefly the privilege of quitting his job in order to go look for another just as bad." This western icon was in actuality an impoverished wage earner, subservient to the monopolistic corporate elite who quickly assumed economic control of the West.

Until quite recently, the Old West was seen as male turf, both written by and focused on men. A new breed of historical scholars, many of them women, have dug deeper, and more realistic images of frontier lifestyle and difficult day-to-day realities of the place have begun emerging. Isolation, alcoholism, abandonment, emotional neglect, dysfunctional families, impossible odds and almost assured failure were the realities facing many real-life families on the frontier.

The new Western history is less ethnocentric and sees more central roles for a wide range of minorities. Native Americans, Hispanics, Blacks, Asians and other ethnic groups now are recognized as having been major and resilient players in the frontier chronicle. The new Western historians are less inclined to view Indians in a predictably negative light *(Dances with Wolves)* and try to understand a racialism that was more complex than a simplistic Indian-white dichotomy.

> **There is a generations-long debate within the social sciences over the role of nature versus nurture.**

Western environmental historians have placed the Bonanza West image of limitless resources in a more critical context. Economic gains in the "winning" of the West now are seen as having taken an enormous environmental toll, some of the costs of which still are being paid. Species extermination including that of the buffalo, introduction of weeds, destruction of biotic resources by livestock and lumbermen, pollution of water and air and recontouring of natural landscapes in pursuit of gold, silver and copper have amounted to nothing less than a war waged against the Western environment.

Writing in her already classic *The Legacy of Conquest*, historian Patricia Nelson Limerick suggests the idealized frontier is an American creation myth. Like any myth, this one doesn't have to be based on firmly established facts.

The long-term impact of the new Western history on Americans', and indeed the world's, perception of the West is not yet clear. Initial evidence suggests resistance to questioning established Western beliefs and images. The spring 1991 opening of "The West as America: Reinterpreting Images of the Frontier," at the Smithsonian Institution's National Museum of American Art, created a furor and clearly illustrated the deep-seated nature of a religious-like devotion to Western mythology. Unorthodox captions for classic paintings in the impressive collection of 164 Remingtons, George Catlins, Charles Russells, N. C. Wyeths and other masters sparked a chorus of criticism from Western senators. Senator Alan Simpson (R., Wyo.) reported he was "shocked" and Senator Slade Gorton (R., Wash.) thought the iconoclastic interpretations of these paintings "amounts to knocking the whole Western experience..." At a hearing of the Senate Appropriations Committee it was made clear to the Smithsonian's secretary that use of government funds (this exhibit was funded entirely with private funds) for such defamation of the American character was not to be tolerated.

Outside the venerated halls of Congress, the revisionist historians' growing chorus seems to have little impact except in university History of the American West classes. Friday and Saturday night urban cowboys at The Horseshoe in Billings have not yet traded in their dancing duds, there has been no loss of interest in authentic "Montana Broke" jeans (once worn by real Montana cowboys) at the Whisky Dust haberdashery in New York City, and the Montana state flag still provides a backdrop for seven-nights-a-week country and Western music performances at Good

Time Charlie's Western bar in Kumamoto, north of Tokyo. Long-established belief systems do not change readily and it is unlikely that Americans, or for that matter the world, will anytime soon abandon this almost sacred and century old, West-centered creation myth. Until that does happen, Montana will, for many, remain the epitome of that magically seductive and mythic land.

A state of synergism

Synergism, "the simultaneous action of separate agencies which, together, have a greater total effect than the sum of their individual effects," helps explain Montana as place. There undoubtedly are a variety of ingredients in this Montana elixir, but the two most potent constituents may be nature and the mythic West. In Montana, people and these two active ingredients come together unlike in any other place in the West. From the pine-clad hills of the Powder River country to Charlie Russell's Square Butte mesa settings to the mountain-shadowed Mission Valley, one can sense this collaborative coincidence of the physical and mythical West.

Although this Montana synergism is a statewide phenomenon, the power of place seems nowhere more potent than in the Broad Valley Rockies, that section of western and central Montana with the distinctive mix of spacious valleys interspersed among and adjacent to precipitous mountain ranges. Covering less than a third of the state, this globally rare open mountain landscape is home to the majority of Montanans. Nowhere else in the Rockies are so many people immersed and interspersed *within and among* the Rocky

Mountains and its distinctive complement of eastern outliers.

There is a generations-long debate within the social sciences over the role of nature versus nurture. How much of who and what we *Homo sapiens* are is a result of genetics and how much is the consequence of our cultural milieu? It is interesting to contemplate how such factors might relate to Montana's power of place. Especially thought-provoking and controversial is the possible role of primordial links to the natural environment.

Geographers once assumed that people living in certain types of natural environments, such as mountains, coasts, deserts or steppes, were putty in the hands of nature to be molded, right down to their very personalities, by the physical setting. This doctrine of Environmental Determinism, now viewed as embarrassingly naive and simplistic, was widespread among American geographers as recently as the early 20th century.

According to environmental determinists, mountain dwellers were expected to be conservative and uncomfortable with change, characteristics acquired from the rugged configuration of the surrounding landscape. Inwardly focused on their own world, they were expected to have little time or concern for the goings-on in adjacent regions. A suspicion toward strangers, extreme sensitivity to criticism, superstition, strong religious feelings, and an intense love of home and family were other presumed traits among mountain folks. The difficulty of life in such a rugged setting meant that residents naturally would be industrious, frugal, provident, and peculiarly honest and endowed with strong muscles,

unjaded nerves, iron purpose, and disinterest in luxury. These qualities may characterize some residents of Montana's Broad Valley Rockies, but few geographers today would suggest they are directly and solely attributable to the region's mountainous setting.

Far-fetched as it sounds, perhaps residents and visitors who feel a rush, a natural high and empowerment with mere proximity to the Broad Valley Rockies can, in part, thank humankind's family tree. Archaeological evidence suggests the earliest members of the human family, the small-brained and big-jawed australopithecines, first appeared about 5.5 million years ago on the savannas of East and South Africa. Based on early 1990s reinterpretation and more accurate dating of a previously discovered skull bone from Kenya, our genus *Homo* has been around for at least 2.4 million years. For almost all of these millions of years and 100,000-plus generations, human survival depended on closeness to nature. In terms of human evolution, the Agricultural and Industrial revolutions, which portended fundamental shifts in human-nature relationships, were last-second developments. It would be naive to think that a few thousand years' veneer of civilization alone explains the human species. What transpired during the previous millions of years certainly impacted the creature, but how, and what could that possibly have to do with Montana place lovers? Let's speculate.

Citing ideas expressed by John H. Falk and writing in *The Experience of Place*, Tony Hiss suggests we humans may be genetically programmed to feel most at home in grassland. In our evolutionary hearth area of East and South Africa, unobstructed

vistas and a savanna setting were the norm for millions of years. Does this explain our penchant for grass and why we have lush front yard lawns and not huge piles of rocks or fields of sand beyond our picture windows? Are we trying to mimic what was for so long our home turf? Research even has shown that hospital patients whose windows overlook grassy areas heal more quickly than those whose views are brick walls.

Although cropping has replaced much of the native vegetation and a long history of overgrazing has meant an invasion by sagebrush in many sections, the lowlands in the Broad Valley Rockies are grasslands. But many places, including most of North Dakota, are steppe environments, yet they lack western Montana's strong power of place. Although many North Dakotans may have strong emotional ties with that state's open landscape, few would deny that the feeling is not exactly universal. Other factors must be involved.

British geographer Jay Appleton has noted two additional human environmental preferences that may be relevant: prospect and refuge. In pre-modern times an ability to scan large areas and see great distances (prospect) had obvious survival benefits. Similarly, a refuge, or hiding place, would be another, perhaps critical, site attribute. In Montana's Broad Valley Rockies even low flanks of island-like ranges provide ideal vantage points for viewing the adjacent grassland, and nearby mountainside pine forests furnish requisite concealment. Interestingly, the high premium building sites in the region are panoramic view lots on the flanks of the mountains nestled in the lower limits of the forest.

Looking across a cultivated section of the Shields River Valley to the Crazy Mountains.

Montana's open mountains landscape also scores highly for what University of Michigan research psychologists Stephen and Rachel Kaplan call "legibility" in their book *Cognition and Environment: Functioning in an Uncertain World*. They think it is possible that humans have a genetic-based preference for open spaces that are easily comprehended and invite reconnaissance, but are sufficiently heterogeneous to

afford landmarks. Western Montana's spacious, open valleys and always-within-sight mountain ranges would seem to combine to offer great legibility. Is it possible that we have a primordial pre-programming to feel reassured and at home in places with this prized complement of landscape features?

Early humans probably were grasslands foragers, scavengers and hunters. In that

preagricultural world, subsistence depended on what nature provided. The more diverse the plant and animal communities, the greater the potential range of foodstuffs. Continuing with this human animal perspective, is it possible that our hunting progenitors have left us with an instinct for ecologically varied environments, those with a more assured life-support system. If so, the Broad Valley Rockies have additional "natural" appeal.

Forested highlands within the region add significantly to what otherwise would be a more homogeneous grasslands environment. Rather than just a grass-dominated plant community with its complement of fauna, mountain ranges add a third dimension and a vertical succession of distinctive life zones. Back in the valleys, riverside riparian zones add still more ecological variety to this section of Montana. As any good present-day hunter knows, the ecotones, or edges of contact between major plant communities, are among the most prolific for wildlife, both in terms of variety of species and individuals per species. Accounts of early explorers seem to suggest this was exactly the case in pre-white Montana. Perhaps our long lineage as hunters and gatherers has phylogenetically programmed us to perceive environmental variance positively.

If Robert Ardrey *(The Territorial Imperative)* and others are correct, humans are territorial creatures, needing to possess and belong to a certain section of earth space. If so, what more ready-made territory than Montana's Broad Valley Rockies. Any good territory should .have clearly delimited boundaries—what better and more obvious limits than the encircling mountain ranges? In addition, these spacious valleys are about as generous as they can be and still be visually taken in with the unaided eye. Perhaps it is this instinctual territorial imperative that makes residents of this part of Montana feel so at home in their Gallatin, Big Hole and Helena valleys.

Montana's Broad Valley Rockies is not the only section of the Rocky Mountains with this combination of environmental factors. Primordial placeness may be just as powerful for the few thousand residents and seasonal tourists of such areas as Colorado's mountain parks or northeast Oregon's Wallowa Valley, but no place approaches western Montana's valleys for total area of coincidence or the number of year-round residents.

The potency of this Montana place cannot be explained by nature alone. Residents and visitors also are cultural creatures, conditioned and influenced by their contemporary society. Most residents probably would agree that part of the personality of this place stems from its natural beauty, but beauty is a cultural appraisal, subject to change. Mountains, for example, have not always been viewed romantically in western society. It was not until well into the 1800s, and following the European lead, that the American notion of mountains as splendor became widespread. Prior to then they were seen as forsaken and foreboding. Works of landscape painters and poets, a growing belief that the divine was manifest in nature, improved transportation and accessibility and other factors combined to help reverse our perceptions of mountains. By the 1880s English writer and art critic John Ruskin could write that "Mountains are the beginning and end

of all natural scenery." A hundred years later most western Montanans probably agree. Today we visually take in the Mission Range or Crazies or Spanish Peaks and our culture tells us they are breahtaking and inspiring, and for us they become breathtaking and inspiring.

Cultural conditioning probably also helps explain the active role of the Old West in the Montana mystique. Despite recent works by revisionist western historians, the mythic West still looms large in the minds of Americans and others worldwide. Alive and well in Montana is the perception of an idealized West, home of a free and rugged individualism most symbolized by that western icon, the cowboy: self-sufficiency, optimism, honor, and where hard work is rewarded and good prevails over evil. It adds a defining and positive component to the regional identity and the personality of the place.

Natural beauty, the cowboy/Old West complex and at least some elements of a phylogenetically proper place characterize all sections of Montana to some extent, but nowhere are they more pervasive and reinforcing than in the Broad Valley Rockies. Is it possible that the human habitat appropriateness helps to explain the comfortable and strong sense of home feeling so common among residents, and that more culturally related feel-good perceptions of that nature and the Old West ambiance help to energize locals? The spiritually lifting potential of the region is apparent to many, especially to former residents who periodically return for too-short visits. Clearly it is a high energy environment that stimulates the senses, the imagination and creativity.

Perhaps the most tangible evidence of the empowering potential of the place is its rich literary tradition. Add up the literary activity of neighboring Idaho, Wyoming, North and South Dakota and it is questionable that the total would be comparable to Montana's. What is even more amazing is that this tradition is essentially a phenomenon of the Broad Valley Rockies and immediately adjacent areas. Well known authors with ties to the region in recent years include Ivan Doig, Norman Maclean, Mary Clearman Blew, Thomas McGuane, William Kittredge, Richard Brautigan, David Quammen and the list goes on and on in contemporary fiction alone. The heft and girth of the monumental *The Last Best Place: A Montana Anthology* is in keeping with the scale of accomplishments.

Many sensitive and creative people seem to be fed by the power of this place and quite understandably literary migrants have set up shop in this region where they, too, can tap into the nurturing and energizing environment. Evidently one does not have to be born of this place to benefit: the place seems to invade the aliens.

Perhaps it is this instinctual territorial imperative that makes residents of this part of Montana feel so at home in their Gallatin, Big Hole and Helena valleys.

THE PHYSICAL REALM

Montanans live closer to nature than most other Americans and, not surprisingly, many have a special interest in their natural world. In many other parts of our nation the depth to which Big Sky residents seek understanding would be considered scientific and statistical overkill. Montanans don't just want to know the name of the mountain range on the horizon, they also are eager to know something about its geologic formation. Since most state residents qualify for a weather-endurance merit badge, it is no wonder they have a keen interest in this ever-present feature of the physical environment. Forests here aren't just trees, they are ponderosa pine, alpine fir, Douglas fir and other species, and Montanans take note of how the forest blend varies from place to place. Combined, aspects of the physical stage also help explain much of what makes Montana such an endearing and distinctive place.

Geology

Montana is a state with a dual physiographic personality: Rocky Mountain Montana in the western third and Great Plains Montana to the east. The complexity of the state's geologic evolution shows on a wall-size geologic map. It shows each major rock unit with a different color or pattern and uses heavy black lines to indicate faults, or major fractures, along which rock units have moved. In Great Plains Montana the pattern is rather simple, with sections thousands of square miles in area shown with the same color or shading. This indicates extensive tracts covered by the same rock unit, still lying flat and undisturbed right where it was deposited tens of millions of years ago.

In Rocky Mountain Montana the pattern is anything but simple. On the map the region is a jumble of colors and irregular shapes. Rather than lying in nice flat layers covering large areas, these rocks have been severely folded, faulted, thrusted and intruded by molten rock from below. The result is a complex regional geology on which geologists thrive. To them it is a 10,000-piece jigsaw puzzle made even more challenging by a third dimension. Investigations to unravel the region's complex geologic evolution have resulted in more than a thousand published reports and articles.

Even at a general level, the story of Montana's geologic evolution is a fascinating one that at times sounds a bit like Ripley's "Believe It or Not." Ideas on the evolution of Montana and all of North America have changed dramatically over the last quarter century as notions previously laughed at are gaining acceptance. Contemporary theories refer to such phenomena as splitting and drifting continents and spreading sea floors, all of which may have a direct bearing on the state's geologic history.

Precambrian

We can pick up our brief overview of Montana's geologic development about one and a half billion years ago during the Precambrian geologic period, the time span that includes rocks older than 600 million years.

It now is assumed that the earth's outer shell, its crust, and the upper layer of the mantle immediately below, consist of a number of rigid plates. The number, as well as the size and shape of plates, evidently has changed through geologic time, but now totals about twelve. These plates are in constant, imperceptible motion, drifting and carrying the continents along with them. They sometimes split or collide with one another, generating forces that can produce mountain ranges and volcanic activity.

Deep in the distant past of the mid-Precambrian, the micro-plate of which Montana was a part, split in two. Most of Montana was just to the east of the line along which the plate separated, and became a part of the eastern fragment. The two plates drifted apart allowing the sea floor of the Pacific Ocean and a new plate to form in the widening space between them. The section that pulled away from Montana may now be a part of the Siberian section of Russia. The plate of which most of Montana was a part drifted in the opposite direction for eons until about 290 million

Sandstone in Makoshika State Park is composed of material eroded eons ago from the Rocky Mountains as they rose hundreds of miles west of here.

years ago when it collided and merged with other drifting continents to form the gigantic land mass of Pangaea which itself split and separated into our present continents.

There was no Idaho or Washington one

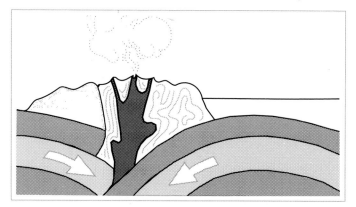

When the earth's plates collide, one usually buckles downward, causing uplift and crumpling of the overriding plate. Convergence of plates is associated with mountain building, deep-sea trenches, volcanoes and earthquakes.

and a half billion years ago; Montana was located on what was then the west coast. This Precambrian sea reached deep into Montana, submerging everything west of its shoreline, which ran approximately through Browning, Choteau, Lewistown, Roundup, Three Forks and Dillon. Rivers emptying into the sea deposited sand, silt and mud in near shore areas, and carbonates precipitated out of the ocean waters. As these bottom sediments accumulated just off the edge of the new continent, the floor of the marginal sea evidently subsided, thereby permitting an extra thick accumulation. In what is now far-western Montana and was then a belt 120 miles out at sea, the subsidence was greatest and accumulation thickest.

Since deposition, these water-laid sediments have lithified into rocks including sandstones, shales, mudstones and impure limestones, and in many areas have been compacted further and altered into harder forms, especially quartzite (previously sandstone) and argillite (previously shale). Abundant fossil mud cracks, ripple marks, raindrop impressions and casts of salt crystals suggest this depositional environment definitely was not a deep ocean. More likely it was a shallow sea or perhaps even a tidal flat that was alternately wet and dry. Its limestone rocks now contain fossils of primitive blue-green algae (stromatolites) that attest to the presence of organisms that must have been exposed to the air much of the time during their growth, possibly in slimy green algal mats on mud flats more than a billion years ago.

These Precambrian-age sedimentary rocks are referred to collectively as the Belt Series. Nearly all of Montana west of Drummond and Glacier National Park is underlain by them. These usually somber colored rocks of reddish-purple, gray, brown and green are easily recognizable on mountain sides and in road cuts throughout the region. With a possible thickness of several miles in the far western fringe of the state, it is easy to see why they so dominate the landscape. In fact, some of the region's mountain ranges—including the Purcell, Cabinet, Mission and Sapphire ranges—are composed almost entirely of these rocks.

Paleozoic

During the Paleozoic Era, which includes the time from the end of the Precambrian some 600 million years ago up to 225 million years before the present, Montana was probably rather low, flat and featureless. Mountains were not yet a part of the landscape. Rocks dating from this span of time tell of a region over which seas repeatedly advanced and retreated—what geologists call transgressions and regressions.

In Rocky Mountain Montana at least 25 different Paleozoic rock units are recognized and named. They now have a combined thickness of from 5,000 to 10,000 feet. Limestone deposited under these seas is the most abundant rock type. It can be seen as thick layers of light-gray cliffs on many of the mountains from southwestern Montana north to the Sawtooth Range. The popular and bold Chinese Wall in the remote backcountry of the Bob Marshall Wilderness is made up of these limestones.

Farther to the south the gray cap of the Bridgers is also Paleozoic limestone. This same 330-million-year-old formation towers as gray cliffs on both sides of the narrow gap through which I-90 passes just east of Bozeman Pass. In addition to limestone, western Montana's Paleozoic rock includes thick layers of sandstone and shale. Geologists especially are interested in these rocks because most oil and gas discovered in Montana has been associated with them.

Mesozoic

Relatively peaceful conditions of leisurely transgressions and regressions of Paleozoic seas were shattered by dramatic developments in the subsequent Mesozoic Era, between 225 and 65 million years ago. The faces of western and central Montana underwent monumental transformations. Forces of unbelievable strength left the previously flat-lying layers of Belt and Paleozoic rock folds contorted and actually standing on end. Huge slabs of these rocks miles in thickness were moved about like toy cars and slid distances of 80 miles and more. Molten material from deep within the earth punched its way up from below, and belching and spewing volcanos added to the drama.

It was a collision, of sorts, that terminated Montana's geologic tranquility. The first rumblings of change date from approximately 170 million years ago when the Paleo-Pacific plate and the North American plate converged just to the west of Montana. Since the crustal material of the oceanic plate was more dense, it buckled under the western, continental edge of the North American plate. Like the front edge of an automobile after a head-on collision, the edge of the overriding continental plate was shortened, crumpled and lifted upward. This marked the beginning of the formation of Montana's first Rockies.

It has been estimated that the compression generated by this collision shortened the blanket of sedimentary rocks in western Montana from west to east by no fewer than 75 to 100 miles. Previously flat sedimentary rock layers buckled into folds up to 25 miles wide and originally up to 5 miles high. These crinkled and inclined layers of rocks can be seen throughout Rocky Mountain Montana. In places, previously horizontal rocks now stand vertically and others have been completely overturned.

Compressive forces also deformed rocks by faulting. The most impressive of these were the large overthrust faults that fractured weak or brittle buried rock layers and shoved large sheets up and over, onto adjacent rocks. Western Montana's most celebrated is the Lewis Overthrust, which carried eastward a huge 1,000-plus-square-mile sheet of layered rock at least six miles thick. Perhaps moving from as far away as northern Idaho, it eventually came to rest atop what is now Glacier National Park. This gigantic thrust sheet originally included Belt rocks at the bottom, mantled by progressively younger Paleozoic and Mesozoic sediments. Erosion has long since stripped away the fairly thin covering of Paleozoic and Mesozoic rocks from the top of this displaced slab and has cut deeply into the older and harder Belt rocks below, etching out the peaks that now tower above the park. Conspicuous and resistant 9,056-foot Chief Mountain on the northeastern edge of the park is a large island mass of Belt rock. It was once part of the thrust sheet and was stranded when erosion removed the interconnecting Belt rock.

Overthrusting of rocks occurred in a broad section of western Montana north of a line extending from just east of Glacier National Park south through White Sulphur Springs, the northern end of the Bridgers, Whitehall and Dillon. Nowhere within this region has overthrusting produced a more unique mountainous landscape than in the Sawtooth Range south of Glacier. High north-south–trending ridges and parallel, intervening valley troughs give the natural landscape a wave-like appearance. This topography results from once horizontal and layered slabs of rocks having been faulted into relatively short slabs and then thrust up or slid over those to the east. The rock formations now stand up at a high angle, stacked sideways like a tilted deck of cards. Each linear ridge and valley marks the upturned edge of a rock unit, ridges corresponding with more easily eroded strata (often shale).

Upward migrations and intrusion of molten material from deep within the earth, and even Mount St. Helens-like volcanos, played a part in the evolution of the region's first mountains, the Ancestral Rockies. To understand their presence we must return to the collision of the Paleo-Pacific and North American plates. You may remember that, while the lighter continental edge of North America rode over the oceanic plate and was uplifted, compressed and crumpled, the heavier oceanic plate buckled down and descended into the earth's mantle. Rocks drawn down in this subduction zone eventually began to melt as they moved deep into the earth. High temperatures and pressure altered the oceanic plate as though it were in a gigantic pressure cooker. Some rock melted and produced molten rock, or magma. Because it was lighter than its enclosing rock, this magma rose, but not all of the molten material reached the surface. Some cooled and solidified into granite thousands of feet below ground, forming large bodies called batholiths. This happened under a large area between Butte and Helena 70 to 80 million years ago. Erosion has stripped away overlying rock and exposed the 60-by-30-mile Boulder Batholith. Its now-irregular landscape of boulders and spires (the result of much more recent erosion) dominates the mountainous terrain between these two towns and is easily visible

Previously flat sedimentary rock layers buckled into folds up to 25 miles wide and originally up to 5 miles high.

GEOLOGY

Top left: Algal stromatolites, the oldest known fossils on earth, at Grinnell Glacier in Glacier National Park.
Top right: The Devil's Slide near Gardiner reveals uptilted rock strata.
Bottom left: Granite outcrop of the Boulder Batholith.
Bottom right: Fossilized leaf from the ocean floor that now is the Terry Badlands.

along Interstate 90 on Homestake Pass east of Butte.

In places molten material reached the surface, where some flowed or blew out through volcanos. During the emplacement of the Boulder Batholith, a field of large volcanos developed on the surface. Erosion has long since destroyed the outline of perhaps once classic volcanic·cones, but lava that poured from them still blankets sections of the area with up to 10,000 feet of basalt. These volcanos spewed ash that drifted far to the east and can be identified in 70-million-year-old rock in extreme southeastern Montana.

Batholiths and smaller intrusions pushed up under other sections of Montana and have been exhumed. These include the Tobacco Root Batholith in the north end of the Tobacco Root Mountains, the Philipsburg Batholith, those in the Pioneer and other ranges. Many of them, by no coincidence, are home to most of Montana's ghost towns and present-day mining districts. The majority of Montana's metal-bearing ore deposits owe their existence to such intrusions. As great masses of molten material pushed upward they cracked and fissured the enclosing host rock through which they moved. Superheated "juices," with high mineral concentrations produced by cooling and crystallization of these deeply buried bodies, were squeezed into the fissures. There they deposited the ores as vein fillings that have yielded billions of dollars worth of gold, silver, copper and lead.

For some, Montana is at its scenic best just east of the Rockies' main ranges where island-like mountains and highlands add visual variety to the landscape. Here forest-clad sentinels rise above surrounding plains adding interest to one of the most unique sections anywhere in the North American plains. South Dakota has its Black Hills and Wyoming its Devil's Tower, but nowhere else in the Great Plains is there such a mountain-studded landscape. To residents of the area the names are familiar—the Little Rockies, Highwoods, Bear Paws, Big and Little Snowies, Judiths, Moccasins, Sweetgrass Hills and more. Often referred to as Rocky Mountain outliers, their evolution is linked to the same forces that produced the main range to the west.

Recent dating of associated rocks suggests that, beginning in the late Mesozoic and continuing into the early Cenozoic Era (60 to 70 million years ago), molten material from great depth was forced upward toward the surface in the areas that now constitute the Judith, Moccasin and Little Rocky mountains. This flood of viscous magma worked its way up through layers of sandstone and shale and other sedimentary rocks, but did not reach the surface. Instead, at varying depths, it spread laterally between adjacent layers of rocks before solidifying. These irregularly-shaped to circular intrusives, called laccoliths, were blister shaped and usually less than a few miles across.

Today these hard igneous rocks are exposed in each of the three mountain ranges. Since their emplacement, a continual regional uplift, linked to the ongoing evolution of the Rockies, accelerated erosion and stripped away more easily eroded overlying sedimentary rocks. Because of their resistant nature, they now stand out as highlands.

Each of the higher peaks in the Judith Mountains is an unearthed laccolith. Granitic Judith Peak at 6,428 feet is the highest, but others also exceed 6,000 feet. Such names as Crystal Peak, Porphyry Peak and Gold Hill are indicative of the mineralization associated with these laccolith formations. The Judith Mountains are peppered with abandoned mines like the New Year, Spotted Horse, Whiskey Gulch and Old Glory. Mineral production was sufficient in at least two areas to justify the development of Giltedge and Maiden.

Rising to more than 5,500 feet, two thousand feet above the surrounding plains, the Little Rockies have intrigued and lured people for centuries.

Rather than a single range, the Moccasin Mountains, just west of the Judiths, are actually two detached highlands, the North Moccasins and the South Moccasins. South Peak, at 5,420 feet, is near the center of the southern intrusive body. North of Warm Spring Creek the highest peak in the North Moccasins rises to 5,581 feet. The early 20th century ghost town of Kendall and other abandoned mines in the North Moccasins are evidence of mineralization in that area.

To the northeast, just beyond the Missouri River, are the Little Rocky Mountains, perhaps the most island-like of Montana's mountain outliers. Rising to more than 5,500 feet, two thousand feet above the surrounding plains, the Little Rockies have intrigued and lured people for centuries. For Indians the mountains are sacred, for Kid Curry and other outlaws their canyons meant safe refuge, and for thousands of miners, their gold was a hoped-for ticket to wealth. Like the Judiths and Moccasins, the core of this highland is made up of igneous intrusives formed when molten rock squeezed between other rock layers and fissures. Sedimentary rocks have been eroded from the central portion, exposing the now-dormant laccoliths.

Around the flanks of the highlands are upturned layers of older sedimentary rocks, which had been pierced and pushed upward by the intrusion. These now form a concentric, irregular bull's-eye pattern around the central igneous mass. Some stand up as virtual walls 600 to 700 feet tall. Numerous caves have developed in the upturned limestone rocks on the south flanks of the mountains.

Eastern Montana is clearly one of the most important regions in the world for the excavation and research on the last of the dinosaurs.

South and west of Old Scraggy and other Little Rockies peaks, it is the more scenically subdued plains sections and their ubiquitous and flat-lying later-Mesozoic rocks that have most captured the attention of the world's geologists. The western half of Great Plains Montana is dominated by rocks formed in the Cretaceous (135 to 65 million years ago), the last of the Mesozoic's three periods.

By late Cretaceous time, adjacent mountain-building forces in western and central Montana had caused the Rockies and outliers to begin rising above adjacent areas. As the Rockies rose, a narrow and shallow seaway that cut North America in two began to close. The western shoreline of this Cretaceous sea lapped up on the eastern flank of the evolving Rockies and shifted east and west in response to the mountain building to the west and sinking of the seafloor itself. When the sea advanced westward, marine mud accumulated over what was then the ocean floor of eastern Montana. Retreats of the sea are recorded in non-marine land deposits, including sands that had been eroded from the rising western highland. Transported seaward by Cretaceous rivers, sand was deposited in deltas and on coastal plains. Other material came to rest in continental lagoons, swamps and shallow lakes on the emergent land west of the seaway. These sedimentary deposits accumulated in essentially flat-lying layers that eventually totaled thousands of feet in thickness. In succeeding millions of years, the deposits hardened, the muds becoming shale; the sands, sandstone; and some of the swampy organic debris, coal.

Fossils and bones in these late Cretaceous rocks tell us that life thrived both on the land and in the sea. Remains of warm-temperate and subtropical plants such as palms, ferns and fig trees attest to a much milder and more equable climate than we have today. Coal deposits dating from this period suggest the existence of near-coastal swamps similar to today's Florida Everglades.

Perhaps the most celebrated residents of late Cretaceous Great Plains Montana were the great dinosaurs, which dominated the land, and the marine lizards, which ruled the sea. According to Dr. Michael W. Hager, vertebrate paleontologist and former director of Museum of the Rockies in Bozeman, "Eastern Montana is clearly one of the most important regions in the world for the excavation and research on the last of the dinosaurs." Around the small town of Jordan, the annual summer arrival of a crew of paleontologists from the University of California at Berkeley—locally referred to as "the bone diggers"—is a tradition. Paleontologists continue to comb the region, and extraordinary finds occur on almost an annual basis, making the region one of the world's most important dinosaur digs.

Cenozoic

Over the eastern half of Great Plains Montana, late-Cretaceous strata are covered by sedimentary rocks deposited during the succeeding Cenozoic Era's Tertiary Period, which includes the span of time from about 65 to 3 million years ago. These younger rocks once were more extensive, but later erosion removed many of these deposits from western sections of eastern Montana and, to the good fortune of dinosaur hunters, exposed the underlying, older Cretaceous-age rocks. All Tertiary deposits were non-marine. Dominant layers are shale, sandstone and coal. Most were deposited by slow-moving streams that meandered back and forth across a broad and very gently sloping plain extending eastward from the still-rising Rockies.

The oldest Tertiary strata is the Fort Union formation, deposited at a time when warm and moist conditions dominated the low plains of eastern Montana. Extensive swampy areas and associated standing water provided ideal conditions for the accumulation of organic debris, the necessary raw material for coal formations. Today this is the chief coal-bearing unit in the entire Northern Great Plains and is mined extensively in Montana, Wyoming and North Dakota. Following the early Tertiary, eastern Montana's climate became drier, and by the end of the period the region was a cooler, grass-covered plain similar to what it is today. Layers of interbedded volcanic ash are proof of Tertiary volcanic activity to the west.

As with the Cretaceous-age rocks, eastern Montana Tertiary sediments also have proved to be a veritable treasure chest for paleontologists, providing valuable insight into mammalian evolution. Remains of mammals ranging from small rodents to the diminutive, one-foot-tall *Eohippus,* the "dawn horse"; the primitive ungulate, *Coryphodon;* early camels; rhinoceroses; and mammoths catalog the ascendancy of mammals over eastern Montana during the Tertiary Period.

In western Montana the initial compression and associated folding and thrust faulting that began 170 million years ago was only the prelude to a protracted period of intense geologic activity. This mountain-building episode continued into the subsequent Tertiary Period and probably continued in fits and starts until at least 50 million years before the present.

Volcanos developed in areas including the Madison Range, where such peaks as Lone Mountain (11,166 feet) and Sphinx Mountain (10,876 feet) are remnants of the subsurface plumbing that once fed volcanos. Farther east a large complex of volcanos produced a highland, the remnants of which we now call the Crazy Mountains. To the northwest, volcanos also spewed the thick pile of volcanic rocks that forms the 300-square-mile Adel Mountains between Craig and Cascade.

In south-central Montana the collision of the plates mentioned earlier cracked the earth's crust and squeezed upward large blocks with their veneer of sedimentary rocks. One large block, defined at the edges by faults, pushed upward beginning 50 to 60 million years ago, forming today's Absaroka and Beartooth ranges. Since this

entire highland (situated between Highway 89 on the west and Red Lodge on the east) is one large block of the earth's crust, geologists refer to the entire elevated tract as the Beartooth Range. Most has been stripped of its previous mantle of younger rocks and now only a few remnants sit atop the north portion of the Beartooth Plateau. Rocks on the surface are exposed sections of the earth's crust and are among the oldest rocks discovered in the world. When scientists working for NASA wanted extremely old rocks for their planetary and early crustal genesis studies, they came to the western part of this uplifted and exposed chunk of the crust. In the Absaroka Range geologists found granite-type rock that dated at 3.5 billion years, among the world's oldest known rock.

Although western Montanans think of the Madison and Gallatin ranges as separate highlands, they are part of the same crustal block that was pushed upward like the Beartooth block to the east. Geologic evidence suggests that they and the Beartooth were part of the same large block during at least the initial period of uplift. A fault along the east side of the Paradise Valley apparently developed later, separating the block and allowing the eastern portion of the Madison-Gallatin block to tilt downward, forming the Paradise Valley. This tilting may help explain why the lava flows of 50 million years ago piled up to such depth over the Gallatins—they simply filled in a lower area.

Mountain-building forces also spilled over into north-central Montana. This time, molten material not only reached near the surface, it also flowed out as lava and, in some places, spewed from volcanos. About

50 million years ago, laccoliths intruded in a 25-mile-long arc under the area of the present-day Sweetgrass Hills. Most of these intrusives clustered in three groupings corresponding with today's West, Middle and East Buttes. West Butte, at 6,981 feet, is the highest in the Hills, but East Butte has several peaks above 6,000 feet. South of the main Sweetgrass Hills, Grassy and Haystack buttes, two other exposed laccoliths, rise as lone sentinels 700 to 800 feet above the surrounding terrain.

Reaching 2,500 feet above the plains, the Sweetgrass Hills are visible for a hundred miles on a clear day, and were an important landmark for the migrating Blackfeet Indians. The presence of tipi rings today suggests that they used the slopes of these forested highlands as seasonal hunting camps. Later, in the 1890s, gold-bearing deposits in Middle Butte attracted hundreds of miners. The little-known town of Gold Butte, which developed south of the mines to serve the local population, was short-lived.

Twenty-five miles south of Havre, the peaks of the Bears Paw Mountains punctuate the landscape. They contain the largest area and volume of igneous rocks in north-central Montana. Geologically, their origin is more complex than many of Montana's outliers. Trending east-west through the central portion of the mountains is an anticline, a broad upwarp in the underlying strata. It was bowed upward during the formation of the Rocky Mountains. Piercing these now-exposed sedimentary rocks are numerous laccoliths and other associated intrusives.

Igneous rocks of the central Bears Paw Mountain Arch solidified underground, but rocks to the north and south are extrusives.

MONTANA DINOSAURS

In the world of dinosaur paleontology, Montana is front and center. A string of extraordinary discoveries since the late 1970s

MUSEUM OF THE ROCKIES PHOTO

A triceratops model draws serious attention at Museum of the Rockies.

has made eastern Montana's late-Cretaceous badlands and Montana State University's Museum of the Rockies the epicenter of dinosaur science. Dr. Jack Horner, media-assaulted paleontologist at the Bozeman museum, has been the dinosaur sleuth and guiding force in moving Montana into the contemporary dinosaur limelight. Given worldwide interest in dinosaurs, especially among young people, dinosaur specialist Horner may be Montana's most famous resident.

Eastern Montana has a long history of yielding startling dinosaur finds. In 1902 a fossil-hunting team working in a section of Garfield County north of Jordan made a discovery that shocked the scientific world. The expedition was from the American Museum

in New York City, its leader was noted dinosaur collector Barnum Brown, and their discovery was something that no scientist had ever seen—the remains of the largest carnivore ever to have walked the earth. This was *Tyrannosaurus rex*, the "king of the tyrant lizards." Few at the time even speculated that such a creature ever had lived, but here was the world's first proof, lying just beneath the surface outside Jordan, Montana. One skeleton would have sufficed, but Brown's party unearthed two excellent specimens!

In the last 90 years only six other *T. rex* skeletons have been discovered. Garfield County, specifically the late-Cretaceous Hell Creek Sandstone in the Charles M. Russell Wildlife Refuge area along the Missouri River, has yielded more *T. rex* than any other place on earth. In 1987 while on an outing in the Refuge, Garfield County ranchers Thomas and Cathy Wankel discovered the world's largest and first essentially complete skeleton. Paleontologists from the Museum of the Rockies excavated the specimen in the summer of 1990, and this time the *T. rex* will remain in Montana, at the Bozeman museum. Previously, all Montana *T. rex* were shipped out of state for display in museums in New York City, Pittsburgh and Los Angeles.

Despite the celebrity status of *T. rex* among the general populace, paleontologists know surprisingly little about this creature. A full-grown adult evidently weighed between 14,000 and 16,000 pounds and measured up to 40 feet in length. Upright, they carried their massive heads 18 to 20 feet above the ground. Their powerful four-foot-long, muscle-bound jaws were equipped with dozens of dagger-like, serrated six-inch-long teeth that cut like steak knives. Eight-

inch-long talons on each of their six toes added to the creatures' ferocious image.

Several years' scientific analysis of their remarkably complete and telling specimen should allow Dr. Horner and his staff to shed light on this high profile Cretaceous species. New insight was immediately forthcoming. Analysis of the creature's forelimb and an associated biomechanical study suggest the animal's relatively diminutive, three-foot-long arm was capable of lifting more than 400 pounds. No one knows for sure yet what that means. But Horner and some other dinosaur specialists think the monster-movie image of an aggressive predator is inaccurate. More likely, they think, this was an animal that lived primarily on carrion. Rather than capturing their own prey, they may have been hyena-like followers, which just cleaned up what more efficient species of hunting dinosaurs left behind. If this was the case, the Hulk Hogan-sized arms were not those of a flesh-tearing Godzilla, they simply were used to pick up dead animals.

Revolutionary reinterpretations are Jack Horner's stock and trade. This Shelby, Montana, native rose to international prominence in the dinosaur world in the late-1970s. While hunting for dinosaur bones one summer near Choteau with friend Bob Makela, he discovered a deposit that eventually would yield dinosaur eggs, nests and thousands of juvenile duck-billed dinosaurs and one herd of 10,000 individuals evidently caught in a Cretaceous mudslide. Finds at Egg Mountain, as the site became known, led Horner to deduce that dinosaurs cared for their young in nests, much like birds. Some find his cold-blooded/warm-blooded dinosaur argument equally innovative. Such revolutionary thinking might help explain his

MacArthur Foundation "genius award," a five-year grant that pays him $1,000 for each year of his age.

Although *Tyrannosaurus* was the most famous resident of Cretaceous eastern Montana, other dinosaurs shared this then more tropical world. Like their kin, the duck-billed dinosaurs unearthed at Egg Mountain were up to 25 feet long and probably frequented swampy areas where they fed on lush vegetation. Unable to fend off the large carnivores of the time, they probably sought refuge in deep water. One hunter was *Triceratops,* with its distinctive bony frill and three long horns, one above each eye and the other on the nose. Up to thirty feet long and weighing as much as ten tons, it was the largest of the horned dinosaurs. A *Triceratops* skull unearthed outside Glendive in 1990 was destined for display at Makoshika State Park, while the skeleton will be added to the *Triceratops* skull collection at the Museum of the Rockies.

While *T. rex, Triceratops,* the duck-billed and other dinosaurs dominated life on land, giant reptiles also went unchallenged in the adjacent sea. The most intimidating of these marine lizards may well have been the streamlined *Mosasaurus,* 30-foot-long creatures not unlike the sea serpents of mythology. Bones of these meat eaters have been found beneath the more famous Hell Creek formation.

Older rocks found lower down in eastern Montana's pancake-like Cretaceous sequence of strata also have produced significant specimens. The 1964 discovery of *Deinonychus,* the "terrible claw," is considered one of the world's most important dinosaur finds in decades. Discovered in early Cretaceous rocks outside Bridger, this nine-foot-long creature with a long, rigid tail held out horizontally, stood on two powerful back legs and was only about four feet tall. Lightly built and carnivorous, it was apparently extremely agile. As its name implies, one of its most distinctive features was a five-inch-long claw attached to a third toe. It was held above the ground and was used exclusively for tearing open prey. Fundamentally different from other dinosaur discoveries, *Deinonychus* lends credence to an ongoing argument against the once unchallenged view of all dinosaurs as lethargic, cold-blooded reptiles.

It is interesting that former Montana residents dead for at least 60 million years have become some of the state's best ambassadors and chamber of commerce sweethearts. State dinosaur digs now are not uncommonly funded by the likes of the National Geographic Society, and press coverage routinely means an army of diverse reporters. "Sesame Street" and *Weekly Reader* staff mix with crews for the PBS "Nova" series, *Wall Street Journal* stringers and television crews from almost any major United States city. At times digs have an international flavor with TV crews from Japan rubbing elbows with European reporters and other foreign press eager to tell their readers/viewers back home about the latest Montana dinosaur discovery.

In Bozeman, the Museum of the Rockies has rapidly evolved into *the* center for dinosaur science and a world-class tourist destination. The recently opened Phyllis B. Berger Dinosaur Hall promises to be a popular attraction with almost 200,000 annual visitors. If that doesn't get dinosaur hounds close enough to the real thing, they can opt for museum-organized summer dinosaur digs.

About 600 people per year enroll in the Museum of the Rockies' week-long Makela Dinosaur Field School at Egg Mountain.

Those unwilling to make that long a commitment can take one of the daily summer-afternoon tours of the mountain. To get there, head south out of Choteau on Highway 287 for about three quarters of a mile and turn west on Bellview Road (there is a sign at the intersection for Pishkun Reservoir). The pavement ends in about a half mile, but continue on another 2 miles or so to a "Y" in the road. Stay to the right and you will end up at Egg Mountain about 10 miles farther up the road. The rewards are well worth the trek.

JOHN ALWIN

This 20-foot-tall Tyrannosaurus rex *skeleton, from Garfield County, is the focal point of the Carnegie Museum's dinosaur hall in Pittsburgh, Pennsylvania. Unearthed in 1902, this skeleton served as the basis for the original description of the species in 1905, giving Montana the distinction of providing the world the "type specimen" for* Tyrannosaurus rex.

They spewed onto the surface as molten lava and today form two large volcanic fields geologically more reminiscent of Yellowstone National Park than of most other areas in eastern Montana. The southern field covers approximately 300 square miles and the northern only slightly less. In places this veneer of volcanic material is itself pierced by intrusive igneous rock.

The dikes and laccoliths of the Highwoods have yielded some of the world's best sapphires and are known by mineralogists and gem collectors the world over.

Geologists now assume that some of these intrusives are merely the remnants of subsurface plumbing that fed active volcanos some 50 million years ago. They would have been the conduits through which lava flowed to the surface. Millions of years of erosion have erased the outline of long-extinct volcanos, and today we are left with wide valley areas between fairly low, rounded crests. Still, the mountains rise high enough to justify eastern Montana's only commercial ski area.

To the resident Blackfeet of the 18th and 19th centuries, this landscape evidently suggested the outline of a bear's claw, since that was their name for the mountains. For Chief Joseph and the Nez Perces, Snake Creek on the northeast flank of the mountains marked the end of their 1877 retreat. After travelling almost 2,000 miles and coming within 39 miles of their Canadian destination, the chief and his party were captured by Colonel Nelson Miles.

For the amateur geologist and mineral collector, the Highwood Mountains probably hold the greatest interest of all Montana outliers. Located 30 miles east of Great Falls, they resemble, geologically, the Bears Paws still farther east. They, too, are a group of 50-million-year-old extinct volcanos long since deeply eroded. As in the Bears Paws, there is an associated volcanic field, this one approximately 120 square miles in size. Highwood Peak is the tallest in the range. It rises to 7,625 feet in the center of the volcanic field and may be the remnant of the region's biggest volcano.

Intrusive rocks, those that solidified before reaching the surface, are also exposed in the area. Included are laccoliths like those in many neighboring outliers. Square Butte, ten miles east of the Highwoods, is one of these exhumed laccoliths. Although only 5,680 feet high, it rises 2,400 feet above the surrounding plains and is a regional landmark. Ringed by cliffs, its 2,000-acre flat top is a majestic platform from which to view the surrounding countryside. Designation of the butte by the U.S. Bureau of Land Management as a Natural Area should help to protect this unique feature.

Dikes are another eye-catching intrusive found on the flanks of the highlands. These are wall-like intrusions of igneous rocks that squeezed up through vertical fissures in the overlying sedimentary rocks and cooled before reaching the surface. Stripped of their surrounding sandstone or limestone, these more resistant rocks are left as narrow ridges that radiate outward like spokes of a wheel. The dikes and laccoliths of the Highwoods have yielded some of the world's best sapphires and are known by mineralogists and gem collectors the world over.

Tucked up against the Rockies southwest of Great Falls is yet another, even older, forested highland of volcanic origin. Most Montanans probably would have difficulty naming the Adel Mountains, this 300-square-mile elevated tract. Driving Interstate 15 between Craig and Cascade, one passes through the center of this pile of volcanic material. One peak reaches just over 7,000 feet, but most are significantly lower. Few recreationists seek out these mountains, but those who do are rewarded with fascinating geological features. Weathered volcanic rocks have been eroded into intriguing landscapes such as the Devil's Kitchen, The Pinnacles and The Sawteeth.

Montanans probably are more familiar with the swarm of laccoliths just north of the Adels. Here, in the apex between the Sun and Missouri rivers, a cluster of more than a half dozen intrusives rises from the plains. Among them are Cascade Butte, Haystack Butte, Crown Butte and Shaw Butte, each a landmark. The area moved Charles Russell, Montana's noted western artist, who chose it as a setting for many of his Old West paintings. Flat-topped and symmetrical Square Butte, seven miles south of Fort Shaw, is recognizable in the background of several of Russell's works. For him the landscape captured the mood of an earlier era when range riders or Blackfeet in battle array might have been seen on the horizon.

South and east of the Judiths, several other prairie mountains and highlands project above the Montana plains. Geologically, they are distinct from most of the north-central Montana outliers. One class includes the Big and Little Snowy mountains, the Pryors and the Bighorns. Each corresponds with a broad arch-like uplift in the ancient underlying rocks of the earth's crust, warped upward during the formation of the main spine of the Rockies.

Continued uplift and erosion have opened window-like holes in the overlying sediment to expose the ancient 600-million-plus-year-old rocks in the core of the Big Snowy Mountains. Most of the rocks exposed in the range are sedimentary layers uplifted when the crust rose about 60 or 70 million years ago. We see them today, draped over the mountain's core. Their homogeneous and gently sloping nature is reflected in the Snowys' relatively smooth outline. Although the Big Snowys rise to impressive heights, the crest of the range is rather tame, lacking the large-scale relief associated with outliers farther north.

Between about 50 to 20 million years ago, Montana experienced a period of relative geologic tranquility. Major processes during that span were erosional, as nature worked at reducing the Ancestral Rockies. Material eroded from highlands was carried by rivers and deposited in adjacent lowlands and within Great Plains Montana. As highlands were worn down and valleys filled in, the natural landscape was subdued and may have resulted in a rather flat and featureless Montana by 20 million years ago.

Today's Rockies. The mountains and ranges Montanans know today probably started taking shape about 20 million years ago when, instead of being compressed as was the case in the forming of the Ancestral Rockies, the region quite literally was pulled apart in an east-west direction. A likely explanation for this is an exceptionally high heat flow below the earth's crust directly under the area. This would have caused the overlying crust to rise and stretch. By at least 20 million years ago,

crustal extensions evidently reached the point where north-south running tensional, or pull-apart, faults developed in the crust, breaking it into numerous large blocks. Even though the entire region rose, some blocks rose higher than adjacent ones. Those that rose the most became fault-block mountains while the others became high inter-montane valleys. In some places new pull-apart forces reactivated existing faults and some former highlands experienced renewed uplift.

Block faulting produced the Second Rockies, the ones we see today in Montana. The nature of these fault-block mountains is most apparent in the more linear ranges like the Mission and Bridger. Both ridge-like highlands correspond to the most elevated western edge of elongate and tilted fault blocks. Vertical movement was most pronounced along north-south faults on their west sides, and today their west faces are the most dramatic, rising abruptly above flat valleys. Certainly one of the most impressive sights in Montana greets travelers heading north on Highway 93 as they crest the hill just north of Ravalli. From this vantage point the mile-high west face of the snow-covered Missions seems larger than life.

Some geologists think that the rivers of southwestern Montana once drained out of the state to the south prior to the formation of the Second Rockies. Uplifting associated with the evolution of today's mountains closed former channels and backed water into large lakes which flooded intermontane valleys. The Bitterroot, Deer Lodge, Madison and Gallatin valleys are blanketed with up to several thousand feet of light-colored, Tertiary-age lake beds. They are

composed of the sand, silt and gravel eroded from adjacent highlands and deposited by rivers on the floor of the ancient lakes into which they drained. Lake beds are seen most easily in road cuts or along steep river banks, where their generally light color and loose, soft nature make them easy to spot.

Certainly one of the most impressive sights in Montana greets travelers heading north on Highway 93 as they crest the hill just north of Ravalli.

Material in these sediments reveal much about late Tertiary time. An abundance of ash attests to continued violent and explosive volcanic activity. Fossil remains of camels, four-tusked elephants and three-toed primitive horses not only help date the block faulting that produced the lake beds in which they are found, but also indicate that Montana was then a much drier, even desert-like place.

After millions of years with their southern outlets blocked by high mountain ranges, new northward-flowing drainage channels were cut across lower divides. The new escape channels that allowed water to drain to the north were cut as steep canyons and gorges through the solid rock of former divides. The narrow canyon of the Madison River through the Beartrap area north of Ennis, the constricted Jefferson River Canyon east of Whitehall and the "Gates of the Mountains" through which the Missouri passes north of Helena may have originated in this manner. Although the lakes have long since drained, their horizontal layers of lake sediments have left western Montana's large intermontane valleys with consistently flat floors.

We should be careful not to refer to the Second Rockies in the past tense, since

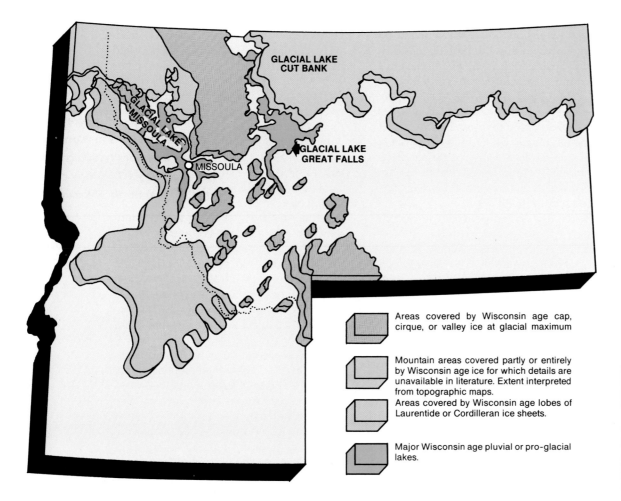

GLACIAL LAKE
CUT BANK

GLACIAL LAKE
MISSOULA

GLACIAL LAKE
GREAT FALLS

MISSOULA

Areas covered by Wisconsin age cap, cirque, or valley ice at glacial maximum

Mountain areas covered partly or entirely by Wisconsin age ice for which details are unavailable in literature. Extent interpreted from topographic maps.
Areas covered by Wisconsin age lobes of Laurentide or Cordilleran ice sheets.

Major Wisconsin age pluvial or pro-glacial lakes.

JOHN M. MONTAGNE, "QUATERNARY SYSTEM, WISCONSIN GLACIATION," FROM *GEOLOGIC ATLAS OF THE ROCKY MOUNTAIN REGION,* 1972

Artistry of the ice

Montana's geologic evolution has continued through the Pleistocene Epoch, which covers most of the last 3 million years. This was a time of major developments in the evolution of the region's physical landscape. A continued uplift of mountain blocks added elevation to western summits, and accelerated stream erosion may have removed hundreds of cubic miles of Tertiary sediments from intermontane valleys and Great Plains Montana. In this epoch, multiple Pleistocene glaciation was one of the most interesting geological processes to help shape the landscape of large sections of Montana.

Both continental and alpine glaciation sculpted Montana. Continental glaciers were gigantic sheets of ice thousands of feet thick covering hundreds of thousands of square miles. The sheet that invaded sections of western Montana during Pleistocene ice ages is known as the Cordilleran Sheet. It formed in the Rockies and Cascade ranges of Canada and spread southward into northwestern Montana, northern Idaho and northern Washington with each glacial period. At its maximum extent in western Montana, portions, or lobes, of that ice sheet reached to just south of Flathead Lake in the Mission Valley and as far down the Swan River Valley as Clearwater Junction. East of the Rockies the expansive Laurentian Sheet pushed southward to the Missouri River and beyond. Alpine glaciation was more of a home-grown phenomenon. Rather than ice invading the state from Canada, alpine glaciers originated within Montana's own mountains, sometimes spreading into adjacent valley areas.

Geologists still are working out the se-

they evidently still are forming. Movement along faults of these great blocks, with valleys dropping down relative to rising highlands, continued through the Tertiary and still is occurring today. This movement generates the earthquakes that periodically shake western Montana and make this region one of the most earthquake-prone in the nation, only slightly behind California.

Alpine Glacial Landforms

Although both depositional and erosional features remain once alpine glaciers recede from an area, those formed by glacial erosion are usually the most striking and easiest to identify.

One of the most common erosional features left by mountain glaciers is the **cirque.** This is a steep-sided, half-bowl shaped depression cut into the side of a mountain by erosion beneath and around the head of a glacier. It is here that snow and ice initially accumulate to sufficient depth to form a glacier and from which the glacier may begin a slow movement down an associated valley. Devoid of ice, these incised basins high on the flanks of mountain peaks are commonly the sites of small lakes called **tarns.** Where the heads of several glaciers have scooped out adjacent cirques around the same peak, it may be left as a sharp angular summit, called a **horn,** once glaciation has ended.

Other conspicuous and distinctive remnants of alpine glaciation are **U-shaped valleys.** Glaciers rarely cut their own valleys, preferring to move down those already begun by rivers. As a large glacier fills and creeps downhill through such a valley it commonly is met by smaller tributary glaciers that flow in from the sides. Once ice melts, the awesome erosive power of the recently retreated glaciers is obvious. Valleys are dramatically altered, with what might have been a winding course replaced by one much straighter. Ridges that formerly extended farther out into the valley are lopped off and left as **truncated spurs.** Narrow river valleys previously V-shaped in cross section are replaced by U-shaped troughs with much wider floors and steep side walls. Since smaller tributary glaciers lack the erosive power of their much larger counterpart in the main valley below, their narrow and less deeply eroded troughs are left as **hanging valleys,** which empty into the main valley high up on side walls. Rivers cascading from these hanging valleys produce some of the Rockies' most scenic falls.

Sharp, serrated ridges are another common and striking landform in glaciated mountains. These sawtooth ridges, called **arêtes,** are formed when erosion by ice in adjacent cirques or valleys wears away and sharpens the intervening divide, just as a rasp hones the blade of an ax.

As they move down valleys, glaciers pick up and push along debris. A pile of material often accumulates in front of the leading edge of the advancing glacier, as it does in front of a bulldozer. Once the glacier reaches its maximum length and starts to melt back, the debris, combined with other material that is deposited by meltwater at the edge of the glacier, are left as a ridge or **end moraine.** As the ice retreats it leaves behind material that has been deposited below the ice forming an irregular surface of low relief called **ground moraine.**

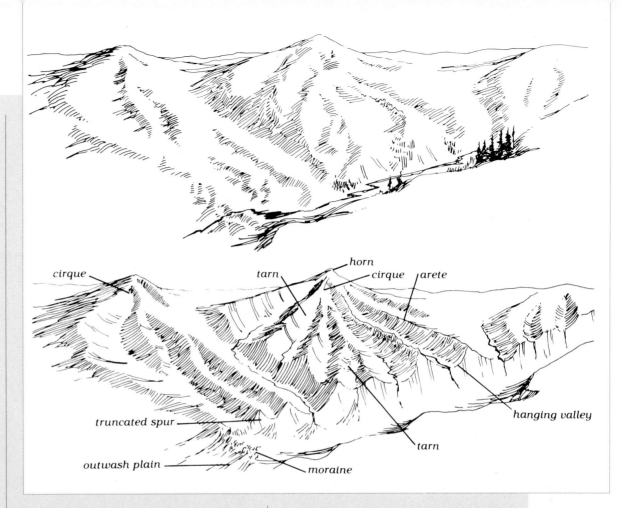

Evolution of the alpine glaciated landscape.

quence and chronology of Montana's continental and alpine glaciation. Whatever the number, interglacial periods separated each glaciation. These were probably times when the climate was warmer and wetter than today and during which glaciers melted. The last Ice Age in the region may have begun about 25,000 years ago and ended as recently as 10,000 years ago—only yesterday in terms of geologic time. Geologists now think that average temperatures during recent ice ages may have been only marginally cooler. More critical was a much heavier winter snowfall and conditions that allowed accumulation to exceed melting. Thus, snowfields persisted and grew from year to year.

During the last Ice Age, and presumably earlier ones, snowfields and, eventually, glaciers developed over many Montana highlands.

Alpine glaciation

As high mountain snowfields thickened, melting, recrystallization and compaction resulted in a metamorphosis of the snow with increasing depth. Freshly fallen, fluffy snow on the surface of the snowfield is underlain by a more compact and granular snow glaciologists call *firn* or *neve*. This is the same kind of granular snow that can be seen in old drifts at the end of winter. At greater depth, compaction further compressed the granular snow until eventually it became glacial ice. When overlying firn and ice reached sufficient thickness, probably at least 90 feet, the bottom layer of ice underwent further deformation and began to spread laterally under its own ponderous weight. Movement down valleys eroded them into troughs and sometimes carried glaciers out into adjacent lowlands to

a point where a warmer climate thwarted further advance and eventually forced the ice to retreat.

During the last Ice Age, and presumably earlier ones, snowfields and, eventually, glaciers developed over many Montana highlands. The largest ice-covered area was the sprawling 60-by-150-mile-long tract in Montana's high and rugged north Divide country. At its maximum extent, this ice cap blanketed the territory from the Whitefish and Swan ranges on the west to the foothills of the Rockies on the east, and from the Canadian border south to the Blackfoot River. In this area that now includes Glacier National Park and the Bob Marshall Wilderness complex, only higher peaks and ridges in the northern section reached above a sea of engulfing mountain glaciers, which spread down into valleys for distances up to 90 miles. At that time this part of Montana must have looked much like sections of Canada's ice-covered high Arctic islands.

Portions of at least two dozen other western Montana highlands also supported glaciers. The largest of these was the complex that covered the higher sections of the Absaroka and Gallatin ranges and the entire Beartooth, spilling over the edges into adjacent valleys. Most other western Montana highlands supported much smaller glacial ice masses, with some of the more extensive of these found on the Cabinet, Crazy, Madison, Tobacco Root and Anaconda-Flint Creek ranges.

The action of these recent alpine glaciers and ice caps added the dramatic scenic sculpting to highlands. Erosion by alpine glaciers sharpens mountain terrain, imparting angular landforms on previously

rounded hills. Glaciated western Montana mountains exhibit all the classic alpine glacial features including cirques, horns, arêtes, U-shaped and hanging valleys and moraines. Glacier National Park is unrivaled as a place to view the spectacular artistry of now-gone mountain glaciers, but other western Montana ranges also display less extensive areas with many of the same features.

Continental glaciation—west

While alpine glaciers and ice caps covered many of western Montana's loftier highlands, a continental ice sheet up to a mile thick invaded the state's northwest corner, filling valleys and smothering all but the highest summits of the Purcell and Salish mountains.

In the last Ice Age the first probing finger-like extension, or lobe, of the Cordilleran Ice Sheet probably inched south into Montana via the Kootenai River Valley just north of Eureka. At that point the Kootenai flows along the bottom of a section of a gigantic steep-sided valley known as the Rocky Mountain Trench. Extending for 800 miles from the Yukon south to Flathead Lake, the trench marks a linear belt under which the earth's crust sank during the formation of the Rockies. The lowland presented the southward spreading ice with its path of least resistance and tended to funnel ice into northwestern Montana.

When the ice lobe reached about as far south as Rexford, evidently it split. A small portion continued up the Kootenai and the main body, called the Flathead Glacier or Flathead Lobe, continued down the Rocky Mountain Trench, passing through the lowland between the Salish Mountains on the west and the Whitefish Range to the east. Glacial *striae,* or grooves gouged in underlying bedrock by harder rocks as they were pushed and dragged along by the overriding glacier, show that the main tongue of ice moved in a southeasterly direction. It paralleled the route of today's Highway 93, passing over the sites of the communities of Trego to Stryker and south through the Olney area en route to the Flathead Valley. As the front advanced southward, even thicker parts of the Cordilleran Sheet followed, crowding the adjacent mountain slopes and eventually lapping onto them. Numerous local mountain glaciers heading in the Whitefish Range to the east flowed down from the highland to join the great Flathead Glacier.

The lumbering Flathead Lobe pushed southward, eventually reaching to just south of Polson where warmer conditions ended a journey that had begun hundreds of miles to the north. Now at its maximum extent, the Flathead Glacier may have had a thickness of 5,000 feet at the Canadian border, and buried the site of Kalispell under 2,500 feet of ice and the south end of Flathead Lake under 850 to 1,000 feet.

The southernmost extent of this ice is marked by the Polson Moraine, a definite ridge rising 500-600 feet above Polson. This is the pile of debris the ice had pushed along its advancing front and left where it came to rest once ice began its retreat. The moraine now serves as a natural dam, holding back the waters of Flathead Lake, which probably occupies a pre-existing, but glacially deepened, basin. Dr. Dave Alt, professor of geology at the University of Montana, thinks the lake fills a basin that marks where a large block of stagnant ice survived for centuries after the end of the last Ice Age. He points to a general lack of other moraines north of here as evidence that the glacier probably withdrew rather quickly, perhaps within a couple of thousand years.

Glacial deposits farther south in the valley tell us that a lobe of ice during the preceding Ice Age may have reached even deeper into Flathead country. Glacial striae just east of the National Bison Range and glacial debris verify that ice reached south to the Jocko River where the thin leading front of the glacier almost encircled the Bison Range, leaving it an island in a sea of ice. Instead of retreating to the north at a steady pace, this glacier evidently backed up haltingly, depositing a series of moraines south of Ronan, collectively called the Mission, or Ninepipe, Moraine. These are much lower and less well-developed than the younger Polson Moraine to the north and constitute a modestly higher belt, with an irregular surface of swells and swales, pock-marked by ponds. Each of these small ponds in the Ninepipe National Wildlife Refuge marks a place where a chunk of buried ice in the moraine melted, creating a depression that has filled with water.

A major extension split from the Flathead Glacier at the north end of the Mission Range and proceeded up the Swan Valley. The north end of the Missions, in the apex of these two glaciers, was buried by ice approximately as far south as Ronan. This explains why the north end of the range is much less jagged than the southern portion, which was sharpened by alpine glaciers. The Swan branch of the Flathead Glacier reached south to Clearwa-ter Junction (intersection of Highways 82 and 200). Cabin owners and other recreationists who retreat to the tranquil string of Swan Valley lakes like Salmon, Seeley, Inez and Alva can thank this glacier for scalloping out these basins and depositing the glacial debris that holds back the water in many.

Glacial deposits farther south in the valley tell us that a lobe of ice during the preceding Ice Age may have reached even deeper into Flathead country.

While the Flathead Lobe pushed south down the Rocky Mountain Trench, other great lobes farther to the west carried the Cordilleran Ice Sheet deep into Montana's northwest corner. The Thompson River lobe pushed up the Kootenai River Valley, continuing beyond its bend to south of where Highway 2 now crosses. Numerous small lakes around Happy's Inn are water-filled depressions left in its moraine, and the Thompson Lakes may be the remnants of a much larger lake that developed along the glacier's margin. A Bull River Lobe spread south along Montana's far-western border area, reaching as far into the state as Bull Lake and perhaps almost to the Clark Fork River.

At its maximum extent, this flood of Canadian ice into northwest Montana reached such a thickness that the Thompson River and Bull River lobes coalesced, smothering all but the highest peaks under ice and linking up with the Flathead Glacier to the east. Glacial striae are etched in the flanks of the northern Purcells up to elevations of 7,100 feet and there are suggestions that ice may have covered everything lower than 7,300 feet above sea level at the Canadian line. At that time, even the highest peaks in the border area, Robinson Mountain (7,539 feet) and Northwest Peak (7,705 feet), reached only a few hundred feet above the ice. Thickness decreased to the south, but not dramatically, and the site of Libby may have lain frozen under 4,000 feet of ice. The dendritic crest of the Cabinets remained as the only extensive area left standing above the Cordilleran Sheet in Montana's far northwest. But even this crest was not free of ice. Sharpened peaks with their associated cirques and U-shaped valleys are tell-tale evidence that although not covered by continental ice, the Cabinets were mantled by alpine glaciers that flowed down to meet the ice sheet, which lapped high up on its flanks on all sides but the south.

The glaciated plains of northern Montana include some of the flattest and most muted terrain in the state.

The Bull River Lobe may not have reached as far south as the Clark Fork River during the last Ice Age, but there is abundant proof that the glacier immediately to the west did. The Lake Pend Oreille Lobe not only reached the river, but also evidently flowed across its narrow valley in the Idaho-Montana border area forming a 2,000-foot-high ice dam. With the river plugged by ice, impounded water from the Clark Fork-Flathead drainage basin backed up, forming a giant natural reservoir called Lake Missoula. Ice-dammed lakes developed in other parts of Montana during the last glaciation, but Lake Missoula is the most famous. The lake's periodic drainage and associated catastrophic floods are of special interest to geologists.

Glacial Lake Missoula. Lake Missoula reached an elevation of almost 4,200 feet above sea level and had a volume of 500 cubic miles. Since its shape was controlled by the pattern of the Clark Fork drainage, its outline was irregular, with arms extending up tributary valleys. The innundated area eventually totalled 2,900 square miles and included all of the Montana section of the Clark Fork Valley to as far east as Drummond, the Bitterroot south to Darby, the Blackfoot to Clearwater Junction, the St. Regis to the Idaho line, as well as the Camas Prairie, Little Bitterroot and Jocko valleys. The Mission Valley also was covered with water lapping up against the southern edge of the Flathead Glacier. The top 700 feet of the National Bison Range was an island in this section of the lake.

A careful look at hillsides in the Bison Range reveals faint horizontal lines that mark former shorelines of Lake Missoula. They can be detected on the west sides of Mount Jumbo and Mount Sentinel, especially when they are emphasized by a dusting of half-melted snow. Lightly colored silt settled to the bottom of the lake and accumulated in thick deposits that still can be seen on hillsides and in road cuts. One of the best exposures is right along Highway 93, on the east side about halfway between Ravalli and Arlee.

The presence of multiple shorelines and layered sequences of lake silts tells geologists that Lake Missoula filled and emptied at least 36 times. A gradual melting back of the Lake Pend Oreille Lobe might have allowed water to flow out slowly, while a rupturing of the ice dam would produce a rush of escaping water. One, and probably many more, of these emptyings was swift and dramatic, and produced landscape features that suggest a flood of catastrophic proportion. Beyond Montana, the bizarre Scablands of eastern Washington are mute testimony to the power of flood waters.

Perhaps the most impressive Montana evidence for catastrophic flooding is the giant ripple marks that can be seen in some areas formerly submerged by the lake. Instead of standing an inch or two high like ripples one might see on the sandy bottom of a river, some of these are made of much coarser gravel and cobble-size material and reach heights of 30 feet! The speed and volume of flows necessary to produce such giant ripples is mind-boggling. One of the best vantage points to see giant ripple marks is from atop Markle Pass, four miles south of the Hot Springs turn-off on Highway 382. When the ice dam burst, water filling the Little Bitterroot Valley to the north rushed through this pass into the Camas Prairie Basin. Looking down on this several square miles of giant ripples at the north end of the Prairie, one can begin to appreciate the volume and speed of water as it raced toward the new outlet.

Continental glaciation—east

The landscape legacy of glaciation also is impressive in sections of eastern Montana. Here, the southern fringe of continental ice that spread outward from an ice cap in the Hudson Bay area of northern Canada, reached into Montana's northern plains. Even though they were at the Laurentian Ice Sheet's southern limits, the glacial ice and associated meltwater had enough power to remake some aspects of the state's physical geography, including realigning the Missouri River.

As the ice sheet spread southward through Canada, it scraped up and pushed along debris. Today scattered across the plains north of the Missouri are thousands of large rocks and boulders that were carried into the state and then deposited when the ice melted. Sometimes these glacial erratics are as large as a car. To geologists, these are especially valuable for determining the glaciers' directions of movement since it is sometimes possible to link erratics with their area of origin. Rock types of some erratics suggest they were transplanted from northern Saskatchewan and northern Manitoba, distances of more than 500 miles.

Northwest of the Bears Paws and four miles east of Box Elder, 3,650-foot Square Butte rises almost 1,000 feet above the plains. The presence of glacially derived granite boulders atop this landmark prove that the ice was thick enough to move over its top. Only the highest outliers in the path of the ice escaped being covered. The Highwoods, Bears Paws and Little Rockies were large and high enough to thwart the southward movement in those areas. Ice lapped up along their northern flanks and, in the case of the Bears Paws, was deflected around the sides. Field evidence is inconclusive, but the tops of the Sweetgrass Hills probably were sufficiently high to protrude above the ice—three islands in a frozen sea.

The glaciated plains of northern Montana include some of the flattest and most muted terrain in the state. Overriding ice not only scoured down and rounded high points, but also left behind glacial material that filled lower areas and contributed to an overall softening of the natural landscape. As the last vestige of ice melted and retreated northward across the border about 10,000 years ago, it left behind a more subdued and flatter landscape. Today's grain farmers of northeastern Montana and the Golden Triangle area can thank this past glacial action for its contribution to the flat to gently rolling land that is well-suited to their extensive and mechanized farming.

In preglacial time the Missouri probably veered in an easterly direction south of Great Falls, by-passing that city site, and flowing from west to east through what is now Sand Coulee. Today tiny, intermittent Sand Coulee Creek looks out of place as it flows east to west through its oversized valley. Judging from its meandering nature, and because its cross-section is similar to nearby stretches of the Missouri, chances are this valley once carried the mighty Missouri.

At the time, the river continued eastward, eventually swinging northward to join its present course near the mouth of Belt Creek, about 10 miles beyond Great Falls. Between there and a point just south of Big Sandy, the preglacial river followed a course similar to the Missouri we know today. But where the present course swings abruptly to the south near its juncture with Little Sand Creek, it formerly continued on a northward course, flowing into the valley that now carries the Milk River just east of Havre. The abrupt widening of the Milk River Valley beginning at this point would thus be explained by its once having carried the flow of the much larger Missouri.

The previous advance of the ice into northern Montana deranged this drainage pattern. At the time of its maximum extent, a tongue of ice reached the Sand Coulee area where it formed an ice dam, holding back the flow of the Missouri. Water backed up, eventually forming Glacial Lake Great Falls. The lake grew to cover approxi-

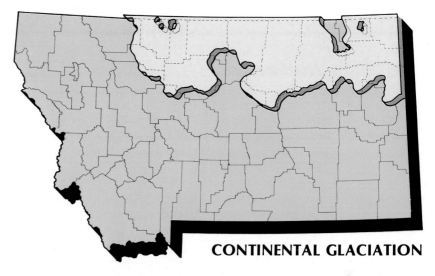

CONTINENTAL GLACIATION

The extent of continental glaciation in eastern Montana.

mately 1,200 square miles, seven times the size of Flathead Lake. It submerged an area roughly bounded by Choteau, Cascade, Belt and Dutton. Located near the lake's eastern shore, the site of Great Falls lay submerged under 600 feet of water!

Blocked by a wall of ice to the north, the lake sought a new outlet. A spectacular spillway developed along the northern flank of the Highwood Mountains, just south of the ice sheet. Vast quantities of water flowing through the area eroded a deep valley up to a mile wide and 500 feet deep. Beyond, the Missouri waters flowed through a new channel that passed south of the Bears Paw and Little Rocky mountains before joining its former preglacial course near Fort Peck.

The melting and retreat of the glacier from the Great Falls area to north of Fort Benton allowed Missouri waters to begin cutting a new and lower spillway. It was at this time that the river's course between Great Falls and the mouth of Arrow Creek, 120 miles downriver, shifted northward and began eroding its present course.

Weatherwise

Weather—especially winter weather—is a frequent topic of discussion among Montanans, some of whom feel proud of their survival in what many Americans see as the nation's icebox. When comedian Jay Leno refers to a frigid state in a joke, there seems to be a better than even chance that that state is Montana. Of late, the Big Sky state even seems to be beating out a more deserving neighbor just to the east. A check of long-term climatic data shows that Montana's cold weather notoriety is not completely justified. Rather than a characteristically uniform and frigid climate, Montana weather ranges from admittedly brisk to a quite moderate Pacific Northwest clime. Striking variation from place to place, not pervasive cold, is the dominant feature.

Montana falls within a broad transition zone between more nearly maritime climates to the west and profoundly continental climates in its eastern plains. The former area is greatly influenced by proximity to the ocean, which heats and cools more slowly than the adjacent land and therefore experiences more moderate temperatures. Winters generally do not get as cold nor summers as hot as places farther inland. In contrast, continental, or land-controlled, climates are far removed from the moderating effect of the ocean waters and the less extreme air masses that originate over them. In the continental interior dramatic seasonal shifts in temperatures between characteristically cold winters and hot summers are the norm.

The highs and the lows

The combination of a relatively northerly location and a situation deep within the continental interior ensures Great Plains Montana a distinctly seasonal climate. More removed by distance and blocking mountain ranges from the moderating effect of the ocean, this region experiences both the state's coldest winters and warmest summers. The northeastern Montana town of Medicine Lake holds the all-time state high temperature record of 117° Fahrenheit, but also has recorded a winter low colder than 40° below zero.

Eastern Montana probably is best known for its low winter temperatures. During winter months it is not uncommon for one of the region's towns to record the nation's (excluding Alaska) lowest overnight temperature. During some cold snaps, Cut Bank probably receives more national exposure than any town in Montana. To many out-of-staters, this Cut Bank Syndrome is extended to include all of Montana.

Bitterly low temperatures often accompany blasts of Canadian polar and Arctic air masses as they push southward out of Canada. The effects are most pronounced in the extreme northeast, where the state's lowest average January temperatures are recorded. Here such towns as Glasgow, Culbertson, Medicine Lake and Wolf Point all experience average January temperatures of less than 10°, and tiny Westby, adjacent to the Montana-North Dakota line, claims the lowest January average at 5.7°. Forty miles away, the 330 residents of Froid (French for "cold") only can guess at their mean January temperature, since the town is without its own weather station.

Winter temperatures gradually moderate in a southwesterly direction and reach their highest in eastern Montana's southwestern corner. Here, Columbus claims a January mean of 22°, Billings and Roundup check in with just over 23° and Big Timber, on the fringe of Great Plains Montana, registers the highest at a balmy 27°.

More ameliorated winter temperatures, in the southwest and northward through such towns as Harlowton, Lewistown, Great Falls and Choteau, can be explained by several factors. Located on the western fringe of Great Plains Montana, these areas are influenced more frequently by moderated Pacific air and, located at higher elevations than most of Great Plains Montana, they often are spared the thermal affront of the bitterly cold air that can blanket topographically lower sections of the Plains.

The term "blanket" is especially appropriate since frigid Arctic air frequently is quite shallow, sometimes only a few hundred feet thick. Because of this shallowness, surface elevations alone may restrict it to the most easterly portion of the state. For eastern Montana slopes gradually from about 5,000 feet at the base of the Rockies to 2,000 feet at the North Dakota line. A several-hundred-foot-thick blanket of cold Arctic air may cover Plentywood, elevation 2,041 feet, but Great Falls, 300 miles to the west and 1,300 feet higher, may be basking in temperatures 30° to 40° warmer.

"Chinook Belt" is the name often applied to this linear region of somewhat ameliorated winter temperatures stretching from Browning south to the Wyoming line. Chinook comes from an Indian word meaning warm wind or snow eater, and it is this wind that temporarily breaks winter's grip on the region. Not just any movement of warm air into the belt is a chinook. A true chinook is limited to warm, westerly winter winds·that have just descended the east slope of the Rockies. Air masses cool and lose moisture as they rise over the Rockies, but then heat up at a more rapid rate on their descent. In Montana the net effect is a modified air mass that is warmer and drier on the east side of the mountains than on the west. The chinook effect is strongest close to the east foot of the Rockies and generally weakens in an easterly direction.

Montana's chinooks have been responsible for spectacular rises in winter temperatures. In fact, the state holds two official national records. The 42° rise in temperature (minus 5° to 37°) recorded at Fort Assinniboine, a former military post (with its own unique spelling) a few miles southwest of Havre, on January 19, 1892, still stands as the 15-minute record. Until January 1981, Kipp, near Browning, held the nation's seven-minute record. That occurred on December 1, 1896, when the temperature climbed 34° . The observer also reported that a total rise of 80° occurred in a few hours and that 30 inches of snow disappeared in one-half day. On January 11, 1981, Great Falls eclipsed this record when the temperature rose an incredible 47° (minus 15° to 32°) in just 7 minutes.

When warming chinook winds are displaced quickly by surges of Arctic or polar air, dramatic drops in temperature are likely. Here again, Montana holds national records. The 100° drop from 44° to minus 56° observed at Browning during a 24-hour period in January 1916 has not yet been equalled. Likewise, the 12-hour record set when the temperature at Fairfield, just west of Great Falls, plummeted from 63° to minus 21° (a drop of 84°) still stands.

As well as helping to explain the somewhat moderated winter temperatures in the swath of territory just east of the Rockies, and sometimes record rises and falls in those temperatures, chinooks also contribute to high average wind speeds. Mention "the Windy City" and most Americans think of Chicago. And yet, that city's average annual wind speed is 10.3 mph compared to the 13.1 mph average at Great Falls. Members of the local Chamber of Commerce probably are not interested in wresting the title of Windy City from Chicago, even though Great Falls really is the nation's windiest metropolitan area.

Although Great Plains Montana winters are cold by most standards, summers are predictably warm. Located deep within the continental interior and far from the moderating effect of Pacific air masses, eastern Montana basks in summer temperatures that often rival those of the Sun Belt states. Regionwide, July and August high daily temperatures average in the mid-80s. Each summer protracted spells of temperatures in the 90s make those who do not have air conditioners wish they did. Miles City checks in with the state's warmest average July monthly temperature of 74.7°, and Glendive is not far behind with its 74°. The

coolest summer temperatures are experienced in the higher outliers where an increase in elevation brings a corresponding drop in average temperatures.

Consistent with a continental location, seasonal temperature variations are dramatic over much of Great Plains Montana. In the far east at Westby, hugging the Montana-North Dakota state line, an average January temperature of 5.7° and an average July reading of 69.5° mean a 63.8° variation. This contrasts with the more maritime 42° differential (January average of 26.5° and July average of 68.5°) at Thompson Falls in Montana's far west.

Chinook Belt is the name often applied to this linear region of somewhat ameliorated winter temperatures stretching from Browning south to the Wyoming line.

As temperatures at these two Montana stations suggest, the maritime–continental contrast between west and east is most pronounced during winter months. It is then that frigid continental Arctic and polar air spreads south out of Canada. While this bone-chilling cold blankets eastern Montana, western Montana often is enjoying milder Pacific air. This explains why overnight lows in eastern Montana communities like Glasgow and Miles City might be 30 below or less, while temperatures in Missoula or Kalispell might not fall lower than a balmy 30° above.

It is not that western Montana is never invaded by frigid Arctic air, it's just that it happens less frequently than on the plains to the east. Higher elevation and the blocking effect of the mountains are not always enough to deflect and keep out the invasions of Arctic air, and periodically they build to sufficient thickness to spill through mountain passes into valleys.

Dramatic drops in temperature often accompany these invasions. Helena experienced a 79° drop in a 24-hour period during a cold wave earlier this century.

Wind and snow still at work sculpting mountains in the Scapegoat Wilderness Area.

Differences between the high pressure associated with Arctic air and lower pressures of the Pacific systems to the west, may result in steep pressure gradients and high winds as more moderate Pacific air is displaced by cold Canadian air. It is these wintery blasts of icy, easterly winds that western Montanans most dread.

Their arrival is accompanied not only by plummeting temperatures and skyrocketing heat bills, but also by the strong easterly gusts that invariably produce the season's worst drifting. To minimize the impact of these blasts, farm shelter belts

in many of western Montana's larger valleys are planted on the east sides of buildings, not on the north as might be expected. Even Missoula, which is considered more of a Pacific Northwest community, has its dignity affronted periodically when so-called "Hellgate winds" funnel frigid Arctic air into the Missoula Valley via the defile of the Clark Fork River (Hellgate Canyon). Similar winds issuing from the narrow gorge of the Flathead River Canyon (Bad Rock Canyon) just east of Columbia Falls have topped 80 miles per hour at Glacier Park International Airport to the southwest.

When the entire state is in the wintery grip of Arctic air, overnight low temperatures in western Montana valleys may approach or even exceed those of plains towns to the east. Virtually all of its communities have record daily low January temperatures of minus 20 or less. Butte's all-time record low is minus 52, Bozeman's minus 43, Helena's minus 42, Missoula's minus 33 and Kalispell's minus 38.

Travel Montana, the state's tourism arm, doesn't brag about it in promotional brochures, but Montana has the dubious distinction of holding the low monthly temperature record in the conterminous United States for six months of the year: January at minus 70, February at minus 66, August at an embarrassing plus 5, September at minus 9, November at minus 53 and December at minus 59. Contrary to what even most Montanans might assume, these low temperature records were not set in places like Cut Bank or Glasgow in eastern Montana; they all belong to stations in western Montana.

The minus 69.7 observed at the 5,470-

foot level of Rogers Pass east of Lincoln on January 20, 1954 still stands as the coldest temperature ever recorded in the lower 48 states. The other five record-setting monthly lows were set at stations in high mountain valleys, with three claimed by the same Riverside Ranger Station between 1924 and 1933. Located just east of West Yellowstone along the Madison River at 6,700 feet elevation, this station might have set the other nine monthly records if it hadn't been abandoned in the 1930s.

The extremely low overnight winter temperatures in western Montana valleys are explained partly by elevation and topography. Temperatures in the lower atmosphere generally decrease with increasing elevation at a rate of approximately 3.5° for every 1,000-foot rise. With many valley floors averaging 5,000 to 7,000 feet above sea level, it should not be surprising that they experience low winter temperatures.

Already-cold overnight readings in high mountain valleys sometimes are accentuated by topography. On still, cold nights even more frigid air from higher up on adjacent mountains may settle into valleys. Cold-air drainage, as it is called, occurs because colder air is heavier, and like water, it moves downhill. This phenomenon, coupled with high elevation, helps explain why such extremely low temperature records are held by valley stations in Rocky Mountain Montana.

Without exception, western Montana communities with the lowest January averages are situated in high, mountain-enclosed basins. Third-ranking Cooke City, hemmed in a narrow valley at 7,600 feet elevation and with mountains rising above

10,000 feet to the north and south, manages only a 13.5° January average. Wisdom, sitting at 6,100 feet in the bottom of the Big Hole Valley, has an average of 12.7°, ranking it second coldest. And the blue-ribbon winner West Yellowstone, at 6,600 feet in the bottom of a high basin in the upper Madison Valley, checks in with the coldest January average at 11.4°. Residents of the Sun Belt must think the Ice Age still lingers in western Montana when, day after day, the national weather report lists West Yellowstone as the nation's cold spot with temperatures bordering on the ridiculous.

Once cold air fills high mountain basins or less elevated and larger lowlands like the Helena and Missoula valleys, it sometimes obstinately lingers for days. Occasionally, even after milder Pacific air has spread over the state and brought warming as far east as the North Dakota line, residents of these western lowlands may have to suffer through several more days of cold. Chillier air remains in valley areas because it quite literally is trapped, held in by warmer overriding air.

In sparsely populated areas, temperature inversions such as this have little consequence other than prolonging cold weather, but in more densely populated valleys they can cause serious air pollution problems. Along with the cold air, car exhaust, particulates and wood smoke are trapped below the inversion and too often reach levels that can be health hazards. With its relatively small size in proportion to population, the Missoula Valley has one of the state's most serious air pollution problems and local government regulates wood stoves and their use. Continued population growth and a reliance on wood-burning stoves are adding to pollution levels in other western Montana valleys as well.

Temperature inversions and the attendant air pollution problems also may develop while the whole region is under the influence of Arctic air. Cold-air drainage may fill valley bottoms with air cooler than overlying air (temperature inversion) and the high barometric pressure that accompanies Arctic air intensifies the problem. High-pressure systems mean heavy, subsiding air movement which increases the likelihood and persistence of cold-air drainage. They also usually mean weak pressure gradients and little chance of the winds and turbulence that are necessary to mix air and flush out valleys.

Most western Montanans don't have to endure the same rigorous winter temperatures as the 913 residents of West Yellowstone or the 100 year-round citizens of Cooke City. Some live in communities with January averages that don't even sound very Montana-ish.

Big Timber's January average of 26.8° is the state's warmest and neighboring Livingston is not too far behind at 25.7°. Farther west in the lower valleys, Januarys are nearly as moderate. Such Bitterroot communities as Hamilton (24.8°) and Darby (25.8°) have helped earn that valley the unofficial title of Montana's Banana Belt. To the north in the Mission and Flathead valleys and west down the Clark Fork, towns have relatively high winter averages by Montana standards. Januarys in St. Ignatius (24.8°), Bigfork (26.1°), Superior (24.8°) and Thompson Falls (26.5°) are all as warm or warmer than in Omaha, Nebraska, Madison, Wisconsin, Chicago, Illinois, or Rochester, New York.

Rocky Mountain Montana is at its climatic best during summer months. Few places can rival it for its nearly ideal combination of warm days, cool nights, gentle mountain breezes and low humidity. Most residents live in valleys where July averages are in the mid-60s. High temperatures typically reach into the 70s and 80s and then drop into the 40s or low 50s at night. Even when daytime temperatures occasionally rise into the 90s, the heat is much more bearable than in the Midwest or on the East Coast where high humidity wilts even the most faithful sun worshippers.

Looking from Hillview onto Missoula— or, at least, onto what is visible during a classic winter inversion.

Higher average elevation and a location less influenced by continental air systems help assure that Rocky Mountain Montana normally does not experience the same hot daytime temperatures as the eastern plains. Certainly one of the most prized climatic traits of these western valleys is their cool summer nights and comfortable sleeping temperatures. A well-known summer visitor of more than 180 years ago, William Clark, commented on this daily temperature disparity while in the Jefferson River Valley in early August 1805. He wrote: "…while we in the valley are nearly suffocated with intense heat of the mid-day sun; the nights are so cold that two blankets are not more than sufficient covering." Today's summer visitors quickly learn why motels make sure guests have extra blankets and that the T-shirt that was fine for daytime outings must be augmented with a sweatshirt after sunset.

Western Montana's large valleys are among the state's driest places. This prevailing semi-arid climate helps explain the extra-cool summertime nights. Once the summer sun sets, the ground begins to radiate heat accumulated during the day. Because of the prevailing dryness of the atmosphere over valleys, there is little moisture in the air to absorb this heat and radiate it back to the surface. Semi-arid conditions also mean that night skies are often clear, with no clouds to help insulate and hold back the heat of the day.

This radiational cooling of valleys begins shortly after sunset and often is accompanied by light breezes of cooler air that drain surrounding mountain slopes and flow in to lift the warmer valley air. Almost like clockwork, light winds begin around 9 or 10 p.m. and provide westerners with a natural air-conditioner. These cool to cold summer nights mean that backyard gardeners often are unable to grow corn to maturity, and green-tomato recipes are sought-after items in higher valleys.

The wet and the dry

The variation in average annual precipitation in western Montana is nothing less than amazing. The region claims the state's driest place—Dillon at 9.55 inches—and its wettest: the higher reaches of Glacier National Park at more than 120 inches per year.

Topography explains the pattern of precipitation and the dramatic variations encountered over quite short distances. Most of the moisture-producing weather systems pass through the region from the west. Pacific air masses moving over western Montana are forced to rise over the Rockies. As they lift, they cool, and their ability to hold moisture decreases. If they rise and cool sufficiently, air masses reach a level where they no longer can retain all their moisture—and condensation and, eventually, precipitation may follow. Such mountain-induced moisture is called orographic precipitation.

Precipitation generally increases with elevation on the windward side of the mountains and reaches its maximum along crests. As air masses move down the east side of the Rockies, they warm and are able to hold more moisture. Subsiding and warming air is not conducive to precipitation and, not surprisingly, lower lee sides of mountains and adjacent valleys in the rainshadow region are predictably dry. Since the Northern Rockies are not just a single ridge, but comprise a series of ranges, the pattern of heavy orographic precipitation over highlands and dry valleys lying in their rainshadow is repeated many times in Rocky Mountain Montana.

In an average year, Dillon (9.55 inches) in the Beaverhead Valley, Helena (10.21 inches) in the Helena Valley, Ennis (11.55 inches) in the Madison Valley and Three Forks (11.7 inches) in the Gallatin Valley each receive less precipitation than such eastern Montana communities as Ekalaka, Miles City and Glendive.

Western Montana valleys tend to be driest in their western half, where the rainshadow effect of the blocking mountain ranges to the west is most pronounced. Precipitation totals increase in an easterly direction where even modest rises in elevation trigger progressively higher amounts of orographic precipitation. This can be seen in the saucer-shaped Gallatin Valley along a 35-mile-long northwest-southeast transect beginning at one of the lowest points in the valley and running up onto the lower flanks of the Bridger and Gallatin ranges. At Three Forks (elevation 4,080 feet) in the western section of the valley, where the rainshadow effect is most pronounced, annual precipitation averages a dry 11.7 inches. Eleven miles to the southeast in Manhattan (4,300 feet) precipitation totals 12.8 inches; at Belgrade (4,500 feet) nine miles farther up the transect, 13.9 inches falls in an average year; ten miles away at the Montana State University campus in Bozeman (4,900 feet) the figure is 18.6 inches; and Fort Ellis (5,200 feet), at the lower slope of the Gallatin Range, receives approximately 25 inches per year. In 35 miles the environment changes from a semi-arid sagebrush- and cactus-riddled landscape to a nearly sub-humid world of moss and pine trees. On the nearby 9,000- to 10,000-foot crest of the Gallatins, precipitation climbs to more than 50 inches per year.

Except in the far west, most moisture falls in the April-through-September six-month period, with May and June the wettest months. Still, orographic winter precipitation is sufficient to pile deep snowpacks on the highlands. Winter snowfall in southwestern mountains like the Crazies, Beartooths, Bridgers and Tobaccco Roots averages between 300 and 500 inches. To the west and northwest these figures rise to more than 800 inches in the Montana portion of the Bitterroot Range and to more than 1,000 inches (more than 80 *feet)* in higher sections of the Missions and Glacier National Park.

Deep winter snowpacks provide western Montanans with excellent skiing at the region's downhill ski areas. Cross-country skiers and snowmobilers are assured deep snows in the high country even in the driest of winters. More important economically is the role this snowpack plays in providing the life-giving waters to irrigated farming in the semi-arid valleys below. Each year, spring and summer snow melt in the high country helps to fill mountain and valley reservoirs and the streams from which farmers and ranchers draw their allotted supply of this critical resource. Statewide, almost 75 percent of spring and summer stream flow comes from melting snowpack.

East of the Northern Rockies, a rainshadow location for Great Plains Montana means most areas receive fewer than 16 inches of precipitation, and vast stretches of the plains pick up less than 12 inches in an average year. Here the pattern of precipitation is much simpler than in Rocky Mountain Montana, and the fairly uniform pattern is broken only by the higher precipitation over outliers. More than 40 inches per year fall on higher sections of the Big Snowy Mountains, and most other major outliers receive more than 20 inches annually. This is also, in part, orographic moisture resulting from cooling air masses, which move into the area and are forced to rise over these topographic barriers.

Warm air rising from these highland areas during warmer months is another factor. Since sloping mountain flanks intercept the sun's rays more directly than surrounding flat land, they absorb more heat. Some of this heat is radiated back into the atmosphere and rises in convection currents from the highlands. Rising air cools and eventually may reach a level where condensation and the formation of clouds take place. This helps explain why, even on hot summer days, outliers commonly have a crown of clouds. If sufficient rising and cooling take place, mountain showers may result. The relatively high 17.5-inch average annual precipitation at Lewistown can be attributed, in part, both to orographic precipitation and to convectional heating.

Like most other arid and semi-arid regions in the world, precipitation in eastern Montana varies markedly from year to year. Annual precipitation in the region rarely equals the long-term average. More commonly, it varies significantly with a grouping of wetter years often followed by a sequence of dry years.

Climatologists and meteorologists have studied this phenomenon, and it now appears that there may be some regularity to this wet-dry succession. Based on his study of eastern Montana precipitation records and investigation of tree rings in the region, Dr. James Heimbach, formerly with Montana State University's Institute of Natural Resources, suggests that a full cycle from below-average annual precipitation to well above, and then back to low, occurs about every 20 to 25 years. Dr. Heimbach thinks this may be linked at least partly to sunspot activity, which itself has a definite cyclical pattern. A better understanding of this precipitation pattern obviously would benefit the region's farmers and ranchers, who could prepare for what may be inevitable drought periods.

Despite these seemingly inevitable inconstancies of weather, eastern Montana farmers and ranchers usually can count on receiving most of whatever precipitation they do get when it is most needed—during the growing season. Long-term records show that all of Great Plains Montana generally gets more than half its annual precipitation during this critical season for crops and grazing. In some areas the seasonal concentration is striking. For example, in just the first three months of the growing season, April through June, such communities as Broadus, Glendive and Poplar receive almost one half of their average annual precipitation.

Cross-country skiers and snowmobilers are assured deep snows in the high country even in the driest of winters.

Weather

Winter as a Montana fact of life:
Right: *Drifted in at forty below on a ranch near Belt.*
Far right, top: *Topping off the antifreeze.*
Bottom: *Easter in Bozeman.*

JOHN ALWIN

GREGG A. HOSFELDT

WAYNE MUMFORD   JOHN REDDY

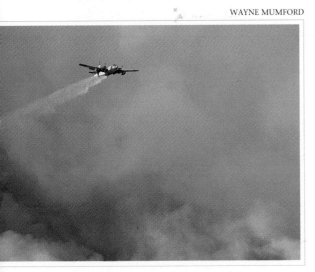

A summer storm panorama includes clouds boiling over mountaintops, lightning that may ignite fires and bring out the slurry bombers, and frequently a rainbow or two at the end.

Vegetative mosaic

Sinuous cottonwood groves along the Tongue River; scrub-pine stands in the rugged Missouri Breaks; ubiquitous grassland-sagebrush plant communities of the eastern plains; a lush mantle of mixed conifers on the slopes of the Little Belts; fragrant cedar groves on the flanks of the Cabinets; fragile alpine tundra high in the Beartooths; and sage and cactus plains in broad southwest valleys—these are just some of the elements in the state's surprisingly varied vegetative mosaic. The picture is much more complex than a forested Rocky Mountain Montana and a grassland covered Great Plains.

Western Montana's subhumid prairie-parkland zone provides some of the state's best non-irrigated grazing.

Although the Montana Rockies generally are thought of as a forested environment dominated by coniferous trees, less than half the region is forest covered. Although the image on page 7 does not show natural tones, the color has been enhanced in a way that clearly differentiates major vegetation types. The dark green of forests easily is distinguished from the valley stringers of green paralleling rivers and identifying large irrigation projects. White areas correspond with elevated tracts above tree line, some tundra covered. Finally, grasslands and sage covered valleys, plains and foothills show up as tan or cream colored.

Zoned by elevation

The vegetative scheme appears chaotic even at this general scale, but the pattern begins to make sense when the factors of topography and elevation are considered.

In a three-dimensional mountainous world, plant communities, as well as climate and soils, are arranged in altitudinal zones, each adapted to progressively cooler, windier and more humid conditions that usually prevail with increasing altitude. Contacts between these layers or zones may be sharp and abrupt, but more commonly they are gradational.

The lowest zone is the semiarid steppe, characteristically treeless except for riparian hardwoods (cottonwood and willow) along stream courses. Western Montana's steppe areas are found in rainshadow settings where annual precipitation may be as low as 12 inches or less. Cactus can be found in places, although various grasses and sagebrush dominate.

East of the Divide, in southwestern Montana, steppe is more extensive than forest. Tucked up in the rainshadow of the main crest of the Rockies and with some places also situated behind local blocking ranges, this corner is one of the state's driest regions. Most sections receive less than 12 inches of precipitation per year, with the driest areas receiving less than 10 inches.

Sagebrush is more common here than anywhere else in western Montana and even more abundant than in many sections of eastern Montana. Not all range experts agree on how extensive sagebrush was in these southwest valleys before the arrival of white settlers, but most acknowledge that overgrazing has led to a heavy invasion by the plant. Present livestock grazing practices perpetuate this condition, but the alteration may predate the arrival of livestock in the region. According to Dr. John (Jack) Taylor, Associate Professor of Range Management at Montana State University, "graz-ing here may have been excessive since the end of the last Ice Age and probably at no time since has this been lush grassland." Large numbers of bison, elk, deer and other grazing and foraging animals must have been lured into these generous, protected valleys by their light to non-existent snow cover. They may have begun a process that has been taken over by cattle and sheep. Taylor points to the sage-covered Virginia City Hill along Highway 287 west of Ennis as just one place that might even be able to support some type of tree cover if not for overgrazing.

The subhumid prairie parkland lies immediately above the semiarid steppe. Its presence is explained by progressively wetter conditions on the flanks of valleys. Vegetatively this is a transition zone from sparse grasses and even some sage at lower levels to more-lush grass and park-like clumps of forest on higher sites, often on shady, north-facing slopes. Western Montana's subhumid prairie-parkland zone provides some of the state's best non-irrigated grazing. The most suitable of these bench lands also are usable for crop production and some have been broken and planted in grain.

Tree cover becomes much more extensive in the next highest, montane forest altitudinal zone. The tree species present in this zone vary geographically and in accord with logging and fire history. The west's montane forest is nowhere more lush and varied than on the wet intermediate slopes of the Columbia Rockies. This is the only place in Montana with commercial stands of moisture-loving trees such as larch, cedar, hemlock and grand fir. Cedar and hemlock cover most humid sites, grand fir occupy intermediate locations and Douglas fir and ponderosa pine thrive in the least humid areas.

The Yellowstone Rockies' and Broad Valley Rockies' montane forestland is less varied and not as lush as that of Montana's far west. Douglas fir is the climax, or naturally regenerating species, although many sites have been replaced by lodgepole pine. Lodgepole has a serotinous cone held closed by a resinous bond that is freed only when subjected to temperatures of at least 113° F. The species therefore is well adapted to seeding itself over newly burned areas. It often comes up as the only tree variety on a burned site and quickly establishes such dense cover that other species cannot get started. The extensive and almost pure stands of fire-maintained lodgepole forests in the mountains of southwest Montana undoubtedly are linked to the region's fire history.

Western Montana's highest forestland falls within a subalpine zone. Englemann spruce and subalpine fir dominate this cool and wet world. Where logging or fire has removed this forest, lodgepole pine, as well as western larch in the Columbia Rockies, has moved in to occupy modified sites.

Above the tree line, a harsh environment of wind, cold and frozen ground rules out the growth of trees except as gnarled and dwarfed individuals in a scattering of protected sites. Here, high elevation creates an Arctic climate and vegetation. This is the alpine tundra zone where slopes are covered by alpine grasses, low shrubs and a surprising display of summer wildflowers—all very similar to those in the vast tundra plains of northern Canada and Alaska.

Western forests

Forestlands may not cover even half of western Montana, but they are basic to the economy and as much a part of the regional identity as the mountains. With large communities such as Missoula, Kalispell, Butte, Helena and Bozeman located in the semiarid steppe and subhumid prairie parkland, surprisingly few residents actually live "in the trees." Nearby forested areas are highly regarded by residents, some of whom are willing to commute long distances to and from work each day for the privilege of living in, or at least adjacent to, the trees of the montane forest or parklands just below. To them a natural, wood-look home in the pines is a western Montana ideal. Bridger Canyon is popular among Bozemanites, as is Pattee Canyon for Missoulians. The forested hills adjacent to Interstate 15 in the Prickly Pear Valley south of Helena have attracted a flood of capital-city workers and have given Jefferson County one of the highest growth rates in the state. Even residents who don't live in western Montana's "Forest Parks," "Mountain Views" and "Blue Sky Heights" are within sight and scent of the region's extensive coniferous forest estate.

With a combined area of about 16 million acres, western Montana's 11 national forests take in the majority of the region's forestlands. In the heavily vegetated northwest corner only a small percentage of Lincoln and Mineral counties is *not* national forest. Across the region, such forest names as Flathead, Deerlodge, Helena and Gallatin are part of the vocabulary of almost every resident.

Passage of the 1960 Multiple Use Sustained Yield Act provided the legal basis for the multiple use of western Montana's and the nation's national forests. Officials must now manage these federal lands for a wide range of often conflicting uses. Timber, water, wildlife, recreation, grazing and minerals must be weighed in forest planning. There probably isn't a single national forest in the region where there aren't ongoing conflicts between timber interests and hikers, snowmobilers and cross-country skiers, or livestock grazers and big-game hunters. Public review and comment are integral elements of the national forest planning process, but that doesn't mean that final management decisions please all.

If western Montana is predominantly shades of green, then eastern Montana is buff, sand, wheat, gold and brown, with accents of green.

Short-grass prairie

Great Plains Montana lies on the western edge of a vast continental grassland that stretches from Texas northward into Canada's western interior. This is the drier side of the plains, and botanists consider most of it part of the short-grass prairie. Vegetative cover within the area is characteristically bunched and sparsely distributed. It clings closely to the ground, intensifying the horizontal dimension and amplifying the sweeping vistas that are eastern Montana. Most of Montana's prairie landscape is dominated by a fairly simple plant community. Vegetation is so uniform that it forces botanists dividing the grasslands into subtypes to consider minor species.

If western Montana is predominantly shades of green, then eastern Montana is buff, sand, wheat, gold and brown, with

DOUG DYE

RICK GRAETZ

JOHN REDDY

VEGETATIVE MOSAIC

Top left:
Mountain ash in autumn color below Pollock Mountain, Glacier National Park.
Top right:
Giant cedars.
Right:
Evergreen forests of the Big Belt Mountains.
Far right: *A sure sign of springtime in the Rockies.*

JOHN REDDY

Top left: Scrub brush near Penney Peak in the Pryor Mountains. **Above:** Pines meet the prairie north of Terry. **Left:** An aspen grove glows autumn gold. **Far left:** Lush spring growth and high water bring floaters to the Smith River.

accents of green. Well before the dog days of summer the flush of green has left most of the prairie. Much to the delight of deer, but to the dismay of nighttime drivers, grasses remain greener along paved highways where runoff increases available water to roadside plant communities.

Howling winter winds drive snow down into the Breaks where it accumulates in massive drifts.

People clearly have put their imprint on these prairie grasslands. Large areas have been transformed into striped grain fields, and formerly weed-free prairie has been invaded by weeds that can be linked to the region's earliest homesteaders. Overgrazing by livestock may help explain the prevalence of sagebrush and saltbush in areas such as the extreme southeast, northern Rosebud County and areas around the Pryors. In the foothills of the Pryors overgrazing by horses, cattle and sheep has altered vegetation even more dramatically. There, scrub, desert-like ecosystems have replaced former semiarid grasslands.

Great Plains Montana is within a large vegetative transition zone between the heart of the plains grassland and the forested Rockies. Accordingly one finds a mix of vegetation from both bordering regions. Eastern Montana may be dominated by grassland, but it is not completely without trees. In fact, there are several different types of forests in the state's eastern two thirds.

The most luxuriant tree cover is found on higher mountain outliers, ecological islands of forests that rise from an engulfing sea of grass. Outliers not only add relief to local topography, they also introduce an obvious third dimension to the vegetative cover. Unlike the main range of the Rockies to the west, most eastern Montana highlands are not high enough for development of alpine tundra altitudinal zones, although summits of the Big Snowy, Pryors and Montana's Bighorns have tundra zones. They also have some subalpine forests of Engelmann spruce and subalpine fir, but most forests on these highlands and other eastern Montana mountains fall within the montane zone. Lodgepole pine and Douglas fir dominate these intermediate elevation forests.

Low highlands sometimes reach into the subhumid prairie parkland altitudinal belt, a transition zone between the forested zones of higher elevation and the grasslands of the semiarid plains. Here vegetation varies from prairie bunchgrass to patchy ponderosa pine. Some forests of the Northern Cheyenne Reservation, the Rosebud Mountains and Custer National Forest outside Ekalaka qualify as prairie parkland.

What might be termed eastern Montana ponderosa pine savanna may be found in areas with a distinctly semiarid climate. These areas are not highlands, so orographic precipitation is not a factor. Such savannas usually get no more precipitation than the 12 to 14 inches received by the surrounding grass-covered plains. This is sufficient moisture to support western wheatgrass or blue grama, but not ponderosa pine. Yet, ponderosa grows and, in some cases, thrives. A zone of pine savanna extends northward from the Yellowstone River between Columbus and Big Timber, and another greets motorists on Interstate 94 between Forsyth and Hysham. This apparent anomaly may have a fairly obvious explanation. Next time you drive by or through one of these savannas, notice how they are virtually always in areas with numerous sandstone outcroppings or fractured clinker formations, "cooked" rock, often sandstone or shale, that lies just above a burned coal seam. Trees grow between the outcrops and sometimes right out of what appears to be solid rock. These rocks absorb little of the moisture from rain or melted snow; most of it is deflected to accumulate in associated soils and debris. This results in a micro watershed that may be several times more moist than precipitation totals suggest and wet enough to support ponderosa pine.

The Missouri Breaks scrub-pine forest occupies the riverbreaks area of the Missouri and Musselshell rivers. Here, ponderosa pine, Rocky Mountain juniper and even Douglas fir mix with wheatgrasses, needlegrass, sagebrush and saltbush. Again, precipitation totals of only 10 to 14 inches annually would seem to rule out tree cover since these trees grow well above the river and its associated water table.

A combination of factors may help explain this scrub forest and the presence of the subhumid Douglas fir. During winters, the huge chasm that is the Breaks acts as a giant snowtrap. Howling winter winds drive snow down into the Breaks where it accumulates in massive drifts. With the warming temperatures of spring these drifts melt and charge the soils and subsurface with huge quantities of water. In places, this soil and other overburden are derived from sandstone and have the capacity to retain large amounts of water, especially when underlain by impervious shale or clay layers. The moisture is available for tree growth during subsequent months. The presence of Douglas fir may be linked to these factors, plus the fact that they grow on north-facing slopes, where shade limits moisture loss to evaporation and transpiration, and wetter ground conditions are more likely.

Floodplain hardwood forests constitute yet another tree element in eastern Montana's vegetative mosaic. Along the Missouri and the Yellowstone and their major tributaries, sinuous and broken lines of cottonwoods add visual and ecological variety to their shores. The floodplain's high water table, seasonal flooding and generally moist soils support the dominant plains cottonwood, as well as box elder, green ash and peach leaf willow, with American elm extending as far up the Yellowstone as Dawson County. For early white settlers within this grassland-dominated landscape, these floodplain forests were often the closest source for timber. Used to build trading and military posts, to fuel steamboats and, later, to erect homesteaders' buildings, corrals and fences, these forests persisted. Now their future is less certain. Increasing control of river flows has reduced or eliminated seasonal flooding which evidently is necessary for cottonwood regeneration.

Above: *George Jacobsen took this picture of home and his first crop on the border of Blaine and Hill counties. Seeds brought in by early-day homesteaders introduced weeds to the prairie, one of many ways humans altered the Montana landscape.*
Left: *When men and horses logged old-growth timber, roading the forests was less severe than with mechanized transport.*

MAKING A MONTANA LIVING

Whether discussing Mongolia or Mozambique, Massachusetts or Montana, it is routine to classify employment as being either primary, secondary or tertiary. A labor force's primary sector takes in all people employed at jobs that involve extracting commodities from nature's storehouse, such as those in mining and forestry, and others that produce desired items by working with nature, such as farming. People engaged in secondary employment work in manufacturing jobs, and increase the value of items by changing their form. Milled grain and other ingredients are combined to produce bread, logs are sawn into more readily usable 2 x 4s and metallic ores are smelted and refined into purer forms. Tertiary employment involves providing services to other people. Everyone from gas station attendant to shoe salesperson, plumber, teacher and dentist falls within this employment category.

When people inhabit an area and set about making a living, they invariably impact and modify the natural landscape and create what geographers call a cultural landscape. This composite of people-induced changes of the natural scene, their imprint, tells much about the inhabitants and their culture, lifestyles, economics, values and relationship with nature. Just like a book, cultural landscapes can be "read" and are so revealing to the trained eye that geographer Peirce Lewis has described them as "our unwitting autobiography."

Western images, Western landscapes

In their *Western Images, Western Landscapes,* Thomas and Geraldine Vale provide a western-specific landscape perspective for defining people's relationship to and interactions with the land. Rather than criss-crossing America's entire western interior in search of landscape variety, this husband and wife pair of geographers opted to use U.S. Highway 89 as a traverse. This historic and scenic route linking Nogales, Arizona, on the south with the Port of Piegan, Montana, on the north was selected as the most representative regional cross-section. After travelling the route on three automobile trips in the 1980s, the authors were able to identify eight distinctive Western landscape combinations. They provide an interesting means for integrating the state's Western images and physical realm, and for tying both to the economics of making a Montana living.

The authors caution that their varieties of Western landscapes/images are not mutually exclusive, that they may overlap and even may be contradictory. Perceptions of the landscapes also may vary markedly from person to person. The eight variants and representative Montana landscapes/images are as follows:

1. **Empty Quarter**—The West as a vast and resource-rich province to be exploited as the East's colony, unable to control its own destiny because of a paucity of population and a lack of political clout. A prime example could be found in sparsely settled Rosebud County, with a just-loaded, 100-car unit train headed east toward a Chicago power plant with low-sulfur coal from the massive strip mining operation at remote Colstrip. In western Montana, mountainside forests pockmarked by clear-cuts would qualify as another example of the West as Empty Quarter.

2. **Frontier**—This is the Old West and the Cowboy West, characterized by what once was and, in many cases, still is long distance between neighbors, combined with dependence on resource extraction. Such landscapes/images are ubiquitous in Montana, from the wooden sidewalks and rustic cityscape with original buildings in Virginia City, to a scene with a cowboy on horseback tending range cattle among the sage and grasslands of Garfield County.

3. **Big Rock Candy Mountain**—Just as for Bo Mason in Wallace Stegner's 1943 novel, *Big Rock Candy Mountain,* the West is seen as a bountiful land of opportunity and a place to achieve the American dream. Landscape elements associated with indigenous wealth are central to this image. These sometimes ostentatious cultural landscapes are more extensive in many other sections of the West than in Montana, where they are perhaps most commonly manifested in up-scale residential neighborhoods. Helena's Upper West Side, with its historic and contemporary

Outfitters packing supplies into the Beartooth Mountains (a classic protected-nature landscape) for their visitors.

mansions of Montanans whose economic ships came in, and fairway-fronting mega-homes in southwest Great Falls' Country Club Addition, are Big Sky examples.

4. **Middle Landscape**—This image is of the West as the ideal setting, the picture perfect, postcard-meriting, utopian blend of cultural and natural landscapes. The landscape viewed from the National Bison Range of the Mission Valley and St. Ignatius tucked in at the base of the towering Mission Range, and the sea-like grain fields of the Triangle region with its complement of elevator-punctuated, cozy little communities with their another-time closeness all typify the calendar-picture prospect of the Middle Landscape.

In our increasingly urbanizing, suburbanizing and humanizing nation, the West has assumed a relatively new role as national reserve for wild nature off limits to intensive development.

5. **Turnerian Progression**—Here reference is to Frederick Jackson Turner and the white settlement frontier so associated with his name. Followed to its most developed state, the "civilizing" process supposedly triggered by the frontier leads to large western cities. Because it has no Los Angeles or even any Seattles or Portlands, this landscape variant has little relevance to Montana.

6. **Desert**—Aridity and scarcity of water over much of the West impose restrictions on land uses and resultant cultural landscapes. Many authors have suggested that dryness is central to the West's identity, one of its defining characteristics. For Vale and Vale this image is one of fragile arid country susceptible to environmental degradation. Although some sections have cac-

ti and residents refer to places as deserts, Montana at its driest is semiarid, not arid. Here there are no Mojaves or Sonorans. Except for small microclimatic sites, Montana has no deserts that are verifiable both botanically and climatically, and this landscape type has limited applicability in the state. A less rigorous definition might allow the driest rainshadow valleys of the southwest and the most moisture-deficient sections of eastern Montana, which average less than 12 inches of precipitation per year, to qualify for this landscape designation. As is common in other arid/near-arid sections of the Western Interior, these areas are dominantly range country, where overgrazing and salinity have been perennial problems for generations.

7. **Protected Nature**—in our increasingly urbanizing, suburbanizing and humanizing nation, the West has assumed a relatively new role as national reserve for wild nature off limits to intensive development. Montana's Glacier National Park, the state's many wilderness and wildlife areas, the National Bison Range and state game reserves all provide excellent examples of Protected Nature.

8. **Playground**—this view of the West is as an expansive and varied playground for the nation and increasingly, the world. Natural, historical and cultural attractions, both indoors and out, are the draw. Condo clusters at Big Sky Resort with Lone Mountain looming large, slip-full docks on Flathead Lake, Butte's World Museum of Mining and the battlefield where General Custer lost—all are Montana examples of Playground-linked landscapes.

Montanans harvesting nature

The first Montanans, its Native Americans, subsisted by hunting and gathering the bounties of nature. For thousands of years this was the only way Montanans made a living—everyone was a primary producer. On a global scale those employed in the primary sector still dominate, with farming the world's number one occupation. In some less developed countries, people employed in agriculture alone account for up to 90 percent of the labor force. But in a very predictable way, employment in primary production begins a pronounced downward trend with the onset of modernization. In some advanced, post-industrial countries that drop doesn't stop until the percentage of primary producers falls to one or two percent.

With about 10 percent of its labor force now engaged in harvesting nature, Montana is no India or Bangladesh, but by U.S. standards its economy does have a relatively heavy dependence on primary employment. This reliance cannot be missed in the state's cultural landscape, where land in farms and ranches accounts for 64 percent of the state's area and cropland alone covers about 28,000 square miles. While agricultural land-use dominates Great Plains Montana's cultural landscape, harvested forest lands and mining-related landscapes are more apparent in the Rocky Mountain section.

Farming and ranching in Montana

Since initial experimentation with farming and stock raising at mission sites in western Montana starting as early as the 1840s, agriculture has been a part of Montana's economic scene and cultural landscape. The picturesque Dutch dairy farming district west of Bozeman, with its neat-as-a-pin farmsteads and scrubbed clean Holsteins—and the sea-like, horizon to horizon golden grain fields of the Triangle region with their complement of windbreak-sheltered farm homes—typify the calendar picture prospect of Montana's agricultural Middle Landscape.

Today, agriculture's importance is obvious from just a few basic statistics. Montana's 24,700 farms and ranches cover more than 60 million acres, second only to Texas in total area, and average a whopping 2,500 acres (4 square miles) each. The 31,000 employed in agriculture generate almost $2 billion annually in government payments and cash receipts from marketing crops and livestock—more than the value of mine and lumber production combined. Montana's agricultural prowess is reflected in the state's early 1990s rankings for barley (2nd), wheat (5th), sheep and lambs (5th), and beef cattle (6th).

Cash receipts from the sale of Montana crops and livestock vary from year to year depending on weather and auction prices for cattle. Over the last decade or so each contributed roughly equal amounts to Montana's agricultural coffers. But an obvious trend developed in the late 1980s with livestock sales consistently outstripping crop receipts.

Livestock. The suitability of Montana for livestock was known even before the initial rush of gold seekers began filling western Montana's dry gulches in the 1860s. Cattle may have been driven into today's Montana as early as the 1830s, but the first large drive of record was Hudson's Bay Company trader Richard Grant's approximately 600 head driven north from southern Idaho's Fort Hall in the mid-1850s. Other owners followed, including the more celebrated Nelson Story and his 1866 herd of 600 Texas longhorns that helped usher in eastern Montana's celebrated and cowboy-crowned open range period. Cattle have been more numerous than people in Montana ever since, with bovines now outnumbering humans by better than three to one. The importance of cattle to Montana is evidenced by the existence of a separate state Department of Livestock, distinct from the state's Department of Agriculture.

The open range may have ended in some sections of eastern Montana as recently as the 1910s and early 1920s, but in the state's cattle country "Range Stock at Large" signs are encountered about as often as stop signs. Here bumpy rides across ubiquitous cattle guards are unavoidable, Stockman's bars and Stockman's cafes are more common than McDonald's, and winning with a prized steer at the county fair is a 4-H member's dream.

Although there are many variants among livestock operations, the Montana cattle industry is dominantly a cow/calf affair. Calves born in the spring are grazed on summer range and grow to 500-600 pounds before they are sold in the fall. Most young animals are trucked to out-of-state stocking operations, especially in such Corn Belt states as Iowa and Nebraska, for additional weight gain before their final feedlot destination and finishing (fattening) on a corn-rich diet. High caloric intake coupled with confinement translates into quick weight gain from 750 or 800 pounds to a desired slaughter weight of 1,100 to 1,200 pounds.

For Montana ranchers, marketing may be the weakest link. Most still depend on order buyers or commission buyers who visit their ranches and make offers on their animals. Others routinely truck their own young stock to out-of-state markets where they seek the best prices on the spot. A few enterprising ranchers have joined to form their own marketing associations. One large southwestern Montana group has been shipping calves directly to Columbus, Nebraska for 25 years. Other smaller groups of ranchers have sent their own agent to the Corn Belt states to establish direct contact with feedlot operators. For all ranchers there always is the more local option of trucking animals to a livestock auction yard in Dillon, Butte, Bozeman, Shelby, Billings or any number of Montana towns.

Greater diversification and larger ranches are two obvious trends in Montana ranching. More ranchers are augmenting cash flows with supplemental yearling operations in which young animals are wintered over and sent to market the following year. As well as raising hay, more ranchers are growing small grains such as wheat and barley to supplement incomes and to help survive the seemingly inevitable down cattle years. If able to overcome a generations-long prejudice against sheep, cattlemen are finding that having their own flock makes sound economic and ecological sense. Sheep, which are able to feed on range too marginal and weed-infested for cattle, allow a rancher to more effectively use available land. They also are about the only means of eliminating some of the most noxious varieties of weeds.

Some Montana ranchers have been able

The Cultural Landscape

About the third week into my geography classes I introduce the cultural landscape by having students step up on their seats and look around the room. By this point in the semester, class members are acquainted with the room and the way it looks. But once they view this familiar surrounding from even this only slightly different vantage point, the room takes on a new appearance. Classroom discussion thus begins with the basic notion that the cultural landscape becomes apparent to those able to develop a new way of looking and a new way of seeing the familiar world around them.

A consideration of the cultural landscape must begin with a brief consideration of the natural landscape that provides the physical stage for the human actors and their landscape modification. The natural landscape is a section of earth space unmodified by the actions of people or their domesticated animals. Here all patterns and processes are of nature and there is no physically detectable evidence of humankind. But as soon as people enter the scene, they set about modifying and altering the land to suit their objectives. In the process of occupying and humanizing the land and making it work for them, people create cultural landscapes.

The conversion process of natural to cultural landscape is much the same the world over, although the specifics of each resultant landscape depend on the modifying group's culture and level of technology. People tend to organize and subdivide land into lots and plots and fields; often borders are marked with fences. In rural areas natural vegetation commonly is eliminated and areas are planted in crops. Houses, barns, sheds and windbreaks; roads, highways and rail lines and a myriad of other features are part and parcel of rural occupancy. An individual sign, drainage ditch or barn is not a cultural landscape, each is but an element in the mosaic of people-affected additions/modifications that, combined, comprise the cultural landscape. Such a pastoral scene, with at least vestiges of the natural landscape, contrasts with even more humanized urban cultural landscapes. Sections of large cities are about as far removed from nature as possible. With property in some central business districts selling by the square foot, land is deemed too valuable to be left to nature—which doesn't provide enough economic return. In such cases, landscapes tend to be dominated by vertical and horizontal concrete and steel.

Landscapes are best viewed from above and that probably is why most real geographers dream of the day when they have their own private pilot's license. I know of many landscape-oriented geographers who refuse to fly commercially except during daylight hours and are prepared to make as big a scene as necessary at airport check-in counters to assure that they will have a forward-of-the-wing window seat.

From the air cultural landscapes are all the more apparent. Checkerboard fields and road networks, strip cropping, irrigated green oases, clearcuts, hamlets, towns and cities all provide silent testimony to humankind's power to remake natural into cultural landscapes. To differentiate between the two, one need only ask, How would this landscape look different if people had never arrived on the scene? Often, the geometry of the cultural landscape, the straight lines and right angles and parallelism and such shapes as squares, rectangles and circles leave little doubt of cultural origins. The color, texture and grain of cultural landscapes also may help differentiate them from nature.

Montana's landscapes run the gamut from pristine natural landscapes to almost totally remade cultural landscapes. But sometimes, even on the ground, it is difficult to differentiate between the two. Natural landscapes are most associated with the state's mountainous backcountry, but even here not all is natural. In sections of the remote Bob Marshall and other wilderness areas, trails, campfires, hunting camps and litter are evidence of people and, in the purist sense, qualify at least in part as cultural landscapes.

In the broad and dry valleys of southwestern Montana what appears to be natural may in fact be subtle cultural landscapes that have been in the making for thousands of years. Over large sections, a long history of periodic burning by aboriginal inhabitants has caused fire-intolerant stands of Douglas fir to retreat upslope and grasslands to expand. Suppression of uncontrolled burning over the last 100 years has allowed Douglas fir to move back into some areas, but a history of overgrazing has resulted in an invasion of these same valley grasslands by sagebrush. Thus impacted by the actions of people and/or their animals, these very natural-looking sagebrush scenes actually are cultural landscapes.

Even tumbleweed, that symbol of the

A contoured stubble field is one sign of humans upon the landscape.

American frontier that adds validity to Zane Grey western scenes and evokes wistful visions of the Old West, is a cultural import from southern Russia. Introduced by settlers in the Dakotas in the late 1870s, the Russian thistle weed quickly diffused through the American West and now is a part of the region's distinctive cultural landscape.

More obvious cultural landscapes include the state's thousands of square miles of agricultural fields. Here domesticated crops such as wheat, barley and hay have replaced natural vegetation and cropping practices including zebra stripe, strip cropping and center pivot irrigation amplify the non-natural nature of landscapes. Nowhere is the humanized aspect of Montana's landscape more apparent than in its largest cities. Here even much of the vegetation is non-native, from the ash and elms to Kentucky blue grass and tulips.

Montana's ghost towns and abandoned farms and ranches provide graphic evidence of the fate of abandoned landscapes. Cultural landscapes can be maintained only with large and continuous inputs of energy. These commonly are in the form of painting and repairs, weeding and other maintenance. Once inputs of energy are cut off, it isn't long before nature sets about reclaiming its former turf. Native plant species quickly begin to re-invade abandoned farm fields and wind, water, ice and snow work at weathering structures. Eventually, the process produces the rustic ghost towns and weather-checked farmsteads so popular with coffee table book photographers. If unchecked, nature's own reclamation project eventually will obliterate most obvious signs of a former cultural landscape and the area will seemingly revert to nature.

to hold on by moving into value-added niche markets. A few have promoted their beef as organic, free of growth hormones and fed on hay grown without use of artificial fertilizers, herbicides or pesticides. Black white-face, or Black Baldies, a Hereford/Angus cross that benefits from hybrid vigor and a resultant more-meat-per-pound of feed, still is the cornerstone of a commercial Montana herd. But even the state's city slickers have been aware of alien cattle on their Sunday afternoon rides. Exotic breeds including Simmental, Salers and Limousin are no longer as novel in Montana. "Everybody's got some exotics" reported Everett Snortland, Director, Montana Department of Agriculture.

Economics have worked against small "starvation units" in the 1980s and 1990s, and many ranchers who have not diversified and/or expanded have been forced out of business. According to Snortland, a 300-cow operation was the minimum size for an economically viable Montana cattle ranch in the early 1990s. Assuming land of average productivity, a 12,000-acre ranch (which could include deeded and leased private and public land) would be the requisite minimum size. Profit-turning ranches range upward in area, with 100,000-acre (150 square miles) holdings not uncommon in Montana's contemporary Frontier Landscape.

In some western Montana valleys, where ranching cattle has been king for more than a century, ranchers' economic challenge is made more difficult by the proliferation of rural subdivisions and second-home developments that occupy land that might otherwise have passed to land-hungry ranchers. Initially, most big spreads

went to usually wealthy and often absentee owners who simply wanted a western Montana ranch to call their own and to which they could retreat during the beautiful three-month summer. These were operated by managers, but making a profit wasn't of prime importance since the main investment was in a cowboy lifestyle. Tax write-offs and rising real estate values assured owners a more than generous final return on investment.

By the 1990s many of these ranches have changed hands several times, and some have been divided into large chunks in turn subdivided into "ranchettes"—parcels 10 acres or so in size, large enough to gobble up vast areas of former agricultural land, but too small to be of agrarian benefit. The recent rash of large ranch purchases by ultra-wealthy, seasonal "cowboys" wanting to buy into an Old West lifestyle removes additional potential and necessary expansion acreage for those whose livelihood depends on ranching.

Cattle and calves are the cornerstone of Montana's sizable livestock industry, generating more than five times the combined cash receipts of all other livestock operations. The state's dairy farming, swine and poultry are not noteworthy on a national scale, nor do they impart an especially distinctive impact on Montana. Among other livestock sectors only sheep and lambs rank in the top tier of states.

Historically, Montana's sheep once far exceeded cattle in agricultural importance, although the sheepherder never achieved the mythic status of the cowboy, and Hollywood stars don't set up Montana sheep ranches. Sheep arrived in large numbers later than cattle, but their numbers increased dramatically until 1903 when the state's flock of almost 6 million ranked Montana number one. Band size declined in subsequent years, with state sheep numbers reaching a 20th century low of just 523,000 in 1983. Competition from cotton and synthetic fabrics, problems with coyote depredations and federal government policies combined with other factors to force many sheep operators out of business. However, in recent years the decline of this dominantly eastern Montana livestock sector has been arrested and numbers have begun to inch upward. Paradoxically, increasing adoption by historically arch rival cattlemen may, at least in part, help explain the turnaround.

With more than 5,300 Montana ranchers dependent on 26 million acres of federal grazing land in the state, Montana interest in federal policy has been more than casual.

As Montana livestock operators look to the future their concerns often focus on national policies that have direct impact on their livelihood. Lately, grazing on federal lands has been the focus of a political storm. With more than 5,300 Montana ranchers dependent on 26 million acres of federal grazing land in the state, interest within Montana has been more than casual.

Critics see the leasing of federal grazing land as both an economic and ecological disaster. In the early 1990s ranchers leasing Forest Service and Bureau of Land Management (BLM) land were paying just over $1.90 per animal unit month (AUM), or the amount of grazing for a cow and calf, or five sheep, per month. Private lease rates are more commonly in the $9.00 to $11.00 per AUM range. Opponents claim below-market rates, which cover only a third of the grazing program costs, make this a gigantic government give-away program.

Criticism doesn't stop there. Opponents point to serious environmental damage linked to overgrazing, destruction of streambanks, water pollution, accelerated erosion and adverse impact on wildlife, including endangered species. At the least, critics demand a steep increase in grazing fees to non-subsidy levels, and some want domestic livestock off federal lands entirely. Writing in an article entitled, "Even the Bad Guys Wear White Hats: Cowboys, Ranchers, and the Ruin of the West," author Edward Abbey sums up much of the more extreme viewpoint. Of cattle he writes, "Almost anywhere and everywhere you go in the American West you find hordes of these ugly, clumsy, stupid, bawling, stinking, fly-covered, shit-smeared, disease-spreading brutes. They pollute our springs and streams and rivers. They infest our canyons, valleys, meadows, and forests." One solution he suggests: "we open a hunting season on range cattle." A longer version of Mr. Abbey's essay was presented as a speech at the University of Montana in April 1985. Obviously Edward Abbey was not a prime candidate for the Montana Stockgrowers Association's "Man of the Year" award!

Ranchers and their organizations—including the venerable Montana Woolgrowers Association (est. 1883) and Montana Stockgrowers Association (est. 1884)—counter with the argument that comparing federal and private leases is like comparing apples and oranges. Kim Enkerud, Natural Resources Coordinator for the Montana Stockgrowers Association, points out that permittees must shoulder many additional non-fee costs when using federal lease lands. These include water supply improvements, fencing, doctoring and "riding on" cattle, all included in private lease fees.

Ranchers argue that they have been making good progress in rangeland improvements and working to correct environmental damage, some dating back a century and more to the open range era. Public lands ranchers see this attack as a frontal assault by outsiders on their lifestyle and the historic lifeblood of the West.

Cereal grains. Just as cattle dominates the livestock sector of Montana agriculture, cereal grains, most notably wheat and barley, account for the overwhelming majority of cash receipts from crops. In recent years receipts from the marketing of wheat alone easily have exceeded the dollar value of all other crops combined. Montana produces some of the nation's best wheat, enough each year to fill a train of more than 45,000 grain hopper cars stretching for a length of 500-plus miles.

Montana produces large quantities of both winter and spring wheat. Winter wheat is planted in late summer or early fall, germinates and sends up tender green shoots before cold weather sets in. The plant lies dormant during winter, but resumes active growth with the warmer days and longer hours of sunlight in spring, and is ready for harvest in the summer. In contrast, spring wheat is planted in spring and harvested in late summer or early fall. If farmers have a choice, they opt for winter wheat, which rewards them with consistently more bushels per acre.

Commercial grain farming requires a lot of land, attested to by the fact that commercial grain farms in the state generally run more than 3,000 acres in size. Since mechanization is essential, the flatter the land the better. Thanks to the leveling action of Pleistocene continental glaciation, the northern section of Great Plains Montana has plenty of the flattish land so prized by grain farmers. Every county in the state harvests some wheat, but the lion's share of production comes from the north-central counties, Montana's Golden Triangle, and the state's northeast corner.

On a continental scale, eastern Montana's wheatlands are considered part of a large international spring wheat region that stretches from the Dakotas and western Minnesota, northward to the southern Canadian Prairie Provinces and spilling back south into the U.S. to include Montana's far northeast corner and the Triangle region. A closer inspection shows that despite its international affiliation, the Triangle region is a major winter wheat producer.

In most sections of the northern Great Plains, winters are too severe for young wheat plants to survive. But in Montana's eight-county Golden Triangle region a favorable combination of topographic and climatic factors and newer, hardier varieties have allowed plantings of higher yielding winter wheat. Tucked up in the northwestern corner of Great Plains Montana, this region is far enough west and high enough in terms of elevation to be spared the impact of many shallow Arctic air masses that move south each winter out of Canada and blanket topographically lower areas farther to the east. Additionally, a protective covering of snow is usually present, which helps insulate young plants from extremely low and potentially killing winter temperatures and winds. In addition to winter wheat, the Triangle also produces much of Montana's

barley, the state's number two crop, and about half its spring wheat.

Globally, major dryland grain farming areas are in semiarid environments: climatically transitional zones between better watered areas where more financially rewarding crops, especially corn, can be grown, and country too dry in average years to permit even alternate-year cropping of grains. Montana's wheat- and barley-producing districts are no exception. In both of the state's prime dryland grain growing districts, annual precipitation averages a relatively dry 11 to 15 inches. However, as with other arid and semiarid parts of the world, the lower the average annual precipitation, the greater the year-to-year variability. For example, the long term average precipitation in Havre is 11.17 inches; the town received a wet 16.18 inches in 1989 but only 4.99 the following year.

Since the first dryland farmers broke virgin prairie sod in the late 1800s, grain growers in eastern Montana have had to contend with the inconstancies of weather. Drought has been the most persistent scourge. Rather than just one dry year followed by a normal or wet year, a grouping of wetter years followed by a sequence of dry years seems to be the norm. Historically, the wetter periods spawned oversettlement and, just as predictably, the drier years brought a population exodus. The natural landscape of deep-rooted, short-grass prairie in these semiarid plains had adapted to the inevitable drought; but the cultural landscape of shallow-rooted cereal grains fares less well. Holding on and riding out the dry years has been a prerequisite for Montana grain farmers for generations.

When nature cooperates and they are given a fair chance to do what they do best, Montana's grain growers produce wheat that is synonymous with quality and is in demand in the world marketplace. Montana exports about 70 percent of its wheat, most shipped to the Orient from Pacific Northwest ports. Because of its high protein content, American buyers are willing to pay a premium for Montana wheat. The higher protein content means bakers need add fewer ingredients to dough, and the associated higher gluten content makes for good rising qualities. Millers rely on Montana wheat varieties to blend with lower protein wheat from other areas.

Because of its high protein content, American buyers are willing to pay a premium for Montana wheat.

Depressed and seesawing grain prices have forced Montana's cash grain farmers to diversify and to experiment with new crops. Just as livestock growers have adopted some additional cropping, many of the state's grain growers have moved toward a hedging of their bets with somewhat more diversified operations that include livestock. Montana's hog and pig production, long centered in the state's grain growing districts, may have special appeal since on-farm production provides much of the animals' feed requirements. Greater diversity has always been the case in mixed farming districts peripheral to cash grain farming areas where such factors as rougher topography and poorer soil have necessitated more mixed farming operations. Now, once exclusively cash grain operators are learning the value of a more diversified agricultural base from these outlying areas.

RICK GRAETZ

Huddled against a winter storm and waiting for the pickup truck bringing hay bales.

Alternative crops are playing an increasingly more important role in Montana's agricultural economy and are adding variety and sometimes new colors to the state's characteristically golden-grain cropping landscape. Canola, a variety of rapeseed in the mustard family, is one of the more obvious and perhaps "loudest" new crops. Its bright yellow flower is an increasingly common sight in rural Montana.

In our health conscious society, canola—which contains the lowest level of saturated fat and highest level of unsaturated fat of any edible vegetable oil—appears to be a promising crop. As an added bonus, it can be planted and harvested with the same equipment already in use by grain farmers, so it can be adopted with a minimum of changeover expense. Other alternative crops include buckwheat and various nitrogen-fixing legumes including chickling vetch, chickpeas and field peas.

Montana mining

Most Montana historians consider mining in the state to have begun with the 1860s gold strikes, an idea somewhat akin to assuming that Columbus discovered America. Both ignore the role of Native Americans. Indians had been mining for thousands of years in Montana before white miners struck colors at Grasshopper Creek in the summer of 1862.

According to Dr. Tom Roll, Associate Professor of Anthropology at Montana State University, mining by aboriginal Montanans may date back at least 10,000 years. Using today's industry terminology, they practiced quarrying or open pit mining. Their primary objective was chert, a hard rock that these Stone Age hunters could flake into sharp-edged knives, points, scrapers and other tools.

Professor Roll reports that prehistoric chert quarries are common throughout mountainous sections of Montana where tectonic forces have brought the host limestone rock to the surface. Camp Baker quarry outside White Sulphur Springs is one of the most spectacular, with excavations up to 50 feet across and 20 feet deep. On the southern Montana plains, Indians quarried chert-like porcelanite, a baked and metamorphosed clay deposit cooked and hardened by a burning, underlying coal seam. Prehistoric Montanans also quarried soapstone, which they worked into delicate-looking steatite bowls and smoking pipes, and color-rich ores including hematite (red) and limonite (yellow) for pigments.

Placer mining. With the arrival of white gold seekers in the 1860s, mining took on an entirely new character and importance to the regional economy. Following the waning of the California gold fields in the 1850s, miners fanned out into other sections of western North America in search of the precious yellow mineral. One northward advancing prong of the western mining frontier carried miners into the dry gulches of Montana's southwest. While en route to new diggings in the Salmon River country of today's Idaho, John White and a small group of prospectors made the celebrated discovery along Grasshopper Creek that would usher in a new era of Montana mining. The rush was on, commercial mining had begun and Montana would never again be the same. Bannack, Virginia City, Central City, Nevada City and other communities appeared in quick succession. Within two years the densely settled mining district several miles square may have had as many as 10,000 residents.

Montana's mining rush was based on placer mining, which initially entailed working river-deposited sediments with pans and sluice boxes to extract gold nuggets and flakes. This type of mining has little staying power and most of the communities it spawned declined as quickly as they blossomed. As the most promising and easily worked deposits were exhausted and new strikes were made in other western Montana gulches, gold-crazed and transient miners pulled up stakes and moved on to the next dig. The pattern of placer mining boom-and-bust was repeated in hundreds of western Montana valleys in the 1860s and 1870s. In most cases the size of the deposit and the number of footloose miners involved were not sufficient to qualify their temporary encampments as towns.

The pattern of placer mining boom-and-bust was repeated in hundreds of western Montana valleys in the 1860s and 1870s.

Hard rock mining. As the placer phase of Montana mining waned, the territory entered a new and more permanent hard rock, or quartz, mining era, which continues to the present in modified form. Rather than relying on nature to strip away the undesirable host rock and water to transport gold flakes and nuggets to easily worked streambeds, the newer variety of miners dug shafts to access the ores, and built mills to extract the desired minerals. The transition from placer to hard rock mining was not universal or immediate. Some towns almost disappeared before the traditional sluice box of the placer miner yielded to the more sophisticated mills, smelters, and other heavy equipment necessary to crush and treat mineral-bearing rock.

The change to hard rock mining and a shift to the recovery of silver and copper resulted in major changes and help to explain the maturation of Montana from a territory to a state. Wandering individuals and loose small groups of the placer mining phase were replaced by greater population permanence and corporate structure. The new mining required significant capital expenditure, much of which came from the East. Hard rock mining expanded the economic base. Lumbering accelerated to meet the needs of mining and refining companies. Mine shafts had to be shorn, steam-operated hoists and pumps fueled, ores roasted, and structures built. Farmers and ranchers profited from the more stable local and regional markets for their products.

In most cases Montana's new metals mines are within known, historically mined areas, some with histories dating back to the 1860s.

Although more than one historian already has written the epitaph of western mining, don't tell the thousands of Montana miners that mining is just a thing of the past. What to some looks to be a collapse may more accurately be described as a change, characterized by rationalization and modernization. Admittedly mining's future did look bleak in Montana, when on June 30, 1983, mining was officially suspended at Butte, easily the state's most famous mining town. But since then metal mining in the state has experienced a revival.

Gone are the days when each shift change set loose an army of single miners who flowed down hillsides by the thousands in pursuit of manly forms of rest and relaxation. Today, the state's average new-breed metals miner works at a nonunion mine that employs 150 to 350, commuting to and from work in a pickup or Subaru or mini-van just like the rest of us. Much of the mining mystique is gone; it's just a job that, in the early 1990s, pays about $10.00 per hour.

Almost all of Montana's metal production comes from mines with start-up dates in the early 1980s or later. Major contributors include ASARCO's Troy Mine south of Troy (1981-copper/silver), the Golden Sunlight Mine near Whitehall (1983-gold/silver), Montana Resources' open pit mine at Butte (1986-copper/molybdenum), the Stillwater Mine near Nye (1987-platinum/palladium/rhodium/gold), the Montana Tunnels Mine south of Helena (1987-lead/zinc/gold/silver), the C.R. Kendall Mine north of Lewistown (1988-gold/silver), the Mineral Hill Mine at Jardine (1989-gold/silver) and the Beal Mountain Mine west of Butte (1989-gold/silver).

In most cases Montana's new metals mines are within known, historically mined areas, some with histories dating back to the 1860s. Operators have returned to the formerly abandoned Wickes, Sheepeater, Siberia, Rimini and other historic mining districts with improved techniques and new economics. One key is economies of scale. Rather than operating a number of small-capacity mines, new mines move much greater quantities of ore per day. Large capacity, controlled labor costs, and efficiency reduce production costs per ounce and mean lower-grade ores become economical to work. On-site ore process-ing adds economic efficiency to many new mines, although environmentalists cringe at even the thought of cyanide leach pads a million square feet in size. In the mineralized zones of western Montana's Rockies, prospect trenches, open pit mines, slag piles, and cyanide leach pads add to the region's current Frontier and Empty Quarter landscapes.

New, relatively large metalliferous mines, some already in the permitting and development stage, are on-line for the 1990s. Additionally, hundreds of exploration projects are underway in western Montana with primary exploration targets of gold and copper. Some efforts are hobby scale, but others are associated with such mining heavyweights as ASARCO, Phelps Dodge, Cominco, Kennecott, Newmont and Homestake Mining. Metal prices and the health of the national and global economies will determine whether Montana's metal mining boom—which saw the value of metals production increase from $262 million in 1987 to $407 million just three years later—continues well into the 1990s.

Nonmetallic minerals. Industrial minerals are the Rodney Dangerfield of the Montana's nonfuel minerals mining industry—like the comedian, they "get no respect." Gold, silver, platinum and even copper have a special aura, but such industrial minerals as phosphate, talc, limestone and cement generally do not engender a great deal of excitement. Collectively this less-than-glamorous group generates about $30 million worth of production, with only talc being of national significance. One cut-and-fill and three open pit operations near Ennis and Alder employ a total of 300 and rank this southwest corner of Montana as one of the world's premier talc producing regions. The fine white powder has many uses in lubricants, in paper manufacturing, and in its most familiar form as talcum powder.

Coal mining provides only about a third the number jobs as metallic minerals mining, but it generates about the same gross production value as metal ores. Unlike the latter, which are widely distributed throughout the state's western and central mountains, 99-plus percent of commercial coal production is concentrated in a small section of the south-central Montana plains. Six large strip-mining operations at Colstrip, Decker and south of Hardin produce low sulfur, subbituminous grade coal, mostly for export to other states.

Oil and gas exploration and production generally is considered the fourth sector of the state's mining industry. Montana is no Texas or Louisiana when it comes to annual production, but the state recently ranked 14th among oil-producing states and 20th in gas production. Despite persistent and often environmentally controversial exploration efforts in western Montana, the eastern plains remain the center of state oil and gas production.

Montana's first major commercial oil activity dates to 1922 and the discovery of the extensive Kevin-Sunburst Field, just south of the Canadian border. During the 1920s, with its classic Big Rock Candy Mountain Landscape, that area dominated the state's still-young petroleum industry. By 1926 it accounted for almost 85 percent of Montana petroleum production.

The decade of the 1930s saw first wildcatting—and then the number-one state ranking—shift to the new Cut Bank Field.

Rapid development there was linked to higher grade oil and money-rich corporations, including the Montana Power Company, which owned huge acreages. In 1936 the Cut Bank Field climbed to the state's number one position, a title it could claim until the 1950s, when large discoveries were made farther east near the Montana-North Dakota border.

Extreme eastern Montana is located on the western flank of a gigantic, international, subsurface geologic structure called the Williston Basin. Underlying layers of sedimentary rocks in this area are gently inclined, dipping slightly toward the east and the center of the basin. Such a flank location can be an ideal place to look for upward migrating oil and gas. If suitable reservoir rock is present to act as a "sponge" to hold the hydrocarbons, there lies the makings of a wildcatter's dream come true. By 1960 the new fields in Montana's edge of the Williston Basin dominated state oil and gas statistics.

Statewide crude oil production peaked in 1968 at 50 million barrels, with the established Sweet Grass Arch and Williston Basin, and a newer Bell Creek Field southeast of Broadus, accounting for most of that. It has been declining ever since, totaling just 20 million barrels in 1990.

Natural gas production has remained surprisingly stable since the mid-1970s. Based on current production rates and proven reserves, Montana has about 12 years' reserve of crude oil and a 21-year supply of natural gas.

Eastern Montana's short-lived energy boom of the late 1970s and early 1980s may have caused Sidney and other energy-linked towns to temporarily burst at the seams with growth, but high hopes, an influx of Texas and Gulf Coast roughnecks, and a flurry of drilling activity did not usher in a new hydrocarbon renaissance in eastern Montana. On the contrary, it has been downhill since 1981, with the oil price collapse of 1986 only adding to the downward spiral and out-migration of people from boom-turned-bust regions. The number of exploratory wells drilled, a good indicator of hydrocarbon health, plummeted from more than 200 in 1984 to about 50 in 1990. The corresponding drop in employment was almost equally precipitous, falling from over 3,600 in 1985 to as few as 1,500 in 1990. Montana's oil and gas industry may rebound, but only with the return of adequate and more stable crude oil prices.

Harvesting the forests

It is the skidders, choke setters and log scalers called for in want ads in Kalispell's *Daily Interlake,* the *Missoulian,* and other timber country newspapers, those who go out into the state's forests and harvest trees, who make up the primary sector of forest-related employment. These are the workers who produce the logs that will be transported (tertiary employment) to mills, where they will be converted into lumber, plywood, pulp, paper, etc. (secondary employment).

Working in the woods is a tradition some western Montana families pass from generation to generation. It is skilled, backbreaking work that is sometimes dangerous, but pays relatively well by Montana standards. Such jobs currently are hard to come by. Montana's forest related employment always has been cyclical. Recessionary times and high interest rates cause

*Skilled,
back-breaking,
and dangerous
work: logging in
western
Montana.*

America to cut back on home construction, which translates into poor demand for building materials and hence unemployment in Montana's timber-dependent communities. The 1980s and early 1990s seem to have had more than their share of unfavorable wood products markets.

The U.S. Forest Service's "Timber Cut and Sold Report" shows that timber harvest on Montana's national forests declined from 624 million board feet in fiscal 1987 to just 350 million board feet four years later. According to Charles E. Keegan III, Director of Forest Products Industry Research at the University of Montana's Bureau of Business and Economic Research, even an increase in housing starts may not be enough to bring back lost harvests and lost jobs.

Timber availability is the key, and Keegan feels both a projected decline in harvest from private lands and low levels of sales from national forests will limit availability and result in shortfalls. National forest officials point to several factors that contribute to low timber sales, including appeals and court decisions, old growth timber management requirements, threatened and endangered species considerations, harvest histories, and the increasing costs of putting together sales.

A reduced harvest from Montana's national forest lands and a downsizing of the state's entire timber industry have serious survival implications for timber dependent families. Repercussions on some local economies will be devastating. In the early 1990s, Lincoln, Sanders and Mineral counties, all major timber producers, were plagued by the state's lowest per capita income levels and unemployment rates of 12 to 14 percent. Evidently the economic picture may not improve any time soon and, in fact, may get worse.

While some lament reduced timber sales and the resultant ripple effects through the state's socioeconomic fabric, many environmental activists applaud the prospect of stabilized forest ecosystems, with fewer clearcuts, less road building and what they see as new potentials for more sustainable development.

Montana manufacturing

America's traditional Manufacturing Belt is nowhere near Montana. It takes in an east-west swath of territory extending from Boston, New York and Baltimore on the Atlantic Seaboard west to St. Louis and Chicago, includes such industrial clusters as Pittsburgh, Buffalo and Detroit. For more than a century it has been the undisputed center of our country's factory-based economy. Montana is about as far as you can be from this heartland and, not surprisingly, factory jobs never have dominated the state's economy.

Still, manufacturing has been a key contributor to Montana's economic development. A tiny population, by national standards, has meant there never was a large local market for Montana's manufactured products. The key to economic success was serving more distant and much larger markets.

Montana is not home to steel, automobile, refrigerator or television factories. Since the first wheat was milled into flour at St. Mary's Mission in the Bitterroot Valley in the 1840s, Montana's manufacturing has centered on processing locally extracted or produced commodities for export out of state. Natural resource commodities such as logs and ores have a relatively low value per weight and generally are unable to be economically transported great distances in their raw form. Transportation innovations over the last century have helped reduce the economic friction of distance, but it still makes sense to reduce the bulk of Montana's natural resources and ship out at least semi-processed products with a much higher value per weight. It would be economically impractical, for example, for unprocessed ores from the Golden Sunlight Mine outside Whitehall to be shipped far with just 0.054 ounces of gold in each ton of rock hauled out of the pit.

Arrival of multiple railroad lines meant a transportation revolution in the 1880s that linked resource-rich Montana with the outside world's hungry markets.

Metals processing

Historically, factory employment, especially in metals processing, was a critical factor in Montana's late nineteenth century economic take-off. Arrival of multiple railroad lines meant a transportation revolution in the 1880s that linked resource-rich Montana with the outside world's hungry markets. Overnight, factory employment in metals smelting and refining operations generated thousands of jobs.

In the 1880s as copper production at Butte soared, a smelter (the world's largest) was constructed at nearby Anaconda to process the ore unearthed by the world's greatest copper producer. Within a few years, that one factory employed more than 2,000 men, much greater than the 1,200 employed in all Montana primary metals manufacturing in 1991. In the 1880s and 1890s there was additional ore processing in Butte, Great Falls, Philipsburg and other communities that added thousands more manufacturing jobs. Expansion of mining and associated metals processing powered an expansion of Montana's economic base and fueled additional state manufacturing employment, especially in lumber and food sectors. The demographic consequence was a stunning 500 percent increase in Montana population between 1880 and 1900 to 243,000.

Today, by all measures, lumber and wood related manufacturing is the largest piece in Montana's factory employment pie.

Metals processing of Montana-produced ores still is part of local economies in Butte (Weed Concentrator) and Columbus (new platinum group smelter) and at dispersed locations in association with many of the state's newer mines, but the two largest metals processors rely on materials mined outside Montana. At Columbia Falls, a privately owned aluminum reduction facility employs 750 in converting Australian and other overseas-produced alumina to aluminum ingots. In East Helena a lead smelter that dates back to the booming mining and refining 1880s, and that once handled primarily Montana ores, provides jobs for almost 300 workers who now smelt South American ores.

Wood products

Today, by all measures, lumber and wood related manufacturing is the largest piece in Montana's factory employment pie. The industry is represented by operations ranging from father-and-son, back- yard-sized sawmills in many western Montana valleys on up to large mill complexes in the Missoula area, Columbia Falls, Libby and Thompson Falls that produce pulp and paper, plywood, fiberboard and lumber.

Yet here too, the trend is one of decline, most markedly in the last several years. Charles E. Keegan's projection of a possible 25 to 30 percent decline from 1989 employment levels in Montana's timber processing industry within 5 to 10 years appears to be right on target. Final figures for 1991 show that the number of jobs already had dropped by 13 percent to just 7,400.

Add in factory employment in food and kindred areas, printing and all other manufacturing and the 1991 Montana average employment in secondary areas totaled 21,700; ten years earlier that figure was more than 25,000. While some sections of the American West and South, the Sunbelt, have gained some manufacturing jobs of late, Montana is one of the exceptions. Here, percentage losses in factory employment are more reminiscent of Manufacturing Belt states where almost 2 million factory jobs have been lost.

Why hasn't Montana benefited from this dispersal of factory employment and registered manufacturing job gains? There is no single answer, but several recent developments have a direct bearing.

Postindustrial economy

As nations move into a postindustrial phase, manufacturing employment drops. This has occurred in Japan, Germany and Australia, and that is just what has been happening in Montana. A postindustrial employment shift is possible because of an increasingly interconnected global economy. A stroll up and down any Montana supermarket aisle, a visit to a downtown hardware store or a window-shopping trip to a local mall, will bring home the fact that essentials and luxuries of our daily life now come to us from all over the world. One of the obvious trends, which accelerated in the 1980s, was a shift of manufacturing overseas to lower–labor-cost countries, in some cases to just across the border in Mexico.

Multinational corporations, which provide much of the glue for this new global economy, take a worldwide view of operations. For the town of Anaconda, that view proved to be costly. Named after its "parent" company, the Anaconda Copper Mining Company (later Anaconda Minerals), Anaconda was a classic company town. Beginning with its inception in 1883-84, the town's commercial life centered around the massive Anaconda copper smelter complex. In 1977 corporate Anaconda ceased after it merged into the Atlantic Richfield Company (Arco), a Los Angeles based transnational corporation. In September 1980, all 1,000 employees at the smelter got their pink slips, informing them that their jobs would end with the June closure of the century-old smelter. Overnight, this community of 12,000 lost 80 percent of its payroll. The same year the company shut down its Great Falls copper refinery and wire mill at a cost of 550 well-paying jobs, but Arco was not yet finished writing off its Montana operations. Three years later its suspension of copper mining at Butte eliminated an additional 700 jobs and left Montana's mining capital without any mining activities for the first time in the town's history. In three short years Montanans were rudely introduced to a downside of the new global economy and transnational corporations that view Anaconda or Great Falls or Butte no differently than some place in Chile or Zambia.

Footloose industry

In postindustrial societies not all manufacturing ceases, but rather traditional smokestack industries are, to a certain extent, replaced by fewer jobs in newer, cleaner, high tech facilities where workers are more likely to wear white lab coats than hard hats. California's Silicon Valley is one of the best American examples of an industrial region based on the new American factory. Semitool, Inc. of Kalispell perhaps best illustrates this new breed of manufacturer in Montana.

Ray Thompson returned to Kalispell in 1979 and established Semitool, a manufacturer of a rinser-dryer used in the production of computer chips. Employment at his new plant rose to 50 by 1983 and totaled 192 in 1992. Sister company Semitherm was started in an adjacent building in 1985 and now employs an additional 25. Such employment might go unnoticed in Seattle or even in Spokane, but in Kalispell the pair of sibling companies is one of the largest private employers.

Thompson had the option of returning to Montana because his planned business was a classic example of a "footloose" or amenity based industry. Unlike many of Montana's traditional manufacturers that must locate close to low value per weight raw material sources or near major market areas, footloose industries can locate almost anywhere they choose. About the only location requirements for most are regularly scheduled airline passenger service, air courier companies such as Federal Express, and phone/fax service. Limited and high value per weight material inputs can be economically assembled at such locations and high value per weight products produced can be shipped long distances economically, even by air in some cases. Such firms tend to locate in high amenity areas where both owners and employees can benefit from a presumed higher quality of life.

Kalispell, a comfortable community with a very manageable population of 12,000, in a beautiful northwest Montana valley just minutes away from Glacier National Park, Flathead Lake and thousands of square miles of national forests, is about as high amenity as it gets. Bozeman and the Gallatin Valley, which already have lured some footloose manufacturers, offer many of the same high amenity attractions. Access to Montana State University is an added draw. The Helena Valley and the Missoula area are two other prime candidates for new footloose investment.

Thus far no western Montana valley has earned the title of Silicon Valley North. Competition for such clean industry is fierce and competitors literally number in the thousands. Semitool's Ray Thompson isn't overly optimistic on the potential for high-tech in general in western Montana. "Right now our image isn't conducive to outside investing," he said, adding that, in some people's eyes, "Montana is equal to Siberia." Many are convinced the state's heavy tax burden is a detriment to new investment. Given even modest tax relief and encouragement, footloose style manufacturing (including high tech) based on plants that employ from ten people to a few hundred, just might be the next stage in Montana's evolving secondary sector.

Providing a service

As manufacturing employment decreases in postindustrial economies, there is an equally predictable growth in the tertiary sector. In the early 1990s state employment in a broadly defined tertiary or service sector, as opposed to primary and secondary, accounted for 9 of every 10 Montana wage and salary jobs. And during the decade of the 1980s, while employment was dropping in such areas as mining and manufacturing, employment in the services was growing by the tens of thousands of new jobs.

Among service employment, it is not the jobs in law offices, EXXON stations, Sears stores or Wendy's that are distinctly Montanan and help distinguish the state from North Dakota or Alabama. It is the state's tourist industry that is more distinctly Montanan and that draws in a sizable amount of "new" out-of-state dollars.

Montana's spectacular scenery, national parks, wildlife, fishing and Old West tradition are a powerful draw for out-of-staters and, not surprisingly, nonresident travel is an important component of Montana's economy and one of the fastest growing. About 5.5 million out-of-staters visit Montana's Frontier, Protected Nature and Playground landscapes annually for pleasure and non-business reasons. The University of Montana's Bureau of Business and Economic Research's 1991 Outlook reports the state's nonresident travel industry employed an estimated 15,700 full- and part-

WILD WEST WORLD:
A MONTANA FANTASYLAND?

Remember Clark Griswold (Chevy Chase) and his family racing across the country in the family station wagon to visit Walley World in National Lampoon's film *Vacation*? If a group of Montana-based dreamers' plans materialize, Griswold families from throughout North America will be joined by planeloads of European and Japanese tourists at a 47-square-mile Wild West World theme park in Montana sometime in the 1990s.

Wild West World, Inc. is a Wyoming corporation licensed to do business in Montana, and mega-business based on commercialism of the mythic Old West at the world's largest theme park is just what they expect to do.

Plans for the Disneyland-dwarfing scheme already are several years old in the early 1990s, and the corporate board of directors hoped to open gates for business in the middle of the decade.

Specifics on a probable location are hard to come by, but the project prospectus mentioned proximity to both Billings and Yellowstone National Park. Access to an airport served by major carriers and to Yellowstone's millions of annual visitors obviously were prime site requirements.

We're not just talking about another Frontier Town or Roadside Boa Constrictor attraction. This project is ambitious enough to have made Walt Disney blush, something in keeping with the West's own megalophilia. Perhaps the most amazing feature of this Gargantuan development is a 295-foot tall, precast concrete and steel cowboy, taller than any Billings skyscraper, almost 150 feet loftier than the Statue of Liberty and easily the world's tallest statue. An inside-the-cowboy elevator is planned to whisk visitors up to an observation deck, perhaps at about the belt buckle level. Even from that high vantage point it is unlikely one could visually take in all of this sprawling "Old West" attraction.

According to Tom Llewellyn, Billings developer and WWW, Inc. CEO, "Visitors to Wild West World are going to be able to live the life of the Old West." Scattered about the property will be six to twelve ranchettes, actually dude ranches, with bunkhouses, central dining halls, corrals and all the other accoutrements. Dudes would be able to partake of daily rodeos, nightly brandings and hayrides, just like real cowboys!

The less adventurous might opt to board at one of what is assumed will be multiple first-class hotels at the theme park.

Board member and Lolo resident Wes Spiker reports that an 1800s-style steam locomotive would convey tourists between widely dispersed attractions, each replicating a specific Old West time and place.

Plans call for a small Western town replete with false-front buildings, saloons, livery stable, shoot-em-ups and other Dodge City staples. "Fort Big Sky," Indian encampments, a mining camp and other attractions are designed to make the Old West "come to life." A 5,000-acre wild game preserve stocked with buffalo, elk, deer and antelope is planned, and additional thousands of acres will be set aside for Native American culture and artifacts.

If a portion of the project happens to include a section of an Indian Reservation, casino-style gambling may add to visitors' Western experience. When combined with midway rides and cotton candy and a herd of western-style shopping centers, it is assumed that tourists will hole up at Wild West World for several days. Clark Griswold, welcome to the Old West.

time workers in 1989, up almost 25 percent in four years. In 1991, out-of-staters exchanged $815 million for their Montana experience.

Travel Montana, the tourist promotion branch of the Montana State Department of Commerce, does an excellent job of producing colorful and glossy booklets and flyers extolling the virtues of a Montana vacation, and even maintains a toll-free number for travel information. While some neighboring states' travel promotion budgets have been shrinking, Montana's has been growing, in large part because of the 1987 state accommodations tax. At least 90 percent of the revenues generated by that tax must go to promote travel. Each year the tax contributes additional millions to the state travel promotion budget, which totaled $5.7 million in fiscal 1991-92. Compared to neighboring states' budgets this is a respectable total, but still is tiny in comparison to such states as Texas ($26 million), Illinois ($25 million) and Hawaii ($23 million). Luckily for Montanans employed in the travel industry, the state is not a hard sell.

Steve McCool, Director of the Institute for Tourism and Recreation Research at the University of Montana, points out that much of the travel promotion effort over the last ten years has been to remedy Montana's previous lack of image. Evidence suggests they have achieved their goal. He can report that "Right now Montana is hot."

A 1990 study of nonresident travel and tourism by McCool and others at the Institute provides interesting statistical insight into this Montana growth industry. For instance, most out-of-state tourists come from Washington (13 percent), followed by

California (11 percent) and Alberta (8 percent). Highway travellers spend an average of 4.4 days in-state and most typically stay in a developed campground. In a recent year about 82,000 out-of-staters made 445,000 visits to downhill ski areas, coming mostly from Alberta (20 percent), mountain-deficit North Dakota (16 percent) and Washington (14 percent). World-famous fishing lured 157,000 anglers (median age 47) who stayed about 3 days before returning home to California (19 percent), Washington (10 percent), Colorado (6 percent), Alberta (6 percent) and other more international abodes.

Montana in a global economy

Innovations in transportation and communication have made possible a global space-time convergence that seemingly has brought all places in the world closer together—the shrinking world. Quicker and more efficient modes of transportation including containerized shipping, doublestacked trains, swift cargo ships and near-instantaneous telecommunications and faxes have prompted references to our collective global village. The key to economic success in this changed world is thinking internationally and that is just what has been happening in Montana with increasing regularity.

The early 1980s write-off of Montana by Arco introduced many Montanans to the downside of global thinking and an increasingly internationalizing Montana economy. But there also is abundant evidence in the state of the great potential upside for Montanans who think and plan globally and participate in the world economy.

Montana's agricultural commodities

Casting in the canyons of the Dearborn River.

GARRY WUNDERWALD

have plugged into the world economy for generations; the challenge today is to find new overseas markets for traditional products and to develop new exportable items. Both the state's ranchers and farmers have reason for optimism.

Thanks to persistent efforts by Montana's congressional delegation, Japan liberalized beef imports in April 1991. This should bode well for Montana cattle producers. The Japanese beef tastes are quite particular and different from American's lean-beef preference. The challenge for Montana beef exporters is to learn how to satisfy the Japanese, who are willing to pay up to $80.00 per pound of well marbled beef. Serving this lucrative market has meant a bit different geography. Rather than being sent to Corn Belt states for finishing, Japan-bound cattle commonly are shipped directly to California. As well as having an abundance of suitable feed crops that produce the requisite white animal fat (as opposed to the undesirable yellow fat of corn-fed beef), California also is closer to the market. The Japanese demand chilled beef, which limits the days available for shipment, distribution and shelf life in Japan. Operating-room style slaughtering conditions, which limit contamination by bacteria, add extra "fresh" days.

Montana beef has an excellent international reputation for high quality and purity. That repute is critical to quality-conscious Japanese who also are being courted by other beef producers, especially in Australia. Perhaps that reputation is why Japanese investors purchased a large cattle ranch outside Dillon in the late 1980s. Zenchiku Land & Livestock Company, a wholly owned subsidiary of Zenchiku Company of Japan, produces beef for the Japanese market. Its several Japanese cowboys have garnered extensive national media attention in both countries.

Internationalization has become the order of the day for many other state manufacturers.

Montana crops have been marketed internationally for generations. Most of the state's annual $300 to $400 million in wheat exports go to Japan, South Korea, Taiwan and the Philippines, and the majority of the $10 million in barley exports is destined for Saudi Arabia and Algeria.

Today efforts are underway to expand exports to traditional trading partners, and to move on to open now-untapped markets for Montana staples such as wheat and barley, as well as new export crops. Mexico and Brazil, for example, are potential overseas markets for barley. Alfalfa hay, widely grown in Montana, may have promise as a sizable export item if compressed into more transportable hay pellets, already a major agricultural export in adjacent states and provinces. Some Montana farmers have begun raising new specialty crops specifically for foreign consumers. Kabocha squash and buckwheat are two current classic Montana examples. Both kabocha, a fancy buttercup squash, and buckwheat, combined with wheat flour to produce noodles, find a ready market in Japan.

Mining and metals processing in Montana also have entered an increasingly more global phase. It is South American ores that provide raw materials for the East Helena smelter, and the Columbia Falls aluminum factory relies on Australia for alumina, or semi-processed ore. Until 1992, most copper concentrate produced in Butte by Montana Resources was shipped to Japan for refining; beginning that year, some was destined for processing in China. The new platinum group smelter at Columbus produces barrels of concentrate (matte) so rich in precious metals (800 ounces per ton) that they can be economically air freighted to Europe for refining in Belgium.

Internationalization has become the order of the day for many other state manufacturers. Two very different Montana companies are representative of the state's new breed of Montana-scale transnationals. Missoula-based Real Log Homes, Inc. has enjoyed an excellent East Asian market for their pre-cut log home packages for years. In 1992 the Japanese market was serviced by its dealer network with outlets in Tokyo, Saitama, Nagoya, Okinawa and near Kobe. High-tech Semitool of Kalispell is equally committed to international sales, and maintains offices in Cambridge, England; Munich, Germany; and Paris, France.

International tourism is another obvious potential Montana growth area for the late twentieth and early twenty-first centuries. Improvements in air transportation and greater disposable income in the world's more developed countries, many with citizens who earn enviable lengthy vacations, should translate to more international tourism. Overseas visitors to Montana—that is, excluding our Canadian cousins—already total between 35,000 and 40,000 per year. Most are drawn to the state by the promise of spectacular and wild nature and an authentic Old West experience—ubiquitous Montana commodities. In an attempt to garner the greatest possible return on investment, Travel Montana has concentrated its efforts in working with key tour operators, wholesalers and travel agencies, and by participating in high-visibility international travel trade shows. Japan, Taiwan, the United Kingdom and Germany have been the primary target countries. Glacier National Park, Yellowstone National Park, cowboys, Indians, wildlife and wide open spaces make travel experts bullish on Montana's future as an international tourist destination. Greater cultural literacy, and simple steps such as foreign-language menus in restaurants and souvenir shops stocking Made-in-Montana products rather than exclusively those Made in Taiwan or Made in Hong Kong, should help assure that prospect.

Assisting Montanans and their economic transition into the global present is official policy for Montana state government. In 1990 a new position of International Affairs Coordinator was created to serve as the liaison for the governor's office in all international matters. Among the many charges of the state's International Affairs Office are diplomatic contacts, hosting foreign visitors, arranging for foreign trade missions, and promoting international education. The Office also works with the International Business Program at Montana State University to publish the international newsletter, *Montana Global*. The quarterly describes itself as "A Newspaper Dedicated to Montana's Future in the Global Marketplace."

In 1992 Montana maintained four overseas trade offices in Tokyo and Kumamoto, Japan; Taipei, Taiwan; and most recently, Calgary, Alberta, Canada. All offices are legislatively mandated and funded by three entities: manufacturing, agriculture and tourism. So as well as helping Montana companies and organizations find markets and distributors for their products in each country, the state's overseas Trade Offices also work closely with Travel Montana and actively promote Big Sky international tourism. The Taipei office is the major reason why Taiwan is home to more foreign Montana tourists than any country other than Canada.

The Pacific Rim, including neighboring Canada, offers Montana special economic potentials. The geoeconomic center of the world economy now is in the process of shifting from the Atlantic nations to the Pacific Ocean and its bordering nations, the so-called Pacific Rim. Montana and the entire western United States are strategically situated to participate fully in what has been heralded as the Pacific Century. The Rim's fast growing economies, burgeoning populations, expanding wealth, and the dearth of natural resources in many western Rim countries have attracted the attention of globally-focused Montanans. As the economies and societies of this nascent world mega-region become more inexorably intertwined, Montana should benefit from its Pac Rim membership.

In the pre-railroad era Montana firms including Baker & Co. and T.C. Power & Bro. made small fortunes freighting between Fort Benton, the head of steamship navigation on the Missouri River, and the southwestern Canadian prairies. The transborder trade in buffalo robes and bootleg whisky may be gone, but Montana has entered a new contemporary period of Canadian trade. Thanks in large part to the 1989 Free Trade Agreement between the United States and Canada, Montana is benefiting from closer economic ties with our neighbor to the north. Canada, not Japan, is America's number one trading partner. And to the benefit of Montana, Canadian-American trade flow is shifting westward with the increasing economic tilt of both countries toward the Pacific Rim. Three major north-south continental trade corridors are developing to service this increased Western transborder interaction. The central one directly involves Montana. It runs from Edmonton and Calgary, Alberta, in the western prairie provinces southward through Montana and then bifurcates with branches continuing on to Gulf ports and the Southwest/Los Angeles.

Thanks in large part to the 1989 Free Trade Agreement between the United States and Canada, Montana is benefiting from closer economic ties with our neighbor to the north.

Back in Montana, significant first steps already have been taken to facilitate transborder commerce. Since late 1991 trucks travelling Interstate 15, the major Montana-Canada link, have been able to make a money- and time-saving single weighing/inspection stop at a jointly operated inspection station at the Sweetgrass–Coutts border crossing. South of the border along the 36 miles of interstate to Shelby, Montana, Canadian trucks have special exemption from state of Montana vehicular weight restrictions. This enhances Canadian accessibility to the Burlington Northern's main east-west rail line and the Shelby intermodal facility, capable of moving containers to and from trucks and rail cars. In return, Montana truckers have special permission to run extra long rig combinations in Canada.

TROUT

TOM DIETRICH

The term Blue Ribbon trout stream is a Montana original. In 1959 a committee of four state and federal biologists devised a

Trout patiently growing at the Montana State Fish Hatchery south of Lewistown.

classification scheme for the state's fishing streams. The end product was a map on which each class of stream was highlighted by a different color. They adopted county fair ribbon colors, awarding a blue shading to their Class 1 rivers or streams, those of national as well as statewide value. Even though the committee did not apply the term "blue ribbon," it eventually became common usage.

Providing residents and tourists with a guide map to the state's best fishing was not the intention of the committee. The primary objectives were public education and stream preservation. By the late 1950s Montana long had boasted of its 32,000 miles of well-stocked fishing streams. Committee members felt such a widespread notion was dangerously misleading and likely to encourage a false sense of security and complacency. If the state actually had that many miles of high-class fishing streams, what difference would it really make if "just" 20 or 50 miles were lost a year. The committee's objective was to devise a ranking and to convey, for the first time, the relative value of the state's recreational stream fisheries.

Since this resource does not lend itself well to dollar-value assessment, there had been a tendency for it to be undervalued in the planning process. The stream map identified and gave long-overdue recognition to the state's most prized fishing streams, and showed the public, administrators, and planners that even though Montana may have 32,000 miles of "well-stocked streams," only 410 miles were of the highest Class 1 variety. Armed with this information, residents were better able to seek the protection these waters merited.

The original 1959 classification was based on a quantitative and qualitative assessment of four factors: availability/access, aesthetics, fishing pressure, and stream productivity. Seven segments of six southwestern rivers (Big Hole, Madison, Missouri, Rock Creek, West Gallatin, and Yellowstone) totalling 410 miles were designated Class 1 and shown with blue on the stream map. The revised 1965 map showed Class 1 stream mileage had increased to 452 miles, with the inclusion of 51 miles of the Flathead River north of Flathead Lake the only major change.

In 1980, the Montana Department of Fish, Wildlife and Parks classified state streams in a less subjective, computer assisted program. The Sport Fishery Potential component of this newer classification ranked four factors very similar to those in the original 1959 study. Fish abundance was based on the combination of weight and number of trout and other desirable game or sport fish per 1,000 feet of stream. Ingress, or accessibility, to streams was ranked in terms of adjacent land ownership (public versus private). Assignment of an aesthetic grade was based on an admittedly subjective assessment of natural beauty, with obvious detractions including pollution, dewatering, channelization, riprap (especially cars, old washers and dryers), mine tailings, and busy nearby highways. Finally, use was based on actual or estimated fishermen-days per unit length of stream.

According to George Holton, former Assistant Fisheries Division Administrator (and a member of the 1959 and 1965 Stream Classification committees), trout streams with a rating of 1 in sport fisheries potential are considered Blue Ribbon trout streams. This newer classification identifies 551 miles of Class 1 sport fishery (Blue Ribbon) trout streams. Sections of some previously identified Blue Ribbon streams don't show up in this assessment, but several new streams and other reaches on previously identified rivers show up as Class 1.

It may be Montana's southwest trout streams—the Madison, Beaverhead and Big Hole—that are the state's best known international "personalities." Fly rods have been named after them, innumerable articles and ads in publications like *Field and Stream* and *Fly Fisherman* have extolled their virtues, and more than passing mention in books on the world's great trout fisheries has imparted a magic ring to their names among fishermen worldwide.

Those who have donned waders to test their skills in these waters include the likes of presidents and Hollywood glitterati. Many a mere mortal in the region has come face to face with the great and near great on these rivers and found himself engaged in conversation on the salmon fly hatch or the appropriateness of a muddler versus a woolly worm.

Stunning mountain settings are part of the lure of these rivers, but more critical to the reputation of each is its high fertility. One key contributing factor is widespread limestone and dolomite rock deposited by oceans more than 60 million years ago. Rivers and their tributaries passing over these rocks pick up calcium, magnesium, and carbonate. This makes rivers highly alkaline, a chemical condition that encourages phytoplankton—minute, floating aquatic plants that form the base of the food chain for river life. Additional nutrients include phosphorus and nitrogen washed in as by-products of agriculture and leached from the rich soils of grassy meadows contributing more "fertilizer." The net result is an extremely fertile water capable of supporting an abundance of aquatic insects on which trout subsist. Fish thrive like cattle in a feedlot, and some eat their way to record size. Modest stream velocities, favorable pool-to-riffle ratios, streambank cover and suitable water temperature further enhance the sport fishery potential of many reaches.

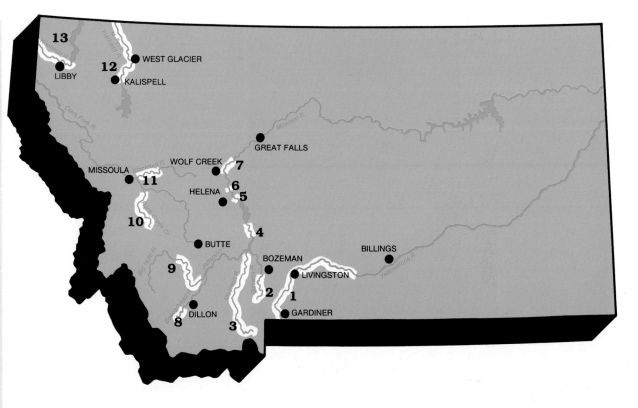

Includes all trout river segments with a "1" (highest) rating for "sport fishing potential."

1.	Yellowstone River	Yellowstone Park to Columbus
2.	Gallatin River	Spanish Creek to Gallatin Gateway
3.	Madison River	Yellowstone National Park to mouth
4.	Missouri River	Toston Dam to Canyon Ferry Reservoir
5.	Missouri River	Canyon Ferry Reservoir to below Canyon Ferry
6.	Missouri River	Hauser Dam to Cochran Gulch
7.	Missouri	Holter Dam to Sheep Creek
8.	Beaverhead River	Clark Canyon Reservoir to Grasshopper Creek
9.	Big Hole River	Wise River to mouth
10.	Rock Creek	Forks at Rock Creek to mouth
11.	Blackfoot River	Clearwater River to mouth
12.	Flathead River (North Fork and main stream)	Canadian Border to Foys Bend
13.	Kootenai River	Libby Dam to Kootenai Falls

Information mapped from Montana Department of Fish, Wildlife and Parks, 1980.

From a national transportation perspective, Montana always primarily has been a transit region, a place that had to be crossed to get some place else. This is reflected in the dominant east-west grain of

MONTANA HISTORICAL SOCIETY

As soon as it was popularized, the automobile revolutionized tourism, as here at Two Medicine Chalet, Glacier National Park.

most major transportation lines from the early Northern Pacific, Great Northern and Chicago, Milwaukee and St. Paul railroads to Interstate 90 and Northwest Airline's routes. Increased Canadian commerce introduces new spatial forces that should mean a strengthening of north-south linkages. Although peripheral in an American

national market, Montana becomes much more central, even a crossroads location in a unified North American market area.

A recurrent theme in western historiography is the West as plundered province, the East's natural resources colony. Proponents point to the lack of sufficient political clout to protect our own interests and extensive federal land ownership—by the Forest Service, Bureau of Land Man- agement, National Park Service and other federal agencies—that removes local control over up to 90 percent of total area in some western states. The so-called Sagebrush Rebellion of the 1970s was mainly an anticolonial insurrection. Late and popular Montana historian K. Ross Toole's 1976 book, *The Rape of the Great Plains: Northwest America, Cattle and Coal,* is in this genre of western history. The role of the West as Wall Street fiefdom is undeniable, but this function clearly has varied over time and space. Anyone familiar with the princely

power and controlling role of the Anaconda Company, "The Company," in Montana's history cannot deny the key role colonialism played in the state's economic development.

The Montana economy and making a Montana living may be at a crossroads stage. Such firms as Model Log Homes, Inc. and Semitool illustrate that Montana can compete with manufactured products in the world market. And there is ample evidence that smaller-scale, even cottage-sized operations, also can do quite well serving a national and global marketplace from a Montana base.

But old ways die hard in Montana as elsewhere and there may be a tendency to fall back on export of low-value raw materials. Such a system is reminiscent of the classic British colonial system in which colonies produced the raw materials, which were shipped to the mother country for processing and manufacture. Expensive, value-added finished products were then sent back to the colonists for purchase. Will Montanans just become the tillers of soil, hewers of trees, and diggers of ores for the Japans, Taiwans and South Koreas and then be required to buy the pricey foreign manufactured goods made with their own natural resources? Will Montanans be content as low-paid motel maids for the world's wealthy having a good time in Montana, while other residents struggle to maintain the live-in wild and Old West diorama so much in demand?

In 1990 Montanans earned an average of 82 percent of the national per capita income, ranking the state 39th. That is an improvement from 1985 when the state bottomed out at 42nd, but a long way from the 1960 rank of 27th. Few residents probably would consider average income levels as the sole or most important measure of well-being, but bouncing along in the bottom quartile of national income levels since the early 1980s has taken its toll on Montanans. The influx of well-heeled out-of-staters has tended to bring home the fact that many Montana families have failed to keep up economically. Unfortunately, social/economic stratification between the haves and have-nots is becoming a more obvious fact of Montana life. In the 1990s hourly wages of $5.00 to $7.00 just aren't enough to raise a family. A neocolonial status within a new global economy probably is not the solution to making a Montana living and sharing in the wealth of the twenty-first century.

MONTANA HISTORICAL SOCIETY PHOTOS

Above: An Alta Deem photograph from 1914 shows a homestead family hard at work obtaining free-of-charge coal from a surface seam.
Left: Axel Olsson, farming south of Joplin in 1912, was proud of his non-irrigated potatoes. For size comparison, he placed an egg in the pile on the ground.

REGION BY REGION

This place, Montana, is immense. Although it can be considered in its entirety, the state's regional richness is most apparent when studied on a more intimate scale.

There is not just one Montana. Topography, geology, climate, vegetation, soils, peoples, history and happenstance have combined to foster a distinct tapestry of many Montanas. State highway maps do not locate or identify the Far West, Historic Core or Central Montana, nor do roadside markers announce when you enter the Big Dry or Yellowstone Country, or when you leave the Triangle or Hi-Line. These regions are perceived to exist—by their residents and others—not because of official designation and delimitation, but because people sense the places have identities of their own and shared features that set them apart from surrounding areas.

FAR WEST

The Far West is the closest thing to the wild, woodsy, mountainous image most out-of-staters have of Rocky Mountain Montana. Except for the roomy and essentially continuous chasm of the Rocky Mountain Trench that runs southward from Whitefish through the Flathead, Mission, Missoula and Bitterroot valleys, almost all of this region falls within the Columbia Rockies. Outside of these more generous and populated lowlands, valleys are nar-

row, and mountains shrouded by lush and varied forests dominate the landscape. Designated and de facto wilderness areas, national forest lands, winding backcountry roads through sparsely settled areas and small and closely knit communities, the whine of chain saws and the roar of logging trucks, huckleberry and lupine fields and occasional moose browsing in roadside streams fit preconceived notions of a picture-postcard Montana.

This is a region in conflict and transition, and the outcome of this unfolding drama is of national importance. On the most general level the clash is one of land use, but that immediately expands to include history, economics, environment, recreation and myriad societal dimensions. How much of the Far West will be maintained in a near-natural state and how much will be exploited and developed?

Depending on one's perspective, the situation is made better or worse by the fact that the Far West is overwhelmingly managed by the federal government. While federally controlled lands in some eastern Montana counties total as little as 3 percent of area, no county dominantly within the Far West is less than 50 percent federally-owned. Among Far West counties, percentage of public domain runs as high as 82 percent in Mineral and 73 percent in both Lincoln and Flathead. Even though residents of Libby, Whitefish, Hamilton and

other Far West communities like to think of the surrounding millions of acres of national forests and other federal lands as their front yard, they more correctly are America's back yard. And what is or isn't done with these lands, in large part, reflects national sentiment, which may be at odds with the wishes of the majority of residents in Libby, Whitefish or Hamilton.

A timber treasury

If Montana is to contribute to the nation's and world's supply of wood and wood products, this section of the state would contribute the lion's share. The Far West's forest estate mantles almost the entire region outside of the large trench valleys and below the high-mountain alpine zones. Both Lincoln and Mineral counties are more than 90 percent forested, and neighboring counties are not far behind. This is Pacific Northwest Montana, where the state's most ameliorated climate and an abundance of precipitation mean a forest cover that extends across valleys and over most mountain crests. In narrow valleys cleared for agriculture, engulfing forests are at the ready to re-invade at the first opportunity.

Forest lands in the Far West have no equal in Montana. The growth potential of commercial forests is classified on the basis of cubic feet of wood growth per acre per year. Sites designated Class V, the low-

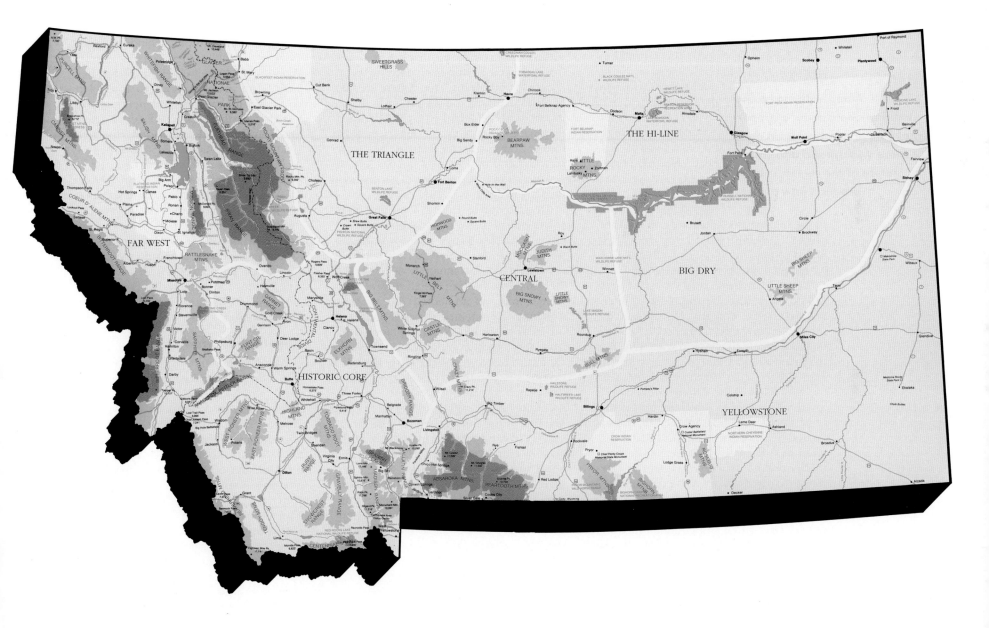

est, produce only 20 to 49 cubic feet of wood per acre per year, while Class I yields more than 165 (an average single-family, wood-frame home contains about 900 cubic feet of wood). The 2.4-million-acre Kootenai National Forest in the far northwest ranks first in the state with a total of 38 percent of commercial forest in the highest Class I and II. Flathead National Forest, another Far West forest reserve, has a corresponding 28 percent of the highest two categories. In contrast, only six percent of the Lewis and Clark, and zero percent of the Gallatin and Custer national forests are so designated.

Along with increasing internationalization, a drop in employment numbers is an even more widespread and critical feature of the region's wood products jobs picture.

Not only are these most westerly forests prolific, they also are the most luxuriant and diverse in Montana. Moisture-loving trees like the western red cedar, western hemlock, grand fir, western white pine and mountain hemlock add to species mix. The Ross Creek Cedar Grove Scenic Area on the west flank of the Cabinet Mountains is an excellent spot to sense the productivity of the state's most exuberant forests. Spared by the devastating fires that swept western Montana early in the 20th century, this popular 100-acre grove still harbors forest monarchs. Giant red cedars up to 12 feet in diameter and 175 feet tall, and towering hemlock and white pine produce a dense cover and a cool, humid, dark and aromatic world. Farther north a few woodland caribou, an extremely rare species in the lower 48 states, may still subsist on their requisite diet of lichens that grow only on spruce and fir in old-growth forest.

Timber harvest on Kootenai National Forest alone accounted for about half the harvest on all Montana national forests in the early 1990s. Felled trees from that forest feed mill complexes that range in size from unnamed, one-man enterprises to large mill complexes. Tree cutters in other Far West national forests, on more than a million acres belonging to Champion International and Plum Creek (legacies of the former Northern Pacific Railroad land grant of 1864) and other much smaller private holdings produce the raw materials that feed mills region wide and beyond.

Despite downsizing, mill employment still is critical to the regional economy. At Libby, the 625 jobs associated with Champion International's plywood and stud mill are central to this community of 2,532. The 700 Champion International jobs at their Bonner mill, an additional 700 at Stone Container's Frenchtown paper mill and other wood products employment comprise the largest component of Missoula County's sizable economic base. Flathead County's economy has been even more dominated by wood products employment. In 1992 the 800 jobs at Plum Creek Manufacturing's integrated sawmill-fiberboard-plywood complex in Columbia Falls and 130 employed at the F.H. Stoltze Land and Lumber Company in the same town were key contributors to the valley's economy. Other mills and log home plants from Eureka to Darby generate additional hundreds of jobs in both the forests and factories.

Increased international linkage to the global economy is a common trait of the Far West's wood products manufacturers. From Stone Container's Kraft linerboard factory west of Missoula, about 12 percent of production (the flat surfaces for both sides of corrugated cardboard) is exported to Pacific Rim nations including Japan, Taiwan, the Philippines, Ecuador, Mexico and Canada. Increased exports don't necessarily mean more Montana forest harvests. A shift to greater dependency on recycled cardboard has reduced the need for Montana-produced virgin fibers. In 1992 the mill consumed 450 tons per day of old cardboard collected from as far away as Winnipeg, Canada and Denver, Colorado. Across town at Champion's Bonner facility, up to 8 percent of plywood production is shipped to Germany and Northern Europe for use in cabinets and furniture. Most is the company's "Satin Ply" variety of fancy plywood, with its veneer of guatambu wood imported to Bonner from the temperate forests of Paraguay in central South America.

Fewer wood-products jobs

Along with increasing internationalization, a drop in employment numbers is an even more widespread and critical feature of the region's wood-products jobs picture. Forest-related employment, a traditional cornerstone of Far West economics since the 1880s arrival of railroads and boom of the Montana economy, is in an obvious downward spiral. For mills without their own forest lands, the situation had deteriorated most rapidly in the early 1990s and few, if any, expected the situation to reverse. "Plain and simple," said Russ Miller of F.H. Stoltze, "it's the Wilderness Bill and environmental appeals that have choked off the log supply," and caused the Columbia Falls-based firm to reduce its Far West employment from 320 in 1990 to just 160 two years later. Such employment loss is commonplace regionwide and, this time around, most assumed losses will be permanent.

Increasing mill efficiency and mechanization account for some job loss, but reduced access to public timber lands is the primary factor. Joel Holtrop, Forest Supervisor for the Flathead National Forest, summed up what he sees as a period of difficult transition. "American society and Western Montana are at a time of changing expectations of the role of our national forests. There always will be a place for some traditional forest production, but other uses such as wildlife habitat, wilderness and recreation are being viewed as increasingly important." Joel is one of the new breed of forest supervisors who are at the helm as America shifts gears to a growing recognition of aesthetic and other environmental values and the necessity of a transition to an emphasis on more sustainable forest ecosystems.

Contemporary Flathead National Forest issues illustrate the changing currents and new expectations. The 2.3-million-acre Flathead stretches from the Canadian border west of Glacier National Park southward down the west side of the North Continental Divide Ecosystem for more than 150 miles. Almost 48 percent of the forest had wilderness designation in early 1992; 2 million acres is habitat for grizzly bear and must be managed with that endangered species in mind. Additionally, 1 million acres currently are leased for oil and gas exploration, but exploration has been held in abeyance pending environmental analysis.

The central issue on the Flathead is timber harvest: how much, where and the requisite roading for removal of timber. And it isn't just recreationists/environmentalists versus timber interests. Most snowmobilers, four-wheelers and bikers, and some hunters, think a road density of 1 mile of road per square mile of land mentioned in the forest plan would be just fine. Other hunters, environmental activists and hikers are aghast at what they see as an unthinkable road spacing. Within this multi-sided debate the Flathead National Forest managers must weigh traditional extractive uses of the forest, such as logging, with a changing western Montana economy and a growing dependence on tourism, retirement and unspoiled nature. As Montana's Far West national forests begin to be managed more as national resources that just happen to be in western Montana, local economic concerns will not be ignored, but they must take a back seat to American concerns. In the Far West's timber-dependent communities, high unemployment rates, increased alcoholism, more incidences of domestic violence and other maladies of a social fabric under stress may be unfortunate temporary consequences of this transformation.

The transitional nature of this time span probably will be obvious to all when we look back from 10 to 20 years into the future. A challenge for Far West residents is to roll with what many see as the initial punches while a winning strategy is plotted.

Environment as investment

Dr. Thomas Power, Chair of the University of Montana Economics Department, presents a convincing non-extractive stratagem for "use" of western Montana's national forest in an often reprinted 1989 Forest Watch article entitled "Avoiding the Passive/Helpless Approach to Economic Development." Professor Power pointed out that 40 to 50 percent of all personal income that flows into Montana communities does not come from wages, salaries and profits. It is generated by incomes from

There always will be a place for some traditional forest production, but other uses such as wildlife habitat, wilderness and recreation are being viewed as increasingly important.

return on past investments, including pension and retirement, and from government transfer payments, including social security checks. Combined, income from such sources exceeds that from any single industry. In short, he argues that a high quality environment and a nice place to live that attracts and holds residents can be responsible for far more income than even large natural resource processors. Most new Montana jobs of late, he points out, are in the tertiary sector and are linked to self-employment and "taking in each other's wash." A region need not look to outside investment in salary-based extractive industries that leave mountainsides stripped of vegetation, streams a polluted chemical soup or air with a foul-smelling bouquet. The natural environment provided by Montana's national forests, especially in the Far West, may be the region's most valuable economic ace in the hole.

Although Professor Power suggests Montanans stop courting tourists, many others think that, like high-tech manufacturers, tourists represent a clean-industry

Far West

Right: *Mystical lighting on the Kootenai River Falls.*
Far right, top: *Main Hall at the University of Montana, Missoula.*
Bottom: *The Flathead Valley is home to Montana's Christmas-tree farms.*

Left: Symbolic offerings attached to a Medicine Tree in the Bitterroot Valley.
Far left: A powwow dance competitor's feather bustle.
Below: Kayaking is one way to enjoy the Far West's abundant waters.
Below left: Cherries are a major Flathead Valley crop.

alternative at least somewhat consistent with a high quality natural environment. It seems a bit unrealistic to assume that Far West residents will be able to live in splendid, self-centered isolation in some ecotopian paradise. Tourist-related employment is notoriously low paying, but probably will be an increasingly important economic reality in the region. Ecotourism, perhaps promoted in conjunction with Far West Native American cultures, should hold special promise. Glacier National Park would figure largely in such regional planning.

Each year the shores of popular Flathead Lake look more like those of just any other resort lake, and the solitude so prized by some sailors is increasingly difficult to find.

Chances are the new residents that file into Western Montana's valleys, bringing with them their non-Montana income sources central to Professor Power's new road to economic well-being, first fell in love with the place while on vacation in the area. And come they do, with the Rocky Mountain Trench counties of Flathead, Lake and Ravalli among the state's fastest growing in the decade of the 1980s. The pace has quickened in at least some sections in the early 1990s. Steve Powell, Ravalli County Commissioner, reported the influx has reached a "frantic" level in his county and credited the inrush to what he calls an "escape phenomenon." As county commissioner he is well aware of the environmental and social costs associated with such an invasion. Fast-growth symptoms run the gamut from depletion of aquifers and contamination of groundwater to crowded court dockets and bumper-to-

bumper cars on Highway 93. He shudders at the thought of a planned four-lane speedway linking Missoula to Hamilton and what will surely be an expanding bedroom community function for Ravalli County.

Fragmenting the wilderness

A seeming surplus of people overwhelming and adversely impacting the very environmental qualities that drew them to Montana's Far West is not limited to the Middle Landscapes of crowding subdivisions and arrays of 10-acre ranchettes in the Bitterroot Valley. The same process is ongoing in many high-amenity and sometimes remote settings. Each year the shores of popular Flathead Lake look more like those of just any other resort lake, and the solitude so prized by some sailors is increasingly difficult to find on sunny, summer days. Across the Mission Mountains in the Swan Valley, private land development, fences and other human encroachments constitute a gauntlet for grizzlies.

The situation has contributed to a small and declining Mission Mountain grizzly population cut off from historical and perhaps biologically imperative linkage with their more numerous kin in the North Continental Divide Ecosystem. Similar invasion of grizzly country has resulted in a parallel situation along the North Fork of the Flathead River adjacent to Glacier National Park's western border.

Such habitat fragmentation has caused Glacier to create the position of Regional Issues Coordinator. With greater federal emphasis on managing Far West wildlands for wildlands' sake, it has become imperative to consider ramifications of develop-

ments beyond an administrative boundary.

Brace Hayden, the current coordinator for Glacier, views the park as just one piece of a large international ecosystem that runs from Montana Highway 200 at Lincoln northward well into Canada. He can enumerate a long list of outside-the-park developments that have implications for park wildlife and environment. Of special concern are proposed coal mining and coal-fired power generation across the border in British Columbia, timber sales and oil and gas development in the adjacent Flathead and Lewis and Clark national forests, transborder issues with the Blackfeet Indian Reservation and recreational developments on private lands in neighboring areas. A guiding principle for him is that, "You can't manage just one small part of the ecosystem and think you've taken care of habitat needs."

Mining—visible or not

The harvesting and processing of Far West forests have raised the ire of many concerned residents, but the ravaging of Montana's innards and extraction of various ores often have caused a maelstrom of conflict. A recent example is a fascinating compromise effort in the Cabinet Mountains.

Distant from the intrusives and volcanic activity responsible for so much of Montana's mineralization, the ancient Precambrian Belt Series rocks underlying the Cabinets owe their mineral richness to different geological processes. Perhaps 800 to 900 million years ago while still relatively "new" in a geologic sense, the then deeply buried sedimentary rocks still contained entrapped sea water from the extant Belt

Sea. At depths of probably at least several miles, circulating waters dissolved or leached out minerals in surrounding rock and deposited a metallic concentrate rich in copper and silver in permeable sandstone rock units. Subsequent mountain-building forces that lifted these deeply buried stratabound deposits and formed the Cabinets moved these now metamorphosed quartzite layers closer to the surface and within economic reach of miners.

Since 1981, ASARCO's Troy unit underground operation east of Heron has mined a slab-like Belt ore body 7,400 feet by 1,800 feet by 60 feet. In recent years it has produced more silver than any other mine in the nation, and provided prized and relatively high-paying jobs to about 350 workers. Underground mining generally has less visual impact than surface or open pit mining, but there is no hiding this economic activity. Just miles from the federally designated Cabinet Mountains Wilderness, Protected Nature and Empty Quarter landscapes stand in marked contrast.

On the east flank of the Cabinets another mining operation is destined to be a first in the nation. Montanore Mine will extract copper and silver ore from the same Ravalli Formation as at the Troy Mine. But here, in a more conspicuous operation, ore will be taken from Mother Nature by tunnel from under the Cabinet Mountains Wilderness. Expiration of the twenty-year window for hard rock mining provided for in the Wilderness Act called for a unique approach to access the stratabound ore body buried several thousand feet below the wilderness.

The solution for Noranda, Inc. and Montana Reserves Company is a three-mile-long tunnel starting from outside the wilderness boundary and reaching almost a mile into the wilderness at a depth of about 3,000 feet below the surface. In early 1992 the initial decline (inclined shaft) that begins on private land almost has been completed. According to staff geologist Lynn Hagerty, it is destined to become an air shaft once final Forest Service and state permits clear the way for a second adjacent tunnel starting from Kootenai National Forest land. The second tunnel also will be 16 to 18 feet wide and 20 feet high, large enough to allow mining vehicles and other equipment to be moved in and out of the room and pillar mine. After passing through a concentrator in an adjacent valley, the ore will be sent via rail to a Noranda, Inc. smelter in Ontario, Canada.

Mining companies generally are satisfied with this workable, albeit expensive, solution. Wilderness purists are somewhat appeased, but many may find their backcountry experience curiously altered by the knowledge that their favorite mountain is undergoing major surgery while they enjoy her surface solitude. Still another under-the-wilderness mine now is in permitting stage and may be in production by 2000. ASARCO's proposed Rock Creek Mine farther south in the Cabinets is projected to tap an even larger and richer deposit in the same ancient Revett quartzite.

Active and projected mines along with exploration developments by ASARCO, Kennecott, Newmont Exploration and others keep the 200 members of the Noxon-based Cabinet Resources Group (CRG) busy. In predictable Far West Montana fashion, this environmental watchdog organization formed in the late-1970s in response to the proposed ASARCO Troy mine. The Group concerns itself with both logging and mining, but mine exploration, reclamation and associated governmental approval processes have received most recent attention.

CRG is especially proud of its contribution to the state's new permitting system, which provides better enforcement tools. That system resulted in a suspension of drilling at the Montanore Mine site in late 1991 when polluting waters from the drilling were discovered in Libby Creek. Jill Davies of Noxon oversees the Group's mining related water quality activities and has to admit that, "Things are getting better."

Underground mining generally has less visual impact than surface or open pit mining, but there is no hiding this economic activity.

*Mount Siyeb,
Glacier
National Park.*

JOHN REDDY

GLACIER NATIONAL PARK

Alpine and glacially carved Glacier National Park is the state's undisputed, Montana-exclusive tourist attraction. Many would agree that this is Montana's Protected Nature and Playground landscape at its scenic best. This most majestic of Montana places also has an equally fascinating history.

Because of its rugged landscape, harsh climate and isolation, the area of Glacier National Park historically was spared much of the human encroachment that has altered nearby areas. Even prehistoric Indians did not view it as an attractive area for habitation or hunting. For most of the thousands of years of human history this section of the Northern Rockies has been an area to be crossed, a natural barrier and buffer zone between neighboring tribes. It was not until the second half of the 19th century that serious exploration by whites began, and not until almost the turn of the century that the first residents settled within the confines of the present park border.

Writings of early explorers and visitors reveal that the Blackfeet Indians did frequent the eastern fringe of the region for hunting and religious purposes, but they were a plains people and their focus lay to the east on the buffalo-rich plains on which their subsistence depended. Even when tribes immediately to the west of the region looked to the east, they saw beyond the spectacular peaks to the more featureless grasslands. The Kutenai, Flathead and Kalispell tribes of the west slope were once plains dwellers, having been pushed westward, like most tribes, by a great continental chain reaction set off by Europeans farther east. By the time of first white contact their adaption to life in the mountain valleys of western Montana still was not complete, and they relied on regular expeditions back to the plains to hunt buffalo.

Hunting parties of these west-slope tribes regularly traveled over Marias and Cut Bank passes to and from the plains. The importance of these forays outweighed the danger of almost certain attack from their enemies, the powerful Blackfeet, who guarded the western approaches to their territory. The Piegan tribe of the Blackfeet confederacy used the same passes when dispatching war parties to raid west-slope tribes.

Canadian free traders supplied by and operating out of the Hudson's Bay Company and Northwest Company posts at present-day Edmonton, Alberta, may have been the first non-Indians to visit the area that became Glacier National Park. They are known to have frequented the Rockies and may have entered Glacier.

Specifics on the first visit of record come from the journal of Nor'Wester David Thompson. In 1810 Finian MacDonald and two other Northwest Company traders earned the distinction of being the first whites to enter the region when they accompanied an entourage of plains-bound Flathead Indians. MacDonald's party was attacked by the Blackfeet as were most others who dared venture into the area over the next several decades.

The U.S. government's railroad survey of 1853-54 marked the beginning of a half-century of organized exploration and mapping. Washington Territorial Governor Isaac Stevens' charge was to ascertain the most practical and economical route for a possible railway across the northern tier of the country, from the Mississippi River to the West Coast. The segment across the Continental Divide within Montana was the most worrisome along the projected route. The quest to find Marias Pass was unsuccessful, and the defile's whereabouts continued to elude explorers for the next 30 years.

Hunters, prospectors, trappers, timber thieves and official government representatives visited the park area occasionally over the next two decades. Of special interest was the 1874 west-to-east traverse over Cut Bank Pass by two American lieutenants based at Fort Shaw, west of today's Great Falls. Lt. Van Orsdale was moved by the beauty he saw. Nine years later in a letter to the Fort Benton newspaper he suggested the area be set aside as a national park, the first published plea for park status.

The decades of the 1880s and 1890s proved to be monumental years for the area destined to become Glacier National Park. Two significant developments stand out in this critical late-nineteenth century period. First was the initial visit and subsequent involvement of George Bird Grinnell, noted naturalist and editor of the popular outdoor magazine, *Forest and Stream.*

Grinnell made his first visit in 1885 and returned home to write a series of articles on hunting in the area. With his interest piqued, Grinnell returned in 1887 and then annually for years. He developed an affinity for the park area and a close personal relationship with the Blackfeet Indians.

When the U.S. government began negotiating with the Blackfeet in the 1890s for purchase of the westernmost section of the reservation—the portion of today's park east of the Continental Divide—Grinnell was a logical choice to serve as negotiator. The tribe eventually agreed to surrender title in exchange for $150,000 worth of goods and services annually for a 10-year period. The existence of Glacier Park as we know it today would have been impossible without this eastern portion.

Following its purchase in the 1890s the Ceded Strip, like the west side, was incorporated in the gigantic Lewis and Clark Forest Reserve. Grinnell and others continued to lobby for more protection. The 1895 creation of Waterton Lakes National Park across the border in Canada added to the impetus for a similar designation for the adjoining American section.

Grinnell's considerable wealth and influence were major factors in the push for national park status. Some consider him the father of the movement to establish Glacier. Park historians and conservationists point to his "Crown of the Continent" article in a 1901 issue of *Century Magazine* as a landmark publication in the movement.

The other major development of the two-decade period was the rediscovery of Marias Pass by railroad engineer John L. Stevens in December 1889. Two years later James J. Hill's newly reorganized Great Northern railway crested the Continental Divide at one of the easiest locations in Montana. Even though the railroad only skirted the eventual park boundary, it became the dominant factor in Glacier's early development.

The first Glacier National Park bill was introduced in Congress in 1907, but it wasn't until the third try in 1909 that the legislation made it through both houses and eventually was signed by President Taft on May 11, 1910. Major William Logan headed west to assume his position as the park's first Inspector in Charge. The govern-ment's initial appropriation was

$50,000 for the construction of roads and trails, hardly enough to transform Glacier into a "pleasure ground for the benefit and enjoyment of the people of the United

JOHN REDDY

States" as stipulated by the enabling legislation. Developing the national park would be a long-term proposition, one that was helped along immensely in the early years by the Great Northern Railroad.

The 1892 completion of the Great Northern line over Marias Pass attracted far-sighted businessmen who sensed the area's outstanding tourist potential. None was more enterprising than George Snyder, who in the 1890s helped develop the road from Belton (West Glacier) to Lake McDonald, and began steamboat service between the foot of the lake and his newly constructed hotel complex at the opposite end. By the 1890s Great Northern passengers could ride a stagecoach from near Belton to the lake, catch a ferry to the Snyder Hotel and take horseback rides into the surrounding mountain country.

Louis Warren Hill, son of railroad magnate James J. Hill, did even more to develop the park's tourist potential. At least one author sees him as "godfather to Glacier." Hill directed the Great Northern's major and critical involvement in Glacier during its infancy. The company led the way in the 1910s, constructing accommodations, trails, and even some highways, with an emphasis on the east side. Through the railroad's Glacier Park Hotel Company, the younger Hill oversaw the construction of the park's flagship inn, the rustic Glacier Park Lodge in 1913, and the Swiss-style Many Glacier two years later. The importance of Glacier to the Great Northern was suggested by the adoption of the Rocky Mountain goat as a prominent element in their corporate logo—evidently Louis' idea.

As park facilities expanded, so, too, did visitation. The 4,000 tourists of 1911 grew to more than 22,000 just nine years later. One of the biggest boons to tourism was the 1933 completion of breathtaking Going-to-the-Sun Road, Glacier's first and only transpark road. This ribbon of con-

crete snakes up the nearly vertical Garden Wall, rising 3,000 feet before cresting the 6,664-foot summit of Logan Pass. More than a half century after its construction it still is considered an engineering feat.

Going-to-the-Sun ushered in a new period of tourism in the park. Prior to its completion, most visitors toured the park on horseback. A transpark highway opened the interior and gave visitors an opportunity to experience a cross section of Glacier from the comfort of their cars. This appealed to tourists, whose numbers increased dramatically, rising to 53,000 in the year before the road's construction to 210,000 in 1936.

Except for an understandable drop during World War II, attendance has climbed steadily. Annual visitation rose to a half million in 1951, and exceeded a million visitors for the first time in 1969. Park visitation totaled 2.1 million in 1991, with most visitors coming from Alberta (19.7 percent), Montana (16.2 percent), California (9.4 percent), Washington (7.6 percent) and Minnesota (4.0 percent).

Fully 80 percent of visitors see Glacier during the three summer months. Open between mid-June and late October, Going-to-the-Sun Road is the dominant visitor-use facility, and Logan Pass, the principal focal point. This highway and its summit area are especially popular with those having only a day to spend in Glacier, yet wanting to enjoy as much of the park's variety as possible. And short visits are the norm at Glacier, with average stays totaling just 35 hours.

Glacier's visitors are tourists on the move. The average one doesn't spend even a night in the park. In 1991 Glacier's lodges and chalets accommodated just 106,000 overnighters and 250,000 nights were logged in by all campers, including RV'ers. National Park planners differentiate between frontcountry tourists, who stick close to the road, and backcountry tourists, who venture off into the park's extensive roadless regions. For visitors of the frontcountry variety, staying at one of the park's grand old lodges is a vacation in itself. The remarkable "forest lobby" of Glacier Park Lodge with its towering 60-foot-tall trunks, the Swiss decor of Many Glacier Hotel right down to busboys in lederhosen, and the rustic hunting lodge atmosphere at Lake McDonald are uniquely Glacier.

Some purists are convinced it isn't possible to experience the majesty of Glacier on a truly personal and spiritual level without spending at least a night or two under the stars in the serenity of the backcountry. With only 76 miles of paved road and even less unpaved roadway within the park's 1,583 square miles, travel by auto is limited—by design. More than 90 percent of Glacier is roadless and managed as wilderness. It is only accessible via an outstanding 700-mile system of trails. Surprisingly few people camp in Glacier's remote interior, although a steady decline has reversed in recent years. Between 1977 and 1982 visitor nights in the backcountry declined by almost 50 percent to 16,198. By 1991 backcountry overnighter numbers had climbed back to 22,909. Although wilderness camping is not as common as in the late 1970s, one-day hikes into the backcountry are more popular than ever, placing strains on favored trails. Litter, trail erosion and trampling of alpine vegetation is evidence of heavier use. People seem to gravitate toward water features. One consequence has been that some accessible portions of fragile lake shores and streambeds have been adversely impacted. Large numbers of visitors also mean more auto emissions (723,092 cars in 1991) and campfire smoke with attendant air pollution.

No aspect of park management is more emotional than that dealing with grizzly bears. Each grizzly-caused fatality and mauling sets off a flurry of heated dialogue on the park's bear policy and raises questions about the animals' place in the park. To keep abreast, the Bear Management Plan is renewed annually.

Glacier National Park is home to approximately 200 grizzlies, evidently a stable and self regulating population. Contacts between people and the big bear were minimal until the late 1950s after which increasing visitation and greater wilderness use by a backpacking public meant more incursions into the grizzly's domain. Potential for encounters are heightened by the fact that nearly all people arrive when bears are most active.

The basic plan is to keep people and bears apart. A two-pronged program centers on educating and managing people while simultaneously dealing with problem bears. Visitors entering Glacier are cautioned by a bear alert handout and prominent in Glacier National Park signs posted at all six entrance stations that warn "this is grizzly country." Signs are permanently posted at the entrance to auto campgrounds and trailheads. Each group obtaining backcountry camping permits receives oral warning of the hazards of camping and hiking in bear country. The park has a policy of computer logging sightings of grizzly throughout the park and in the adjoining Blackfeet Indian Reservation. Sighting forms are distributed daily and scrutinized for potentially dangerous trends. Sufficient bear activity in an area can lead to temporary trail and campground closures. Frequency of grizzly bear activity in and near Many Glacier and Avalanche campgrounds has meant they have been closed to all but hard-sided camper units. For the safety of backcountry hikers passing through the Many Glacier area, the park provides a fenced, bear-proof camping enclosure.

Glacier enjoys a well deserved reputation as one of the world's outstanding wilderness parks. Its worldwide significance was recognized in 1974, when included in the international Biosphere Reserve system established by the United Nations Educational, Scientific, and Cultural Organization (UNESCO). More recently it has been nominated as a World Heritage Site. The park retains much of the extraordinary quality of primitive lands, flora and fauna for which it originally was created. The 50 million people who have visited Glacier since its designation as a park invariably have experienced a kind of massage of the senses, and have taken with them a spirituality that lingers long after the scenic snapshots have been put away.

HISTORIC CORE

Southwest Montana is the state's historic core of white settlement, the nucleus around which a new outpost of European civilization grew by accretion in this section of America's Far West. Rich in history and blessed by a diversity of natural landscapes and resources, this Broad Valley Rockies' corner of Montana retains a rich and distinct regional identity based on vestiges and legacies of yesterday and a mix of cultural landscapes indicative of the state's most varied economy. By many measures it remains Montana's epicenter.

This was a colorful era of bawdy placer mining camps with their interesting amalgam of brothels and literary guilds, quick riches and dashed dreams.

Contrary to popular misconception, white settlement of the American Far West did not advance in a wave along a single broad front as it had in sections of the East and Midwest. Instead, bridgeheads of white settlement were established in widely scattered pockets separated by great distances and inhospitable territory, and then advanced outward into lands already occupied by Native Americans. According to noted American historical geographer D. W. Meinig, Montana's Historic Core, which he restricts to a much smaller Butte-Helena area, was a Secondary Nucleus during early stages of settlement. Its function was similar to Deadwood-Lead, Boise and Phoenix and less than such Major Nuclei as Oregon's Willamette Valley, Utah's Wasatch Oasis and the Sacramento-San Francisco axis.

A geologic history that included the emplacement of igneous intrusives including the Boulder, Philipsburg and Tobacco Root batholiths and volcanic activity left this region Montana's most mineralized. And it was a quest for the valuable shiny metals, the "Oro y Plata" of the official state seal, that lured and held Montana's first sizable contingent of whites.

Indians were the first to discover gold in the area, perhaps thousands of years ago. The initial date of its rediscovery by white men is clouded. Some say Francois Finley, one of the tribe of half-breed French Canadian fur traders who settled in the Flathead country, should be credited. The story goes that he discovered gold in river sand at gold discoveries at Gold Creek east of today's Drummond, and in 1850 took less than a teaspoonful to the Hudson's Bay Company's Fort Connah in the Mission Valley. Post commander Angus McDonald evidently did nothing at that time, but wrote to his superiors at Victoria when Finley brought in more gold within a year or two. McDonald evidently was told to keep the discovery a secret since fur trapping and hordes of settlers didn't mix.

A party including James and Granville Stuart usually is credited with the first discovery of record. It was the spring of 1858 and the site was the same Gold Creek area. Four years elapsed before serious diggings began and the short-lived and tiny encampment of American Fork appeared at the junction of the Clark Fork and Gold Creek. It never amounted to much and quickly was eclipsed by more major discoveries farther south along Grasshopper Creek and Alder Gulch.

The pace of development at these new diggings was frantic. The flood tide of gold seekers was recorded in the diary of one miner on November 12, 1864, who wrote: "It surprises me to see how rapidly this country improves. First two miles below here is Virginia City, a thriving village with many business houses; then one mile farther down is Central City, not quite so large; then in another mile you enter Nevada, as large as Virginia City; then about a mile and a half further brings you to Junction City. The road connecting these 'cities' is bordered with dwellings on both sides all along, I shouldn't have the patience to count the business places, but can say that the market is so well stocked that all necessities and many luxuries can be obtained in the stores. Recalling that only eighteen months ago this was a 'howling wilderness,' or rather a howling desert…"

This was a colorful era of bawdy placer mining camps with their interesting amalgam of brothels and literary guilds, quick riches and dashed dreams. Some of the characters would fit right into a Louis L'Amour novel. None was more infamous than Bannack outlaw-turned-sheriff, Henry Plummer, leader of a notorious group of desperadoes. The legend of the mining camps' secretive vigilantes and their mysterious "3-7-77" symbol lives on today with this sequence of numbers still adorning Montana State Highway Patrol decals.

While the diffusion of gold placer mining activities to other Historic Core gulches and beyond was still underway, the shift to hard rock mining began. Again, geology guaranteed that this new phase of Montana mining would be centered in the same region. Punching mine shafts and tunnels underground to ore zones and processing of mine production created dozens of new Core communities and meant a second life

for others. Butte, Philipsburg, Granite, Elkhorn, Garnet, Pony, Rimini, Pioneer, Wickes and additional mining centers catapulted the region into global mineral prominence.

The entire Core region shared in the economic coming of the nineteenth century's last third. Helena may have started as a gold mining camp following the historic July 1864 strike, but rapidly evolved into something much more. A fortuitous central location within a fabulously rich mining region, a strategic position astride the Fort Benton-Virginia City Road and proximity to the Mullan Wagon Road linking Fort Benton and Walla Walla, Washington, helped assure Helena's survival long after the last of the local diggings were exhausted. Almost immediately, Helena became the financial hub and wholesale/retail trade center, entertainment node and distribution

Above: In 1862, Bannack in eastern Idaho Territory was the Historic Core region's first gold rush boomtown. Two years later, it became the capital of brand-new Montana Territory.
Left: The Legal Tender mine in the Clancy area of northern Jefferson County.

The Meade Hotel and Skinner's Saloon welcome visitors to Bannack State Park. Montana's first mining boomtown in 1862 and first territorial capital in 1864, Bannack soon was eclipsed by Virginia City.

point for residents in nearby mountain mining towns. Even communities as far afield as Virginia City and Bozeman were within reach of Helena's long tentacles of trade and commerce. By 1870, at a time when neither Billings nor Great Falls existed, when Butte had but 241 residents and Bozeman 168, and after Virginia City's population had dwindled to 867, Helena was the undisputed number-one city in Montana with 3,300 residents.

Transfer of the territorial capital from Virginia City to Helena in 1875 was testimony to its ascendance. Wealth and opulence peaked in rapidly maturing Helena the next decade when the capital assumed the title of "Queen City of the Rockies." Downtown, impressive brick and stone office buildings of the latest architectural styles crowded the winding contour of Last Chance Gulch. Mansard roofs, pediment windows, cornices, gargoyles, and even carved-stone dolphin rain spouts graced handsome buildings where previously more functional and less permanent log cabins and false-fronted frame buildings stood.

In the residential neighborhoods fringing the downtown, mining magnates, bankers, politicians and others among Montana's most wealthy and influential built their mansions. At that time Helena claimed more millionaires per thousand residents than any other city in the nation. Conspicuous consumption was the norm on such mansion-rich west side drives as Madison, Stuart and Dearborn. Helena was clearly the most prestigious Montana address of the 1880s.

Although only 64 miles away, Butte was another world. After a shaky start, it rose to prominence as Montana's undisputed mining capital, a title it would hold for more than a century. Like many other communities in the Historic Core, Butte started as a placer mining camp. It has been estimated that several thousand placer miners worked the Silver Bow drainage during the summers of 1865 to 1867. By then Butte, still a camp, peaked at about 500 residents and had a well-deserved reputation as one of the territory's most disreputable places. The easily worked alluvial deposits were depleted in short order and as the number of white miners fell, the Chinese population rose—a sure sign of the waning of a gold camp. Initial efforts to work quartz deposits on Butte Hill were unsuccessful and, by 1870, the census tallied only 241 in Butte, of which 98 were Chinese. Four years later Butte was just another dying camp with a population that may have fallen below 60.

Just when Butte City's fate seemed certain and its place among the growing list of deceased territorial mining camps assured, this played-out gold camp was reborn. In 1875 it was found that the rich quartz ores on the Hill could be mined for silver and milled locally at a respectable profit. This discovery ignited a second invasion, one that brought larger numbers of miners and a permanence previously lacking. By 1880 Butte was riding high on a silver boom and claimed title to Montana's second largest town with 3,364 residents.

Silver kicked off Butte's second boom, but it was and development of Butte copper that soon catapulted it to a position of world-class mining center. The 1882 discovery of rich copper ores in the legendary Anaconda Mine ushered in a phase of mining that continues to this day and validated Butte's claim to being the Richest Hill on Earth.

Butte was the right place at the right time. The community tripled in population to 10,723 in 1890 largely as a result of its role as supplier of copper to a world in the grips of an electrical revolution. The timing couldn't have been better for maximum growth. With the 1879 introduction of the electric light bulb and adoption of electric motors, demand for copper wire accelerated. Butte took on the traditional copper producing center in Michigan's Keweenaw Peninsula in a vicious price war for national dominance and emerged victorious.

Wealth and opulence peaked in rapidly maturing Helena the next decade when the capital assumed the title of "Queen City of the Rockies."

The 1880s also witnessed the opening salvos in the so-called War of the Copper Kings. No schoolchild in Montana gets much beyond fifth grade without knowing the particulars of this extraordinary 12-year conflict between Butte's first two copper barons, Marcus Daly and W. A. Clark. The clash of these powerful personalities had implications for much of the state and even reached into the U.S. Senate chambers.

Mines like the Anaconda, Parrot, Alice, Colusa and Lexington called for miners, and lots of them. The rosters of the mines and smelters largely were filled by foreign workers who arrived in Butte in droves starting in the 1880s. Almost 24,000 people lived in Silver Bow County in 1890, nearly all in Butte and its environs. Just under half the populace, about 10,700, were foreign born. Prior to the turn of the century, Cornish and Irish dominated among non-natives. Butte's ethnic mix expanded after 1900 with the addition of even more groups, with markedly greater numbers arriving from eastern and southern Europe. By 1920 residents included 1,273 Yugoslavians, 1,229 Finns, 964 Italians and other sizable contingents from more than a score of countries.

No schoolchild in Montana gets much beyond fifth grade without knowing the particulars of this extraordinary 12-year conflict between Butte's first two copper barons, Marcus Daly and W.A. Clark.

The immigrant character of Butte was amplified by the tendency for each national group to cluster, or as described by a local paper in 1910, to "flock together," in ethnic neighborhoods. Rather than a single homogeneous city, Butte became an ethnic mosaic like larger industrial cities in the midwestern and eastern sections of the nation. The sights, sounds and smells of these ethnic enclaves were just like back home in the old country. Despite persistent friction, Irish and Cornish concentrated to the north and northeast of the Hill, close to the mines. Places like Corktown and Dublin Gulch were once as Irish as their names, while northern suburbs of Centerville and Walkerville had heavy concentrations of "Cousin Jacks," the Cornish. Lively and compact Finntown complete with its famous steam bath houses developed somewhat later. Chinatown, with everything from vegetable vendors and laundries to opium dens, occupied an area of several blocks on the south side of the central business district. "Bohunks," Slavic people, eventually dominated the McQueen and Boulevard additions. Suburban Meaderville east of town originally was populated by Welsh and Cornish, but later became known as "Little Italy" and was a mecca for gamblers.

Mining activity and population continued to build and peaked in the years during and just after World War I. Most of the stately masonry buildings of Uptown Butte were built during this period of rapid growth from the mid-1880s to the mid-1910s. The scale and architectural merit of these buildings were consistent with the grandeur and urban sophistication of a Butte that saw itself as *the* burgeoning American West metropolis. No one knows for certain what the area's between-census population was in the late-1910s peak, but local historians estimate there may have been almost 20,000 miners and as many as 100,000 residents. Despite this size and its status as one of the West's largest inland cities, Butte remained an interesting combination of frontier camp and modern, cosmopolitan city.

Growing numbers of miners in the last decades of the 1800s created demand for local and regional food sources. The Gallatin Valley evolved into an early and important food exporting area. Even the fur traders had noted the agrarian qualities of the generous valley. When veteran trapper Osborne Russell passed though in 1838 he commented on its large size and its smooth and fertile nature. Natural fertility was especially good in the wetter, eastern side of the valley where native grasses had contributed to soils rich in nutrients and organic material.

The pace of agricultural development in the Gallatin Valley paralleled the filling of western gulches by gold seekers. Bannack, Virginia City, Nevada City, Helena and other Core mining camps and towns were supplied with some goods hauled up from Salt Lake City or east from Walla Walla, but it made better economic sense to produce grain, potatoes, vegetables and livestock regionally in areas with outstanding agricultural potential like the Gallatin Valley. As early as the fall of 1864, the *Montana Post,* a Virginia City newspaper, could report the Valley was rapidly being filled by farmers. By 1867 Valley wheat acreage had expanded to 8,351 acres and production to 300,000 bushels. In the late 1860s the Gallatin had three flour mills and was the territory's granary, a title it could claim until the agricultural settlement of the eastern Montana plains.

Advent of rail service intensified the Gallatin Valley's agricultural specialization. Irrigated farming greatly expanded, earning it the title "Egypt of America." The Valley was billed as a veritable agricultural cornucopia. At times regional hype may have gone a little far, as was the case in a December 1890 article in a Bozeman newspaper that claimed the average yield of cereal grains in the valley "is much larger than that of any state or territory in the Union, or even the civilized world." The same month an ad in the *Butte Daily Record* referred to the Gallatin Valley as having "no equal for productivity in the world" and as a "dimple in the fair cheek of nature."

As the regional trade and commercial center, Bozeman's initial growth was closely linked to the Gallatin Valley's agronomic attributes. An 1870 population of 168 grew to 2,143 just 20 years later, along with increasing cropland and livestock numbers. The 1893 opening of the Agricultural College of the State of Montana (now Montana

State University), the state's land grant college, ushered in a new era and significantly broadened Bozeman's economic base. Unlike the Core's two other major urban centers of Butte and Helena, Bozeman's early growth was least linked to local mining. Turn-of-the-century coal mining south of Bozeman Pass and in the Trail Creek area east of town was as close as mining got to Bozeman.

Elsewhere in the Core, historical agriculture centered more on livestock, and cropping in many areas was limited to hay. This was especially true in Montana's far southwest corner. Stock growing had a surprisingly early start in the Beaverhead, Madison, Big Hole and other area valleys. During the 1850s and 1860s the region developed as Montana's earliest and most important livestock producing area and claimed some of its first ranches. Initially these were strictly open-range outfits, relying on free and unfenced range. Sensing the opportunity for hefty profits in the 1850s, former Hudson's Bay Company trader Richard Grant and his family were among the earliest to use these dry, rain-shadow valleys with their nutrient-rich range to winter-over and fatten cattle. In the spring they drove their herd south to the Oregon Trail in southern Idaho, where westward-bound pioneers were eager to replace their trail-worn and emaciated stock on terms quite favorable to the Grants. Word of the suitability of southwest Montana range spread in the 1850s and 1860s and others drove in herds from places as far away as Oregon and California.

In the 1850s Johnny Grant, son of HBC trader Richard Grant, moved north into the free grazing lands of the Deer Lodge Val-

*In 1890, when this F. Jay Haynes photograph **(above)** was made, Butte claimed a population of nearly 24,000, and at the peak of its expansion in the teens **(left)** may have had 100,000 inhabitants.*

HISTORIC CORE

Right: Tom Jüngst jumps a cornice at Bridger Bowl Ski Area near Bozeman. **Far right, top:** Butte's Chinese population once was segregated into a Chinatown. **Bottom:** Bonnie Blair training at Butte's High-Altitude Sports Center for the 1899 Olympics, where she gold-medaled in speed skating.

Above: *A hunting camp in the Gallatin National Forest.*
Top: *Sign of the 1990s boom in Bozeman.*
Left: *Boulder's radon mines attract a national clientele.*
Far left: *Above Philipsburg.*
Left top: *Canyon Ferry Reservoir of the Missouri River near Townsend, the Big Belt Mountains on the horizon.*

ley and built his own trading post and ranch headquarters along the Mullan Road. A few years later he moved south and built a new headquarters at present-day Deer Lodge. Grant sold out in the mid-1860s to Conrad Kohrs, a businessman with first-hand knowledge of the potential for profit from beef in nearby mining communities. Kohrs started with a modest operation and built it into one of the largest cattle empires in Montana. In 1870 Kohrs may have initiated the movement of the range livestock industry out of the western valleys and onto the range of Great Plains Montana when, finding his local range fully stocked, he drove a herd into the Sun River Valley. Eventually this early Montana cattle baron owned 30,000 acres in the Deer Lodge Valley and controlled between 1 and 5 million acres of range scattered from western Canada south into Colorado.

The landscape legacies of mining are now one of the region's most distinctive features and are nowhere more impressive than in Butte.

In an interesting historical aside, two early twentieth century Big Hole ranchers are credited with inventing one of the most novel of western agricultural implements, the beaverslide haystacker. In 1910 David J. Stephens and Herbert S. Armitage were granted a patent on their sliding hay stacker. The 30-foot-tall stacking implement relied on a large hay basket that was pulled up an inclined glide surface to dump its generous load into a haystack of 20 and more tons in size. The speed and efficiency for field stacking hay, especially in rough hay meadows, was revolutionary, and use of the beaverslide quickly diffused from Montana's Big Hole Valley into other ranching areas in western America and Canada.

Timber harvests on the forested slopes of the Historic Core's insular mountain ranges also have a long history. Regional lumber requirements for everything from Virginia City sidewalks to supports in Butte's underground mines and open-air ore roasting heaps, and house construction along Bozeman's South Willson, meant local markets and area sawmills.

Tourism also had surprisingly early roots. Bozeman undoubtedly would have evolved into a major Yellowstone National Park gateway city had not the Northern Pacific Railroad built its branch line up the Yellowstone's Paradise Valley to just north of Gardiner, guaranteeing Livingston initial park portal status. Bozeman did develop as the jumping-off point for some of the earliest dude ranching in the state. Around the Historic Core region, hot spring spas have a long history, and hunting forested mountain ranges and fishing outstanding Broad Valley Rockies trout streams have been popular with tourists for more than a century.

In the 1990s Historic Core, legacies of the past are commonplace on the landscape and in the regional economy. The area still has Montana's most diverse economy, although the relative importance of key sectors has shifted in recent years. Mining, once the leading sector, now exists on a greatly reduced scale. Copper mining returned to Butte in the 1980s after several years' absence, and the newer breed of smaller, non-union gold mines continue to sprout in long abandoned mining districts, but current employment levels are minor compared to historical ones.

The landscape legacies of mining are now one of the region's most distinctive features and are nowhere more impressive than in Butte. More than a century of mining has left an indelible imprint on the cityscape that contributes to the community's unique look and feel. Gallow frames, mine spoils, the rapidly filling and mineral stained pit, and the tiny, closely packed homes of thousands of yesterday's miners are prominent elements in this admittedly somewhat obtrusive landscape. The sense of big and brawny Butte is most apparent Uptown, where hulking and dated buildings exude the community's masculinity. In his *Historic Uptown Butte,* an interesting architectural and historical analysis of the business core, Bozeman architect John DeHaas points out that Butte has a metropolitan character lacking in all other Montana cities. Butte definitely is not a Disneyesque restored mining town like so many tourist traps in the West. It's the real thing, where mining history is not limited to a single street or small district; it permeates much of the community and its landscape. Walk the streets of Uptown and chances are you, too, will sense Butte's still-broad shoulders and narrow waist.

The M & M Cigar Store at 9 North Main continues on from yesterday as the grand dame of Butte bars, one of the last of its old-time saloons. It started serving drinks in the 1890s and today may have more regulars than any other drinking establishment in town. Locals don't take out-of-town guests here to impress them with the community's sophistication. It's not one of those Naugahyde and chrome bars with wall-to-wall carpeting, subtle mood lighting and soft background elevator music—it's a Butte institution. In addition to its well worn bar, there is a dinner counter along the opposite wall that provides inexpensive, filling, but by no means fancy, meals 24 hours a day. Fred, son of long-time owner Charlie Bugni, says their pasties are especially popular. The back room is for round-the-clock gambling. Poker and pan players humped over felt-covered tables from yesteryear, a floor littered with Keno cards and cigarette butts, and a wall-size Keno board give the place the look of a real joint.

Environmental degradation of the Butte-Anaconda environment by more than a century of mining and smelting is an unfortunate bequeathal. In the 1980s, sections of Butte, Silver Bow Creek and the area around the copper smelter in nearby Anaconda were declared national Superfund sites by the Environmental Protection Agency (EPA). Environmental and health hazards linked to airborne and river deposition of lead, copper, zinc and arsenic made this one of the nation's most seriously contaminated places. According to Bruce Farling of the Missoula-based Clark Fork-Pend Oreille Coalition, an environmental group focused on the Clark Fork River drainage basin, emergency action had to be taken in Anaconda. There the EPA removed 35 families from Mill Creek within the Anaconda smelter site after high levels of metals (especially arsenic) in soil samples and high concentrations of lead in children's urine called for immediate action.

In Butte the gargantuan Berkeley Pit, the center of Anaconda Company's mining from the mid-1950s to its abandonment in 1983, is rapidly filling. Water, charged with heavy metals from thousands of miles of tunnels that honeycomb Butte's underground, gushes into the pit at an estimated 5 to 7 million gallons per day. The EPA estimates the pit's water level will rise to the point where area groundwater will be threatened by the year 2000 or soon after. A siphoning system that would simultaneously treat and "mine" the mineral-rich waters might be a solution.

The former Anaconda-area settling ponds present another problem. In the past, leaks and heavy flows following thunderstorms have flushed blood-red, metals-charged polluting waters from the ponds down the Clark Fork as far as Milltown Dam just east of Missoula. Health-threatening water contamination has been documented there and a replacement water supply has been developed. From Milltown upstream to Anaconda and Butte, these contiguous Superfund sites constitute the largest Superfund complex in the nation.

In 1983, Montana filed the then-maximum $50 million claim against the Anaconda Minerals Company and its parent company, Arco, for unspecified natural resource damage to the Clark Fork River basin. Superfund studies of damages to surface and groundwater, soil, vegetation and fisheries continue. Rough estimates suggest losses have impacted 100 miles of fishery and 27,000 acres of agricultural land.

Off in the Historic Core's hills, ghost towns are additional, more picturesque landscape legacies of a mining past. Elkhorn, Garnet, Rimini, Pioneer, Granite, Southern Cross and others appear on official state highway maps and draw curious tourists each summer. Most now have at least summer seasonal residents lured by the romance of times gone by. The state-managed ghost town of Bannack draws tens of thousands of visitors annually despite its remote location and gravel road access. The town's two-story courthouse, wood-frame and log homes and two jails still stand. Even Skinner's Saloon has survived, one of the few buildings dating back to the community's first two years. Enough of the town remains to make history believable and allow visitors to become immersed in that past. Although not a ghost town, authentic Virginia City is very much a living museum. Assuring that Montanans and others will be able to continue enjoying these relic communities is one goal of the 135 members of the Montana Ghost Town Preservation Society (Box 1861, Bozeman, MT 59771).

Off in the Historic Core's hills, ghost towns are additional, more picturesque landscape legacies of a mining past.

Agriculture continues to be a major component of Core economics and land use. The region remains dominantly livestock country, with cash receipts from livestock and livestock products almost three times those generated by crops, much from forage crops. More than 400,000 acres of harvested hayland and 400,000 cattle and calves are the cornerstones of the regional agricultural economy. Beaverhead, Madison and Gallatin counties rank numbers 1, 2 and 3 in hay production, and Beaverhead's 150,000 cattle and calves position it first in Montana and among the nation's top livestock counties.

The Paradise Syndrome and search for life in a picture-perfect landscape has ar-

The Gallatin River at Three Forks, where it joins the Jefferson and the Madison to begin the Mighty Missouri.

rived in full force in the Core and is impacting the regional livestock scene. Bozemanite Don Vaniman has been selling Montana ranches and farms for 15 years, most recently through his own Don Vaniman Ranch Broker agency. He reported, "You don't sell many ranches to ranchers any more." Buyers now are movie stars or corporate executive types who are willing to pay an average of $1 million for the right 2,000- to 4,000-acre ranch. According to Vaniman, "You can't really sell an average working ranch—it's got to be right up against Forest Service land and/or have big trout on it." Ranching real estate isn't even discussed in the context of AUM's, or number of livestock that can be carried—"no one cares anymore—what these guys want is to buy into a way of life." Modern-day Ben Cartwrights aren't interested in the inconvenience of riding very far by auto getting to and from their own Ponderosas. Ranch demand drops off in areas more than an hour from airports. Although a $1 million Montana ranch tucked up against the Tobacco Roots or Pioneer Mountains is nothing more than a day-dream for average Montanans, it is pocket change to our nation's growing contingent of super-rich.

Only in Gallatin County do cash receipts from crops approach the value of livestock and livestock products. Hay accounts for the greatest acreage, and even though the Gallatin Valley is no longer the state's granary, it remains an important producer of barley and, to a lesser extent, wheat. With about half of the cropland irrigated, the valley has more irrigated land than all but a very few of Montana's counties.

The Gallatin's most distinctive and prosperous agricultural area is the section centered on Amsterdam and Churchill. Neatly kept homes, finely manicured yards, an occasional miniature windmill in a front yard and names on mailboxes like Van Dyken, Flikkema, Braaksma, and Dykstra are obvious signs that this is a Dutch area, still sometimes referred to locally as the Holland settlement. It ranks as the state's premier dairy region, accounting for about one fourth of all milk cows in Montana, and in recent years has displaced the Flathead area to earn the state's number one potato-producer status.

Timber production on the marginal commercial forest lands of the Core is of decreasing importance. For years below-cost timber sales from the Gallatin, Deerlodge and Beaverhead national forests have been assailed by environmental groups who see much greater economic value in forests as mainstays of the region's growing tourist industry, as habitat for wildlife and as critical headwaters areas for Broad Valley Rockies rivers.

The proximity to Yellowstone National Park and a location at the junction of two interstates alone would help assure a healthy tourist business. But the addition of the region's own attractions, from high quality downhill ski areas such as Bridger Bowl to world famous trout streams, to the ubiquitous mining and other Old West vestiges makes tending to visitors one of the regional growth industries.

The high amenity environment and gamut of outdoor recreation that draws tourists also has begun to attract new employers. The 1988 move of Patagonia Mail Order to Bozeman often is cited as a classic of example of the power of the environment to lure new employers. Most of

the 35 employees handle toll-free calls from throughout the United States and Canada and worldwide mail orders for the company's line of specialized outdoor clothing. Items are shipped out the next day from the company's Ventura, California, warehouse. Patagonia could have located in any place with basic transportation and communications services, but chose this corner of Montana. Similar examples can be seen regionwide.

Word is out on desirability of life in the picturesque valleys of Montana's Historic Core region, but not all areas are considered equal by prospective new residents. Gallatin County's 17.7 percent growth between 1980 and 1990 led the state. Regionally, Jefferson County (12.9), Lewis and Clark County (10.4) and Madison County (9.9) were well above the state-average, 1.6 percent growth rate, but other counties witnessed sizable population loss during the decade. Deer Lodge County lost 17.9 percent of residents, Silver Bow 10.9 and Granite 5.6.

Selectivity has concentrated growth in a few localities, especially suburban areas outside Bozeman and Helena. In the capital city area the Helena Valley north of town has been growing at an impressive clip for more than a decade. Those seeking a more forested setting have moved into areas to the south, in the extreme north end of Jefferson County. New residents of foothills subdivisions like Gruber Estates, Blue Sky Heights and Forest Park Estates have given this largely rural county one of the state's fastest growth rates over the last 20 years. Few seek out building sites near ASARCO's East Helena facility, the nation's eighth-ranking factory in terms of pounds

of toxic pollution, according to a 1990 EPA report.

Outside Bozeman the filling and proliferation of Gardner Parks, Sourdough Ridges, and Painted Hills subdivisions add to population totals. With the average Bozeman home price increasing by more than a third over the last three years, more new arrivals are opting for the less expensive, yet still close-in, town of Belgrade. That community's 46 percent increase in population during the 1980s was second only to 46.3 percent growth in the Bitterroot's presumed polygamist town of Pinesdale.

The 1988 move of Patagonia Mail Order to Bozeman often is cited as a classic of example of the power of the environment to lure new employers.

Bozeman's hot real estate market has helped one local ERA realtor earn number one ranking for sales among the many thousands of company agents nationally, more than once in recent years. Co-worker Mike Money, sales associate with the same ERA Landmark office in Bozeman, described a growing influx of young retirees, educated professionals, and what he called "mobile professionals" such as consultants who travel extensively and can live almost any place with good airline connections. Bozeman is especially popular with arrivals from West Coast locations. Some of those who followed Horace Greeley's advice are now having to backtrack a time zone and at least one mountain range in order to find their Shangri-la.

CENTRAL MONTANA

To its north, the physiographic contact between Great Plains and Rocky Mountains is sharp and distinct, with more subdued land to the east and the jagged Rocky Mountain Front thrust skyward on the west. To its south, the cloud-touching Beartooth Range in Montana's Yellowstone Rockies rises no less dramatically from the topographically more muted lands to the east. In between, in Central Montana, the transition from Great Plains to Northern Rockies is a more gradational affair. Along an east-west distance of 120 miles, Great Plains and Rocky Mountain Montana seemingly overlap in a unique Big Sky collage of natural and cultural landscapes, a Montana microcosm.

Montana in miniature

Everyone agrees that Lewistown is in Central Montana, but how far out in all directions can this region claim title? The notion of a Central Montana region bordered by other Montanas on all sides is a mental construct and its limits depend on the regional basis used and who is doing the defining. For example, heading east out of Lewistown on Highway 200 toward Jordan, not all agree on where Central Montana is left behind in the rear-view mirror and panoramic Big Dry Country begins to engulf travellers. It's a judgment call. At what point does a defining Central Montana landscape of mixed farming—with both grain and cattle—against a backdrop of Rocky Mountain outliers yield sufficiently to the more two-dimensional and thirsty Big Dry rangeland?

Despite the personal nature of such regionalization, it is perhaps only the inclusion of the White Sulphur-Ringling-Crazy Mountains section and the adjacent Little Belt Mountains that would fall beyond the limits of most people's Central Montana. Addition of this far southwest corner is based as much on sense of place as on distinctive landscapes. Here, the high and rugged lineal Big Belt Mountains constitute a barrier and cultural fault line that have encouraged a regional identity that focuses eastward.

Central Montana is Montana in miniature—but not miniature in a micro sense. The place still is of a Big Sky scale and encompasses 14,000 square miles. But within that tenth of Montana the range of eastern and western, past and present, is startlingly representative of the whole state. If a visitor could take in only one of our seven component Montana regions and wanted to experience as much as possible of what makes the Big Sky state so special, this would be the place to go.

The Judith Mountains, Moccasins, Big and Little Snowies, Highwoods, Little Belts, Crazies and Castle Mountains punctuate the landscape and make this the most mountain-studded section of the North American Great Plains. Elevations of highlands range from the lofty and glacially sharpened 10,000- and 11,000-foot Crazy Mountains peaks to the Moccasins with no points above 5,600 feet, to detached and diminutive laccolithic highlands the names of which are known only to locals. The Little Belts are the most extensive tract of highlands and forest, and are home to the states' highest major year-round mountain pass on a through highway, Kings Hill at 7,393 feet. But even in this most expansive highland, mountain outlines are rounded and softened by tree cover that commonly starts part way up on one flank, spreads over the crest and down the mountain's other side. Central Montana valley floors that average at least 4,000 feet in elevation translate into local relief of 2,500 to 3,000 feet in most sections, relatively subdued by mountainous Montana standards. The net result is a diverse physical stage that tends not to overwhelm in either the horizontal or the vertical dimension. Central Montana is on a more human and comprehendible scale than the vertically exaggerated adjacent sections of the Rocky Mountains or the more intense horizontality of the Great Plains. Rather than inspiring the awe that Glacier National Park does, the typical Central Montana natural landscape embraces human residents with a calm and comfortable beauty.

In this region, the grain elevator and cattle are the two most ubiquitous elements in Central Montana's humanized landscape. Few sections of Montana have as balanced a dependence on livestock and crops as the region's core counties of Fergus and Judith Basin. The broader agricultural base cushions those economies from the extreme price cycles that predictably jar highly specialized districts. This is especially true in Fergus County, one of the state's premier agricultural counties, ranking 4th in number of cattle and calves, winter wheat and hay acreage. Wayne Edwards, president of the same Farmers State Bank his grandfather started in Denton in 1929, works with area farmers and ranchers on a daily basis and pointed out, "We're in a fairly strong area here—we're fortunate in that we're pretty diversified—most of our customers do both farming

Campfire Lake on the Gallatin National Forest in the Crazy Mountains.

and ranching." Much of the county is well watered and fertile and although county-wide averages show winter wheat yields of about 40 bushels per acre, Edwards reported that some farmers on north benches commonly harvest 60 to 70 bushels of winter wheat per acre. Less fertile soils and lower precipitation totals mean a greater livestock emphasis in most quarters of Central Montana to the south and east.

Prior to white settlement it was the lush grasses of the Judith Basin country and the forested mountains that were the preferred hunting grounds for Indians and later fur trappers and traders.

With what railroad companies call rationalization and locals consider simple abandonment, national railways have been moving out of the region. The 1980 termination of the east-west Chicago, Milwaukee, and St. Paul line through Roundup and Harlowton left the southern section without local rail service. To the north, farmers refused to give up their most economical link with the outside world. They banded together to save local service when the Burlington Northern discontinued an important market link. The Central Montana Rail, Inc. now operates the 87 miles between Moccasin, Danvers and Geraldine where it links up to BN track. General manager Carla Allen reported that their non-profit operation boasts six locomotives, which collect grain hopper cars at their Geraldine yard for assembly into mostly 52-car unit trains.

Growing cattle and crops has a long tradition in this central region, and is part of the area's classic Montana montage of history, replete with Indian raids, cattle barons, military posts, colorful placer and quartz mining camps, hopeful homesteaders and even ethnic coal-mining communities. Prior to white settlement it was the lush grasses of the Judith Basin country and the forested mountains that were the preferred hunting grounds for Indians and later fur trappers and traders. By the 1870s, whites had started moving cattle onto the luxuriant prairie, probing and testing the suitability of these lands for livestock. To few people's surprise, cattle thrived, and soon large ranches and thousands of head populated the Basin. The well grassed and well watered range drew legendary Montana stockman Granville Stuart, who built the headquarters for his cattle empire at the base of the Judiths. In typical frontier succession, Central Montana white residents demanded protection from Native Americans and the federal government responded by constructing Camp Lewis and, later, Fort Maginnis.

The first major influx of population into the area had to await the discovery of gold in the highly mineralized Judith Mountains. The original discovery was made on the west side of the range in 1880, and a predictable army of prospectors converged on the diggings. Within a year the new camp of Maiden may have had a population of 6,000. The easily panned and sluiced deposits were exhausted quickly, and operations shifted to quartz mining. By 1885, Maiden vied with the valley town of Lewistown for designation as seat of Fergus County. Its case was a valid one since the mining community's population of several hundred made it the largest in the newly created county. But support from stockmen and ranchers in the basin tipped the scale in favor of smaller Lewistown.

Other mining communities came and went among the mineral-rich outliers, including Giltedge, Kendall, Hughesville and Castle, but within a decade upstart Lewistown assumed role as unofficial regional capital. No one expects the new Kendall gold mine, in operation since 1988, to spawn a settlement to rival the Fergus county seat.

Lewistown: center of the center

A group of about forty families of Métis—French Canadian–Indian mixed bloods—arrived from Canada in 1879 at what was to become Lewistown. These immigrants had fled from the western province of Manitoba to their promised land, situated near the Carroll Road, a vital link between Helena and a steamship port on the Missouri above the mouth of the Musselshell River.

In 1881 Reed's Fort, named after the local postmaster and then trading post owner, was built and formed the nucleus of the new community. Other buildings soon were added, including a hotel, blacksmith shop and saloons. For a while the young community was known as "Lewiston," but the spelling was changed to "Lewistown" in 1884. The fledgling community grew in unison with the influx of ranchers and farmers in the last two decades of the 1800s, but lack of local rail service hampered development. The belated 1903 arrival of the Central Montana Railroad rectified that problem, and town population catapulted from 1,096 in 1900 to 6,120 twenty years later, almost equal its 1990 tally of 6,051 residents.

Rapid growth in such a short and prosperous period has left an indelible mark on Lewistown. Abundant use of stone by local

Croatian masons who arrived between 1898 and 1915 adds a permanence and durability to the cityscape. The town has four districts listed in the National Register of Historic Places, all dating from this early-twentieth century building boom. A distinctive Fergus County Courthouse crowns one of these districts. This clock-towered classic was built in 1907 in Mission style—a defiantly indigenous American West design. The historic central business district along 6 or 7 blocks of Main Street is a trip back in time. According to local architect Jeff Shelden, regional architect George Wiedeman returned to the area with post–Chicago-fire styles of Louis Sullivan and other masters and added them to Lewistown's built environment. The 60 to 70 bungalow-style homes on such streets as Hawthorne and Lake in the historic Judith Place Addition are pure 1910s.

Lewistown's centrality within the productive agricultural lands of this Rocky Mountain outlier country and within the state of Montana still helps sustain the community. Considerable local discussion has focused on where the exact geographical center of the state actually lies. It has long been assumed to be in the area, but the precise location depends on which story is to be believed. The most popular one placed it at the exact location of either the bathroom or kitchen drain of the old Dockery House, which was torn down to build the Christian Church. Police Chief Russell Dunnington has heard all the stories, including those that have the audacity to suggest the actual center point isn't even in town, but 14 to 20 miles to the southwest.

New evidence that surfaced in 1982 further fired the debate on "Where?" According to Henry W. Gehl, general manager, excavation work that year for an addition to the Lewistown Park Inn unearthed an intriguing cache that suggests that site may be the state centroid. Workers found a souvenir coin from the Chicago World's Fair, a compass, rusted gold miner's pan, and large rock with a map of Montana scratched on its surface with an "X" over the central point. A parchment document signed by a W. S. found stuffed in a buried hollow buffalo horn "certifies" the distinctive location. The historic treasures now are displayed in a glass case in the new and appropriately named "Center Mark" indoor pool and room complex. Gehl pointed out that a central location within the state, an easy day's drive from any Montana address, makes the Inn a busy convention site for state-wide gatherings.

Roundup's ethnic mosaic

While no Central Montana community can challenge Lewistown's reign as unofficial regional capital, to the south Roundup does command its own second-order hinterland. The town's population has been remarkably stable at around 2,000 for more than 20 years, despite the loss of rail service in 1980. This might not sound like much in most sections of the nation, but in this part of Montana it is borderline metropolis size.

The present town of Roundup got its start when, in 1907-08, the Chicago, Milwaukee, St. Paul and Pacific Railroad built its West Coast extension up the Musselshell River. Subbituminous coal deposits in the Bull Mountains were a major factor in the extension of the railroad's line through the area. The Milwaukee needed Roundup coal to fuel its steam locomotives, since the Bull Mountains field was the only major coal source along its right-of-way between the state of Iowa and the Cle Elum area on the east slope of Washington's Cascade Mountains.

Yugoslavian surnames like Ratvovic, Bublick, and Antonich, and Polish monikers such as Marsinkowski, Cowalski, and Cowalczyk are commonplace in Roundup and have been since early in the 20th century. Descendents of the Eastern Europeans who immigrated by the hundreds to work in area coal mines, they are now part of the ethnic mosaic that imparts a distinctive character to this southeastern corner of Central Montana. Although the major mines are now history, they and their workers have had a permanent impact on the area. At Klein, two large cemeteries on either side of Highway 89 are somber reminders of the hazards of earlier underground mining.

The first major influx of population into the area had to await the discovery of gold in the highly mineralized Judith Mountains.

During the holiday season, *potiza,* a Yugoslavian sweet bread made with a walnut filling, is a local favorite. Long before home wine making came into vogue, many residents of Yugoslavian descent were brewing their extra strong *grappo.* In some cases traditional wedding ceremonies that can last for days still include the custom of pinning money to the dress of the dancing bride.

In the 1990s Roundup functions primarily as a farm, and especially a ranch, service center. The P.M. Coal Mine outside of town is the last remaining operation. This small strip mining operation employs six to

CENTRAL

Right: The Fergus County Courthouse in the center of Lewistown, in the center of Montana.
Far right: The blockhouse at Fort Logan near White Sulphur Springs served in the early 1870s.
Bottom: Twodot is one of several Montana towns named for the brand of a prominent local ranch.

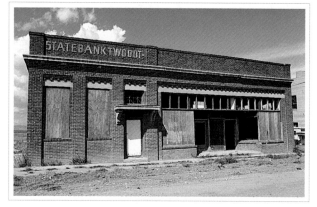

JOHN REDDY

Above: *A pastoral setting for the church at Forest Grove, south of Lewistown.*
Left: *Belt Creek in the Little Belt Mountains.*

eight people; its production of only 16,000 tons per year is one thousandth that of a large eastern Montana counterpart. A projected Meridian Minerals' Bull Mountain mine would greatly expand local production.

Central Montana retains much of the character and flavor of Montana of a generation or two ago.

A location a bit off the beaten path, beyond Interstate 90 and generally east of the heavily travelled Yellowstone-Glacier axis has meant that most people who visit Central Montana do so by design, not en route to someplace else. Perhaps, in part, because of this relative remoteness, Central Montana retains much of the character and flavor of Montana of a generation or two ago.

In the Judith Basin, an early combine heads, threshes and sacks wheat.

*Modern equipment aided
the Gilsky Brothers north
of Lewistown in 1905.
George Carolus photo*

Big Dry

According to locals, the Big Dry appellation derives from Indian place name geography. To northern Plains tribes, it was obvious that this generous prairie region east of the Rocky Mountain outliers and between the Yellowstone and Missouri rivers wasn't just a little bit dry, it was big dry. That semiarid nature is a key factor in explaining why today the 17,000-square-mile territory has a declining average population density of only 0.7 people per square mile, one seventh the already sparse state average.

Most of the Big Dry remains open, sagebrush scented, livestock grazing country.

This is classic *yonland,* distinctive from adjacent *sutland* areas. These terms were introduced by Montana State University rural sociologist Karl Kraenzel in the 1950s to distinguish the two major types of settings in which people live in much of the Great Plains. Sutlands commonly are linear in form and strung out along and adjacent to major river valleys and more heavily used lines of transportation and communication. Larger communities, more dense population and irrigated farming are characteristic of such areas. In contrast, the larger yonland, literally "out yonder," is an area of poorer transportation, smaller towns, much lower population density, ranching and dryland farming.

The Big Dry yonland lies between the Yellowstone River Valley sutland on the south, and on its north are Fort Peck Reservoir and a section of the Hi-Line sutland paralleling U.S. Highway 2, the Burlington Northern Railroad and Missouri River. Circle, with a 1990 census population of 805, is the regional metropolis, and Jordan checks in as second-ranking town with 494 residents. Even though state highway maps locate such "towns" as Mosby, Brusett, Ingomar, Vida and Cohagen, those familiar with the area know such places usually are comprised of a post office and maybe a bar and/or gas "station." The Cohagen Bar constitutes Cohagen's central business district and the Vida Country Club comprises downtown Vida. In most cases, all residents of each community could fit in your family vehicle. Consistent with its yonland nature, the Big Dry has only 40 miles of rail, a single spur line that penetrates from Glendive and dead ends at Circle. This outback region has no scheduled airline or even commercial bus service, none of its own radio or television stations and just one resident medical doctor (in Circle) within its 17,000 square miles.

Livestock and a little wheat

Only in the better dryland farming districts in northern McCone and northern Richland counties is there a persistent cropping emphasis. In this section of the Big Dry, continental glaciation pushed south of the present course of the Missouri River and softened the landscape. Favorable topography coupled with a mantle of fertile soil and adequate average annual precipitation make this corner of the Big Dry an established wheat producer. Predictably cold winter temperatures mean a spring wheat emphasis.

To the west less favorable soil qualities, often rougher unglaciated topography and lower precipitation mean little emphasis on cash grain farming and much greater dependence on livestock ranching. This is especially the case in 5,000-square-mile Garfield County, which epitomizes this section of the Big Dry.

Garfield County farmers do plant about 120,000 acres of wheat in an average year, but cash receipts from sale of county livestock commonly outrank cash generated by crops five to one. Only in the Blackfoot area northwest of Jordan and in the Two Furrow section east of Cohagen—where Russian-German families such as the Pluhars and Halfas have farmed for generations—does a grainfield dominated landscape prevail. Large-scale expansion of wheat acreage by controversial block farming greatly increased county wheat acreage in the last half of the 1970s, but by 1990 the area seeded in wheat almost exactly equalled that planted a decade earlier. Some farmers continue to break former rangeland, especially to square up fields, but evidently new regulations have tempered the wholesale conversion of range into huge unbroken and easily wind-eroded fields thousands of acres in area. Most of the Big Dry remains open, sagebrush scented, livestock grazing country.

With carrying capacity of county land averaging 30 acres per head, and ranging as high as six head per square mile section, ranches tend to be large. Among the 236 operators who generate sales of at least $10,000 a year, the average spread is almost 8,300 acres. The largest ranch, owned by the Binion family of Las Vegas Golden Horseshoe fame, controls about 250 sections, and several other ranches cover more than 100 square miles. The county's herd of approximately 55,000 head outnumber people by 35 to 1 and almost 100,000 head of sheep rank the county number one in the state.

Ingomar, home to a few dozen souls and the Jersey Lilly Saloon.

Jordan Country: Garfield County

Geographers worldwide know of Garfield County because of a classic 1931 article by then president of the American Geographical Society, Isaiah Bowman. He had a special interest in frontier areas and was drawn to what he called Jordan Country by the persistence of frontier conditions. I revisited the same area for a golden anniversary look and publication and found many aspects of life were still "frontierish" fifty years later. In the 1990s many of the early traits persist and the county remains great "next-year" country.

Few now can recollect when there seemed to be a family on almost every section, and four or five neighbors might be seen from a farmhouse window.

At the time of Bowman's 1930 visit, Garfield County had a population of 4,252, most residing on 1,077 farms and ranches. Average farm size was 1,095 acres. A trend of declining population was already underway then. Decades of additional rural depopulation and thinning of populace left a 1990 population of 1,589 and just a quarter the number of farms/ranches, which average eight times the 1930 size. Abandoned and weather-checked homesteaders' shacks and homes attest to obvious initial oversettlement. Some seniors pensively recall the wholesale abandonment of the countryside in the dry Depression decade of the 1930s. Few now can recollect when there seemed to be a family on almost every section, and four or five neighbors might be seen from a farmhouse window.

Dr. B.C. Farrand, the county's single medical doctor at the time, remembers Bowman's 1930 visit. Ninety-six-year-old Dr. Farrand, still a Jordan resident, arrived in the summer of 1925. He helped establish Jordan's first hospital in 1928 and recalled that residents initially were hesitant to use the new facility. He remained Jordan Country's only doctor until retirement in the 1970s. It proved difficult to keep a doctor in Jordan and finally, after a string of temporary postings, the community abandoned the idea. In the 1990s the county is without a resident medical doctor and its previous 28-bed hospital, but participates in an innovative Medical Assistance Facility program being watched by others in the nation. This program gives Jordan a clinic licensed for two beds and is staffed by a physician's assistant. More comprehensive medical care is available 84 miles and a 1½-hour ambulance ride away in Miles City.

For rural residents of 1930, school was an isolated one-room building, staffed by a teacher both difficult to obtain and reluctant to stay beyond one academic year. Garfield County high school students attended class at one of the county's two high schools in Jordan and Cohagen, both of which maintained dormitories for students who lived too far away to commute daily.

In the 1990s the geography of county education is surprisingly unchanged and clearly shows the social cost of space. During the 1991-92 school year, 11 Garfield County rural schools offered grades one through eight. Pine Grove, Kester, Big Dry and seven others were one-room schools with enrollments of four to ten children. Most shacks and log cabins of Bowman's time may have yielded to modular and trailer units, but it still is difficult to find teachers willing to serve in the more isolated sites, where their only contact with other people might be four or five youngsters for weeks on end.

Sixty-four-year-old veteran teacher Aris George has taught at the district's most isolated Ross School in the Musselshell River Valley for two years, but doesn't think he'll be back for a third. "I love the kids, but there is only so much a person can take," said Aris. He is the first teacher to return for a second year in recent history. Four students from three different families in kindergarten, second, fourth and sixth grades made up his class.

Home for Aris is a trailer next to the older log school building, 17 miles north of pavement and Highway 200 at Mosby. Access is difficult, especially when the road is wet: the sharp rocks have damaged his vehicle and flattened even his six-ply tires. Without drinkable water at the school, he has no choice except to make frequent trips to Mosby to fill his two five-gallon pails. According to Aris his school building was without usable indoor plumbing for his first 18 months and all had to avail themselves of outhouses. Aris summed up the situation, "It's a hardship here." He doubted that his annual salary of $7,200 would be sufficient inducement to sign a new contract.

An extensive rural bus system now links many parts of Garfield County with the single high school in Jordan, but large sections are too remote and inaccessible to be included in the service area. To accommodate students from such areas, the county built a dormitory in Jordan in the 1930s. Among the last public high school dormitories in the nation, it was home-away-from-home for about 30 week-day residents in the 1991-92 school year.

Transportation, a problem at the time of Bowman's visit, remains so today. In 1930 Jordanites and those of the surrounding area were eagerly awaiting the arrival of rail service. The previous fall the presidents of both the Great Northern and Northern Pacific had been in town extolling the attributes of their projected line. Neither railroad built through the county, nor did any other, and to this day, the area remains railless. In fact, since the 1980 abandonment of Chicago, Milwaukee, St. Paul and Pacific track and the late-1980s loss of rail service between Circle and Brockway, the entire region is more isolated today than it was in 1930.

Most residents are still, at the least, inconvenienced by poor transportation. Ranchers and farmers have no choice but to truck their commodities to adjacent rail service 67 miles from Jordan at Circle or 84 miles to the sutland city of Miles City. Twice each month residents can ride the community's mini-bus to "Miles." Although it is intended primarily to provide free transportation to senior citizens, others are welcome to go along on the all-day outing for a $5.00 fare, provided there is room. About once a month the same bus makes the 350-mile round trip to Billings; non-seniors' fare is $10.00.

Big Open, big controversy

Back in Jordan at the Hell Creek Bar, the Ranchers, and at other taverns and cafes the width and breadth of the Big Dry, one topic dominates discussion in the early 1990s—the Big Open proposal. It is a Montana version of the Frank and Deborah Popper's controversial Buffalo Commons vision for large sections of the American

Great Plains. Most of the Big Dry falls within what the Poppers would like to see become a gigantic wildlife refuge.

The Montana-specific Big Open concept stems from a paper presented at a 1987 Missoula conference sponsored by the Institute of the Rockies. In his presentation, Hamilton resident Bob Scott proposed that the Big Dry west of Circle and the yonland between the Fort Peck Reservoir and U.S. Highway 2 be converted into a 16,000-square-mile wild game preserve. Since then the initial idea has evolved, but it still

is based on the assumption that most of the Big Open area is unsuitable for production of wheat and beef and should never have been taken from the buffalo. Proponents think farmers and ranchers are fighting a losing battle, one that costs American taxpayers millions in federal government payments annually. Their basic suggestion is that farmers roll up their fences and pursue more ecologically sound and sustainable stocking of the range with native ungulates, especially buffalo. Their incomes supposedly would then blossom as they

Unloading the "emigrant car" upon arriving in Montana, 1913. Homesteaders found traveling with all their worldly in one boxcar an economical way to start the new life. Henry Syverud photo

Big Dry

MICHAEL CRUMMETT

JOHN ALWIN

Top left: *Joyce and Paul Harbaugh start the day on their Jordan-area ranch.*
Top right: *Where Highway 12 meets I-94, a concise statement of the Big Dry's openness.*
Bottom left: *Complex beauties of the Terry Badlands.*
Bottom right: *The Benzien school, Garfield County—all one room of it.*
Facing page: *In the Hells Creek area.*

ROBERT SCHERTING

MICHAEL CRUMMETT

turn their livelihoods to serving wildlife viewers and hunters who arrive to partake of this Montana Serengeti. With economic collapse of area farmers and ranchers unavoidable, supporters see a transition to a wildlife-based economy as inevitable—

Many ranchers have been taking in hunters for decades and others have earned extra income from guiding for just as long.

they want to make sure that like so much of Montana this, too, doesn't pass to the control of wealthy out-of-staters. A fear is that Texas-style hunting ranches owned by multinational corporations will put the entire area off-limits to average Montanans.

Big Dry residents' reaction to the proposal was swift, loud and predictable. Chances are they reacted precisely the same way you would if outsiders told you that your way of life was both wrong and doomed and that they knew exactly what you needed to do to rectify the situation. It didn't help that residents heard about others' plans for them through the national media.

Locals' first questions were, who are these people from Missoula and Hamilton in western Montana and Eugene, Oregon and Boston, Massachusetts who serve on the Organizing Committee for the Missoula-based Big Open Project, and what do they know about the realities of ranch/farm life on the eastern Montana plains? Some of the farming and ranching families in the Big Open area have been part of the local agricultural scene for four and five generations and weren't about to let what they saw as some outside, academic environmentalists tell them what they should or shouldn't be doing.

Dave Huston has ranched in Garfield County since returning from WW II in 1943 and operates a cow/calf operation on about 8,500 acres 45 miles northwest of Jordan. "A plum insane idea" is how he reacted to what he sees as "a monstrosity created by a couple of outside professional agitators." The preoccupation with restocking buffalo perplexes Huston, who pointed to century-old buffalo wallows that still can't be used for cropping. "Buffalo are the hardest thing on range outside of a prairie dog," said Huston. Soil compaction, erosion of topsoil by sharp hooves, and salt from their urine render such wallows useless until repeated plowing pulls sufficient topsoil back over affected areas. He especially resents attempts by Big Open proponents to convince him that he and his neighbors are poverty stricken and in need of economic restructuring. In fact, the most recent figures from the U.S. Department of Commerce show that Garfield County ranks 5th in the state in per capita income, well ahead of Missoula County.

Virginia Edwards, formerly of a ranching family, now lives in Jordan and finds the Big Open proposal equally offensive. She considers it "a bunch of bunk." In February 1992 more than 200 like-minded residents from a four- or five-county area rallied at the new VFW Hall in Jordan in opposition to the plan. Janet Guptill, editor of Garfield County's *Very Own Local Paper,* has been working to keep readers informed and help lead local opposition to the proposal. She is careful not to report everything in her paper because, as she said, "When you're at war, you don't always tell the other side what you're doing."

An early 1992 Big Open Conference at Lewistown (neutral territory?) sponsored by the Missoula-based Big Open Project group, and including ecologists as well as the infamous Frank and Deborah Popper, had to be cancelled at the last minute. Some say it was scrubbed because of threats of violence, others report rumors that buffalo were to be released in the lobby of the Lewistown Park Inn, and some are convinced that it was called off simply because not enough people were willing to ante up the $25.00 pre-registration fee, $35.00 at the door.

In the heat of the battle the strategy seems to have shifted. Charles Jonkel, one of the Big Open leaders, now talks about raising livestock on the *best* range and crops on the *best* farmland and recognizing native wildlife and space as a third source of income on the rest of the land. To a large extent that is already what has been happening in the Big Dry. Many ranchers have been taking in hunters for decades and others have earned extra income from guiding for just as long. In fact, the Jersey Lilly Saloon in Ingomar may be the most famous of all Montana saloons among out-of-state hunters. Still other farmers and ranchers operate on-ranch bed and breakfast businesses and hire out to give tourists wagon rides across the prairie. Many already are engaged in the very activities espoused by Big Open advocates and had been well before the birth of the proposal.

Above: Dawson County homesteaders dressed up for their portrait.
Left: A bumper homestead crop in Dawson County. L.A. Foster photo

YELLOWSTONE COUNTRY

Vast and diverse, Yellowstone Country is both the largest and most varied of our seven Montana regions. Here the mix of natural landscapes is unrivaled: fragile alpine tundra atop the almost–two-mile-high Beartooth Plateau, seemingly endless short grass and sage prairies, colorful badlands, picturesque ponderosa-studded hills, the dramatic gorge of the Bighorn River and the more subdued and sinuous course of the majestic Yellowstone.

Unfettered for its entire length, the Yellowstone is the last of its kind—the sole major free-flowing river in the contiguous United States.

It is the latter river that lends its name to this spacious country. The Yellowstone River binds this place and looms large in its residents' regional identity. A check of phone directories in towns from Livingston to Billings, Hardin, Miles City and Glendive illustrates the reality of this regional affiliation—Yellowstone Properties, Yellowstone Bank, Yellowstone Belaro Speedway, Yellowstone Boys and Girls Ranch, Yellowstone Tavern and even Yellowstone Anesthesia Associates are just some of the place-linked appellations.

Big sister river to the Missouri in terms of average annual flow, the Yellowstone originates in the pristine high mountains of northwest Wyoming, flowing in a northwesterly direction into Yellowstone Lake. Leaving the lake behind, it has cut a tortuous path through Yellowstone National Park's colorful, pancake-like layers of volcanic rocks. Over Upper and Lower Yellowstone Falls and through the beautiful Grand Canyon of the Yellowstone, the river weaves its way toward Montana. It may be the yellow-colored walls of this gorge to which the river owes its name. Entering the state near Gardiner, it soon reaches the spectacular, trough-like and mountain encircled Paradise Valley south of Livingston.

At the northern end of Paradise the river flows through a narrow hourglass-shaped constriction. Dam builders have cast covetous eyes at this site for a potential Allen Spur Dam for almost 90 years. Past proposals have called for a 380-foot dam plugging that narrow gap and a 32,000-acre reservoir flooding the Paradise Valley for a distance of 30 miles. The dam has been an on-again, off-again topic for generations despite the fact that slopes at the site are unstable, underlying limestone bedrock is less than suitable, and the area is earthquake prone. The valley's "Hollywood North" population is certain to join in the loud chorus should power interests once again test Montanans' sentiment for such a project.

For now the stately waterway passes unrestricted through the wind-swept gap at the valley's north end and swings sharply toward the east below Livingston, still a free-flowing river. On to Big Timber, the Yellowstone enters plains-dominated eastern Montana. It flows eastward weaving a sinuous course through a flat-bottomed and often rock-rimmed valley one to three miles wide. Giving freely of its waters to irrigators, urban residents and industrial users, the river moves past Laurel, Billings, Forsyth, Miles City, Glendive, Sidney and a long list of other communities before joining with the Missouri just east of the North Dakota state line. This confluence marks the end of a journey that began 670 miles away. Unfettered for its entire length, the Yellowstone is the last of its kind—the sole major free-flowing river remaining in the contiguous United States.

Along that course it takes on the waters of several major rivers, all entering from the south. The Boulder, Stillwater and Clark's Fork of the Yellowstone deliver runoff gathered from the well-watered and rugged Yellowstone Rockies. The name of the next and largest Yellowstone tributary, the Bighorn, is an approximate translation of the Indian name *Ah-sah-ta*, which referred to the herds of bighorn sheep in its basin. Flowing north out of Wyoming's Bighorn Basin, it carries waters drained from the moisture-trapping Absaroka and Wind River ranges to the west and the Bighorns to the east. In Montana, the waters are captured temporarily in the steepsided Bighorn Canyon behind Yellowtail Dam before continuing northward to confluence with the Yellowstone just east of Custer. The historic Tongue and Powder rivers are the last major tributaries. They deliver water collected from the east flank of the Bighorn Mountains and Wyoming's Powder River Country after passing through one of the nation's most active coal mining districts.

Yellowstone Country is steeped in Old West history. Native Americans had resided in the area for thousands of years when the first white explorers began probing what was to them *terra incognita*. The initial incursion of non-natives, which culminated in pitched battles of the 1860s and 1870s, may date back as far as the 1740s. In January of 1743, two sons of Pierre Gaultier de Varennes, Sieur de La Verendrye, may have become the first white out-

From the Devil's Canyon Overlook down into Yellowtail Reservoir, Bighorn Canyon National Recreation Area.

of-staters to visit what now is Montana. Francois and Louis Joseph had been sent by their father in search of a reputed water route to the Pacific. They fell short of their objective, but reportedly did see the "Shining Mountains" and encountered the "Bow People." The mountains the brothers sighted may have been the Bighorns and the Indians, the Crow, but since their journal of the expedition is sketchy and lacking in specifics on locations, we only can speculate they reached Yellowstone Country.

The Yellowstone River became the water highway for St. Louis-based fur traders and trappers who moved in close on the heels of Lewis and Clark.

It seems likely that other whites visited this region during the next half century. It is not difficult to picture grizzled and buck-skinned free traders drifting south out of the British lands to the north, perhaps outfitted by Hudson's Bay or Northwest Company posts in today's southern Alberta or Saskatchewan. Or others may have worked their way up the Missouri and Yellowstone drainages lured by hopes of huge profits from a virgin fur area. That they evidently failed to leave written accounts of their exploits is not surprising since few, if any, would have been literate. Verbal accounts of their expeditions may have been shrugged off in St. Louis or Edmonton House as just more fur traders' braggadocio. Or perhaps they were discreet and did not reveal their source area so as not to invite competition.

The beginning of documented and systematic exploration of Montana and its Yellowstone Country had to await the arrival of the celebrated 1804-06 Lewis and Clark Expedition. The entourage entered today's Montana from the east just beyond the mouth of the "Roche Jaune," or Yellowstone River, on April 26, 1805. Their westward passage took them up the Missouri. It was on their return trip in the summer of 1806 that Captain Clark led a party out of the Gallatin Valley and over the drainage divide to the Yellowstone River near present-day Livingston. Clark and his party built dugout canoes and floated downriver, enjoying their most comfortable and leisurely traveling of the entire expedition. On July 25 the captain went ashore to examine "a remarkable rock...nearly 400 paces in circumference, two hundred feet high" on which he carved his name and the date. Clark named the distinctive rock Pompey's Pillar, after Sacajawea's child, whom he called "my boy Pomp." Today this riverside sentinel downstream from Billings still sports Clark's etching and has been designated a National Historic Landmark. From this point the party continued downriver, meeting up with Captain Lewis and his party just beyond the mouth of the Yellowstone in mid-August. As the Corps of Discovery moved down the Missouri, the first fur trappers of record moved up-river to the Yellowstone Country.

The Yellowstone River became the water highway for St. Louis-based fur traders and trappers who moved in close on the heels of Lewis and Clark. Manuel Lisa helped lead the way, building Lisa's Fort (also called Fort Manuel) at the mouth of the Bighorn River in 1807. Other forts and trappers followed in succeeding decades. An interesting aside to these early endeavors was trapper John Colter's winter 1807-08 sojourn into today's Yellowstone National Park. His description of these previously undescribed spouting geysers, boiling mud and other geothermal features earned the area the name Colter's Hell.

Perhaps no section of Montana is as steeped in Indian history as these lands of the Yellowstone watershed. Here, in this surprisingly unchanged and still dominantly range country, it is easy to visualize a band of Crow Indians silently moving their encampment beneath a rising dust plume or, atop a rimrock, a scouting party of mounted Sioux silhouetted against a Montana blue sky. It was here among the sandstone outcrops and short-grass prairie that much of the violent clash of cultures that accompanied Montana's Europeanization was played out. Such names as Crazy Horse, Sitting Bull, Lame Deer, Red Cloud, Custer, Miles and Terry, and map features including Little Bighorn, Fort C.F. Smith and the Bozeman Trail were central to regional development and today are given extensive coverage in state history books.

Just as the gradual profile of the Yellowstone River had drawn fur trappers and traders up-river, that waterway's tame valley offered the path of least resistance to the Northern Pacific, which reached the valley from the east in 1881. By the next year transcontinental rail service linked the valley to the outside world and a necklace-like array of railroad developed towns helped lay the foundation for the ascendance of this lineal belt as eastern Montana's premier sutland.

Billings is one of the railroad-spawned communities that sprang up along the Northern Pacific as it snaked through the Yellowstone Valley in 1881-82. The namesake of N.P. President Frederick Billings, the community was designated division point on the new line. The town got off to a slow start, with its 1890 population of 836 well behind young upstart Great Falls (3,979) and even Miles City (956). A decade later, census returns gave no suggestion that Billings was destined to dominate eastern Montana. That year its 3,221 residents meant the community was less than a third the size of rival Great Falls. Billings promoters were undaunted, billing their new town as the "Denver of the Northwest." They were confident it was "The Magic City" and was destined to become the urban focal point in an evolving prairie north hinterland.

Commerce-driven Frederick Billings might well be proud of "his" city's ascendancy. Today Billings, population 81,151 (metro 113,419), is the undisputed regional capital of a 200,000-square-mile, resource-rich hinterland that covers much of eastern Montana and spills over the state line to claim sections of Wyoming and the Dakotas. Historic rival Great Falls checked in with a declining 1990 metro population two thirds the size of Billings'. Now when Jeanne Moller, Director of Business Development at the Billings Area Chamber of Commerce, discusses competing urban centers she talks about such places as Spokane, Washington, to the west and Denver on the south.

Billings' continued economic prosperity has come in spite of economic setbacks in the last half of the 1980s. In fact, the metro population may have peaked in 1985 at over 120,000 just prior to an energy industry crash. Until the mid-1980s Billings was riding high on an energy boom. Even though the area has had three area oil re-

fineries for years, the local energy boom was linked more to its role as a white-collar energy town. Scores of oil and gas exploration/development companies had set up offices in Billings, from which they remotely directed exploration in fields hours away by car. The 1986 halving of crude oil prices drove many energy companies out, with the loss of thousands of jobs. Only from the vantage point of the early 1990s are residents able to look back and declare the earlier energy exodus a blessing in disguise.

The message to the community was clear—either diversify or be ready for another sharp boom-bust cycle. Variety has been the hallmark of subsequent economic development. Fortunately for Billings, it is now of sufficient size to be seriously considered as a major wholesale distribution center. The new and huge NAPA Auto Parts warehouse in the city's southwest is a classic example. Auto parts and accessories from the Billings facility supply outlets in eastern Montana as well as sections of Wyoming and the Dakotas. Traditional varied economic roles also have expanded. Billings remains Montana's major transportation hub. It is the state's largest retail trade center and its two major hospitals make it a regional medical center that draws from a multi-state area. A British-owned sugar mill continues to operate, but the community now is without major local meat packers for the first time in generations. In another sign of the international times, one former packing plant has been acquired by a Korean group that will pro-

duce leather for export. Montana hides can produce the Cadillac of leather—cold weather translating into leather that is both thick and free of damage by pests.

Beyond metropolitan Billings and outside the irrigated farming districts in the

SOURCE: AUDIT BUREAU OF CIRCULATIONS, JANUARY 1992

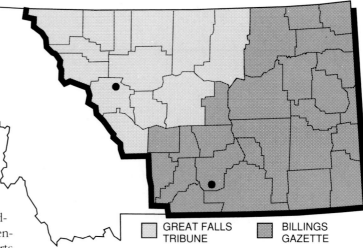

GREAT FALLS TRIBUNE | BILLINGS GAZETTE

The Battle for the Montana Plains by two newspapers, the Great Falls Tribune *and the* Billings Gazette

Yellowstone Valley is the range that produces the cattle synonymous with regional agriculture. Range is still dominant over most of the plains portion of Yellowstone Country, accounting for up to 90 percent of land in farm in some counties. Large ranches that have been in families for generations are sometimes the only evidence of human habitation over broad stretches. Only in the extreme southeast, in Carter County, are cattle outnumbered by sheep.

But in these downriver and backcountry plains areas beyond the Yellowstone River sutland, it is not livestock ranching that imparts distinctiveness to the extensive Yellowstone Country yonland. A combina-

Yellowstone

Billings viewed from the landmark Rimrocks that rise above it.

***Clockwise from left:** Students "driving the drag" in Glendive on a Friday night. The United States Post Office in downtown Powderville. Medicine Rocks. Dressed for the weather at the annual Miles City Bucking Horse Sale.*

tion of coal mining and the Indian presence, the black rock and red man, contribute much to that regional identity.

Coal production is big time in Yellowstone Country. Eastern Montana has vast reserves of surface mineable coal, both lignite and higher BTU (heat content) subbituminous grades, and most of that lies south of the Yellowstone River. Surface strip mining is the standard method used to remove coal in the region. With this type of mining, the overlying material is removed, usually with mammoth draglines, exposing the underlying coal. Seams are essentially flat lying, which makes mining easier, and range in thickness to 50 feet and more. Since the ratio of overburden to thickness of coal layer often is small, these are among the most efficient coal mines in the world. Using draglines and large shovels and trucks, individual miners can produce up to 185 tons per day, many times that of counterparts in Appalachian mines. An added plus is the generally low sulfur content of this western coal, usually a half to a third that of Eastern U.S. coal, which means less pollution when burned.

Large-scale, surface strip mining in Yellowstone Country began in earnest in the early 1970s. This is graphically reflected in state coal production figures (almost all from the region) which show a rise from 3 million tons in 1970 to almost 32.5 million tons in 1979, and then a decline. Most was produced from several large strip mines in south-central Yellowstone Country and was shipped under long-term contracts to

The Crow Tribe is benefiting economically from coal mining and the Northern Cheyenne soon may have their own strip mine.

Midwestern utilities via speedy 100-car unit trains.

The Yellowstone Country coal situation has changed in recent years. In the early '90s annual production has increased to about 38 million tons from the half dozen strip mining operations around Decker, Colstrip and north of the Crow Indian Reservation. According to the Montana Coal Council, the 50 percent reduction in the state's coal severance tax (designed to compensate future Montana generations for the loss of this nonrenewable resource) has been the major factor in this production increase. Long-term contracts now are a thing of the past and coal prices have softened. Neighboring Wyoming provides the stiffest of challenges with its lower severance tax and better grade coal that is more economically mined. Competition for markets is intense and new approaches are called for in the Powder River Basin coal country where overcapacity is a fact of life.

Western Energy, a Montana Power Company energy arm, in conjunction with Northern States Power of Minnesota, has responded by developing a pilot coal-drying facility at their Colstrip, Montana, mine designed to produce "Syncoal." The process reduces the 25 percent moisture content of the subbituminous grade coal to just 5 percent, raises the heat value from 8,800 to 11,000 BTU per pound and increases the BTU–sulfur ratio. The end product should be in demand by utility companies striving to comply with Clean Air Act requirements for emissions at their coal-fired power plants. The savings in transport cost per BTU is impressive. Loaded with syncoal, a 100-car unit train would carry the equivalent of only five railcars of water instead of

the current 25. The higher heat value may open new markets at Midwest power plants designed for higher grade bituminous coal and there is increased talk of expanded overseas exports.

Members of state environmental groups never have been pleased with strip mining of Montana's coal. Large producers, such as Western Energy Company's 13 million ton per year Rosebud Mine at Colstrip, have "disturbed" thousands of acres. Visual impact on natural landscapes is profound. And environmental consequences can extend beyond the actual mine site to adversely affect such things as groundwater and air quality. Socioeconomic impacts on communities can be just as profound. Posting of bonds by mine owners and a law requiring mined land be regraded and "restored to the approximate original contour" and revegetated with a diverse, effective and permanent vegetative cover are meant to minimize long-term environmental impacts.

Coal mining already is linked to Yellowstone Country Indians. The Crow Tribe is benefiting economically from coal mining and the Northern Cheyenne soon may have their own strip mine. North of the Crow Reservation and east of Hardin, within a Crow Ceded Area, the tribe has a majority ownership of coal at the Absaloka Mine. Production began in the early 1970s and today totals about 4 million tons per year. As well as receiving a royalty payment on each ton of coal produced, the tribe, by agreement, receives half of these high-paying mine jobs.

Just to the east, Northern Cheyenne tribal members are grappling with the prospect of their own strip mine in the Tongue

River Valley. According to Edwin Dahle, President of the Northern Cheyenne Tribe, the potential mine area is underlain by billions of tons of very low sulfur coal. With just 60 feet of overburden covering an almost 60-feet-thick coal seam, Dahle reports that theirs would be among the nation's most cost effective operations. Harsh economic realities on the reservation make 400 high-paying coal mining jobs, and additional income from a 165 megawatt coal-fired power plant and two 20-acre greenhouses heated by steam generated from an associated coal dewatering plant, look all the more inviting.

Although carefully planned coal development would help alleviate problems faced by some of the almost 4,000 residents on the 689-square-mile Northern Cheyenne Indian Reservation, it would be no panacea. Difficult socioeconomic realities on the reservation are pervasive and reflect a society-in-crisis situation shared by many other Montana reservation Indians. Despite the Indians' prideful past, the current situation of widespread economic hopelessness and vexing demographics are reminiscent of the Third World. Montana life for many reservation Indians is somewhere other than the escapist Eden it is for many other state residents.

According to tribal President Dahle, winter unemployment peaks at about 80 percent and averages almost 70 percent—underemployment adds to the jobs predicament. Steve Small, Economic Development Director for the tribe, says the economy is dominated by large family-operated ranches and farms, which provide few jobs. At the peak of the summer fire season, unemployment drops to the mid-50 percent range when locally constituted Bureau of Indian Affairs fire fighting crews are off working around the nation. High-paying positions are rare and average per-person income on the reservation is less than half that in most Montana counties. The tribe's Dull Knife College, a two-year institution, starts some students off on academic and professional tracks, but most pursue careers off the reservation. A graduate of the University of Montana, Small is one of the exceptions, a college graduate who returned to the reservation. "A lot of our talent never comes back," he said.

Tribal President Dahle thinks that up to 40 percent of high school aged children are not attending school, an unacceptable situation perpetuated by lax enforcement of truancy laws. Nineteen-year-old Marjorie Bearing, mother of three children, reports that it is not uncommon for 14- and 15-year-old students to become pregnant, with many dropping out of school. According to her, "Most who start out having kids here aren't married." Luckily for Marjorie, her mother stepped in to help with sitting and insisted that her daughter graduate, but many other young mothers are not so fortunate. Wiser from her own experiences, Marjorie realizes that tribal members must contribute to positive change, and she is considering sharing her observations and advice with local high school students. Illegitimacy among young mothers contributes both to the 3.33 percent birth rate, higher than such fast growing less developed countries as India and Egypt, and an infant mortality rate almost twice the U.S. average.

Chemical dependency is rampant on the reservation and tears at the social fabric. "You can't find a family that isn't affected directly or indirectly," reported Charles Bearcomesout, Director of the Northern Cheyenne Recovery Center. Alcoholism remains a persistent problem and today most adolescents seeking assistance also are hooked on marijuana or some additional drug. Even though the reservation is dry, alcohol is readily available in next-door Ashland and at bars just over the reservation border on both the Colstrip and Sheridan highways. Especially troublesome of late has been youths' consumption of Lysol spray, which has been taken off the shelf at the Lame Deer IGA store. Despite the current scourge of drugs, Bearcomesout thinks there is hope now that residents are willing to talk openly about the problem and are no longer ridiculed for seeking help.

Difficult socioeconomic realities on the reservation are pervasive and reflect a society-in-crisis situation shared by many other Montana reservation Indians.

Additional positive change from within the tribal group is linked to a rekindling of centuries-old native spirituality and pride in being an Indian. Increasing efforts are being made to help young tribal members grow up with a clearer sense of who they are and how they connect within a larger universe.

Constructive change also can come from outside the local Indian community, even from Hollywood. After playing a Cheyenne mixed-blood in the movie *At Play in the Fields of the Lord*, actor Tom Berenger sensed a chance to better the economically desperate situation on the reservation. His investment made possible the 1990 start-up of Cheyano Designs. Chief designer Joanna Wabisca, working

JOHN REDDY

Yellowstone Country from one extreme to the other.
Right: *A small cousin of the nearby Skytop Lakes in the Beartooth Mountains.*
Facing page: *Sunset on the Chalk Buttes southwest of Ekalaka.*

TOM DIETRICH

with eight seamstresses and 17 beaders, produces distinctive, high-fashion beaded garments. The lamb suede, cashmere, silk and other creations in the latest fall and spring collections are not available locally—they are strictly for upscale shops, with prices starting at $1,000.

On the adjacent 2,460-square-mile Crow Indian Reservation the controversy sparked by efforts to rename Custer Battlefield National Monument points to unresolved Indian-white conflicts. The name change was ancillary to the main thrust of federal legislation, which called for an Indian memorial at the national monument. In early 1992, the site was renamed Little Bighorn Battlefield National Monument, and plans began for a memorial to help explain the Native American perspective on that late June 1876 clash of cultures. Edward T. Linenfield, author of insightful *Sacred Ground: Americans and their Battlefields,* is not surprised by the national name-change hoopla. After studying battlefields throughout the U.S., he has concluded that "Little Bighorn is the most intensely contested patriotic site in America." Although bullets and arrows are no longer flying, the Little Bighorn controversy suggests that Indian-white symbolic battles still are very much alive in Yellowstone Country and throughout much of the West.

Upcountry, beyond the venerated battlefields of the 1870s Indian wars, are the Yellowstone Rockies, a world apart from Yellowstone Country's pervasive plains quarters. In this mountain- and wilderness-dominated headwaters area, name affiliation perhaps is more strongly linked with the park than with the river. Increasingly, these and other encircling mountainous areas and the core Yellowstone National Park are being viewed as a single, interrelated Greater Yellowstone Ecosystem, linked by geology, geography, biology, botany, shared challenges and possible futures.

Conservationists concerned about the future of this 28,000 square miles of the Middle Rockies have focused their efforts through the Bozeman-based Greater Yellowstone Coalition (P.O. Box 1874, Bozeman, MT 59771). With almost 100 member groups and thousands of individual members, the coalition views this dominantly federally-owned, West Virginia-sized ecosystem as globally unique and significant.

The Yellowstone Rockies portion of the ecosystem faces many of the same confrontations and opportunities as other regions encircling the park. Renewed interest in old mining districts is at the top of current controversies. The new gold-producing Mineral Hill Mine east of Jardine and the platinum-group minerals Stillwater Mine south of Nye may be just the beginning of greatly expanded mining in these mineralized Montana mountains north of Yellowstone. In the early 1990s at least nine other sizable exploration projects linked to gold, copper, nickel and chrome were underway, with drilling and geophysical surveys in southern Park, Sweet Grass and Stillwater counties. Each mine site and prospective new operation, such as Cooke City's New World Mining District, is the center of environmental concerns. Few conservationists' fears were alleviated by news that eagles nesting next to the tailings facility at the Mineral Hill Mine had raised two young.

Hardrock mining is only one of many ongoing resource and land use conflicts in the Yellowstone Rockies. Wilderness, forest roading and harvests, rural subdivisions, wildlife management and habitat fragmentation, air and groundwater pollution, grazing allotments, tourism and recreational developments are some of the additional interwoven and high-interest issues confronting the Yellowstone Rockies. Key to the efforts by the Greater Yellowstone Coalition is public recognition of the entire ecosystems' interrelatedness and the necessity of a sustainable melding of the region's natural system with social and economic systems.

Each mine site and prospective new operation, such as Cooke City's New World Mining District, is the center of environmental concerns.

Above: *Trading fort near where Mission Creek flows into the Yellowstone River east of today's Livingston. W.H. Jackson photograph from the Hayden Survey, 1869-1871.*
Left: *The* Josephine. *In 1875, this steamboat ascended the Yellowstone farther than any other, to near the site of Billings.*
Left top: *Swing ferry at Buffalo Rapids of the Yellowstone River near Miles City. L.A. Huffman photo*

THE TRIANGLE

Draw a line connecting Great Falls, Havre and Cut Bank, then back to Great Falls, and you will have approximated the limits of Montana's internationally renowned "Golden Triangle." This is a classic example of a perceptual, or vernacular region. AAA highway maps do not outline or name it, nor do highway signs announce when you enter or leave. This is a region perceived to exist by its residents and those of the state, not because of official designation and delimitation, but because people sense it has an identity of its own and shared features that set it apart from surrounding regions.

It is the grain elevator, this sentinel of the prairie, a vertical artifact in a horizontal world, that is the regional icon.

The Golden Triangle is Montana's premier dryland grain farming area. Mere mention to most state residents conjures up images of levelish landforms and a distinctive cultural landscape of seemingly endless geometric striped grain fields. This is where towering grain elevators rise from the railroad sidings of even the smallest towns. It is the grain elevator, this sentinel of the prairie, a vertical artifact in a horizontal world, that is the regional icon.

In everyday usage this most productive and prosperous of Montana's non-irrigated farming areas usually simply is referred to as the Triangle. That term has been borrowed here and applied to a somewhat larger area. Included is a belt of surrounding territory in which cash grain farming varies in importance and livestock may be locally more important. In these peripheral areas factors such as rougher topography, poorer soils, and competition with irrigated agriculture limit dryland grain farming.

The core area, the Golden Triangle, has nearly ideal conditions for dryland wheat production. Soils tend to be fertile and well drained. And since the area was glaciated during the last Ice Age, topography is generally flat to gently rolling, ideal for the large machinery essential to this highly mechanized and extensive type of agriculture. As in most all of Montana, precipitation is concentrated during the critical spring growing season, just when young plants need it most.

Older economic geography textbooks show the area as part of a large international spring wheat region that spills south out of Canada. Spring wheats, including durum, are premier crops, but as Triangle residents know, winter wheat is another cornerstone cultigen. In a recent year harvested wheat acreage in the eight-county area totaled 2.2 million acres—more than 3,400 square miles. The Triangle produces about half of Montana's wheat and in many years claims the state's top six producing counties.

Like other dryland farming areas in eastern Montana this region experienced oversettlement in the early years of the century. And like other sections of Great Plains Montana, it also suffered through the difficult years of large-scale exodus in the 1920s and 1930s. But unlike many other quarters, it was able to retain a more dense rural populace owing to the land's greater productivity. Today, even though it is far from crowded, it remains the state's most densely settled rural area of its size.

As in other of Montana's non-irrigated areas, the 320-acre homestead-size farm has long been obsolete. The average size for area cash grain farms is now closer to 2,500 acres and growing. Although large, this is smaller than the minimum required acreage in most other eastern Montana dryland cropping and ranching areas. Most Triangle farms are family owned and operated, with many already having passed through several generations. Operations able to add additional acreage have had a chance to survive; those unable to expand have been the sites for farm auctions.

Still, the area does not approach the Corn Belt or other better watered Great Plains areas for farm spacing and country population. In an average year on these semiarid plains, moisture isn't always adequate to grow dryland crops in the same field year after year. By early this century dry-side Great Plains research had shown that leaving land fallow, or unplanted, and cultivating to control moisture-robbing weeds during summer, built up soil moisture and helped assure a larger crop. Block summer fallowing was already an accepted part of "scientific" dryland farming by the early 1900s, although evidently only a minority of Triangle farmers used fallowing prior to the 1917 onset of drought conditions. Early years of agricultural settlement had been wet ones in the Triangle and pioneering farmers had made the mistake of confusing weather with climate. Fields that produced large yields without summer fallow during wet years were capable of producing only repeated crop failures in dry years. Farmers fortunate enough to make it through the parched late 1910s realized they would have to change their farming practices to better cope with the Triangle's uncertain precipitation.

A distinctive and ubiquitous zebra stripe cropping pattern remains as one of the region's most visible landscape legacies from

Granaries east of Great Falls make a typical Triangle sunset silhouette.

early settlement and agricultural adjustment. Montana historian Joseph Kinsey Howard credits Canadians across the border in Alberta with introducing strip cropping to Montana farmers. According to Howard, Alberta farmers began experimenting with alternate cropping systems during the dry late 1910s. They narrowed the width of their fallow fields, alternated strips of crops and fallow, and oriented strips at right angles to the prevailing wind to minimize erosion. Word of the technique spread south of the border and Montanans went north to check out the new field system. Most liked what they saw and returned home to try out the new geometric approach to farming. Soon strip farming clubs were organized and by 1922 the director of the Montana Agricultural Experiment Station advocated the practice. In the 1930s the Agricultural Adjustment Administration's Montana committee virtually made strip cropping mandatory.

Most Montana wheat is shipped to out-of-state destinations, with the bulk headed for Pacific Northwest coastal ports and the international marketplace.

Another reminder of the earlier times is the close spacing of communities along railroads within the most fertile farming districts. Driving west out of Havre along U.S. Highway 2, one goes through a string of these traditional grain collection towns and their obligatory railside elevators. In a space of only 41 miles, one passes through Kremlin, Gildford, Hingham, Rudyard, Inverness, Joplin and Chester. This close spacing may have made sense in the era of more dense population and horse-drawn grain wagons, but with a thinning of population and improved transportation, it is no longer an economic necessity. Most such small towns are struggling for survival and are now only shadows of their former selves.

For many small grain-handling towns a shift to grain subterminals and unit trains has some serious implications. Lower multi-car grain hauling rates for 26-car trains and unit trains of 52 cars available at only more widely spaced and much larger capacity subterminals, spell the end of many smaller elevators. In some areas rail abandonment (or "rationalization" depending on one's perspective), especially of branch lines, already has left former railside grain collection centers without service.

Area farmers continue to meet for coffee early each morning at local eateries in declining rural farm service centers to discuss such topics as wire worms, saline seep, the relative merits of Neeley versus Redwin winter wheat varieties, and the always unpredictable weather. At Gildford Merc, divided into three sections with hardware on the left, groceries in the middle and an eight-table cafe on the right, farmers at morning gatherings can number into the upper teens. The coffee tab is picked up by the loser in a "10½" card game. Six miles up the road at larger Hingham (pop. 181), the Highway Bar and Service is host to the local gathering, where farmers tend to congregate about 6:30 A.M. out front on the bar side. Around the region, such morning rituals are an integral part of the Triangle agrarian culture.

Changes in grain transportation have been hot morning-coffee topics of late. Gone are the days when most grain growers could select from competing grain elevators. According to Daryl and Joyce Spicher, who farm 4,400 acres south of Hingham with two sons, that community had five elevators run by three different operators 30 years ago, and today has just two elevators owned by the same company. Farmers who question dockage or handling charges and protein assessment of wheat or barley have few options.

Farmers also are at the mercy of the Burlington Northern, which has a monopoly as the Triangle's only transcontinental railroad. Most Montana wheat is shipped to out-of-state destinations, with the bulk headed for Pacific Northwest coastal ports and the international marketplace. Such long-distance conveyance by truck is less economical than rail transport and in recent years has moved only about 10 percent of state wheat. It is the BN that moves most of Montana's wheat, and since the 1980 passage of the Staggers Rail Act and relaxed government supervision over rail rates, many state grain growers have begun feeling like sharecroppers to the BN. For some Montana grain farmers, bypassing the BN entirely, trucking grain to the north Idaho Port of Lewiston on the Snake River and barging it downriver the final 360 miles to Portland is an increasingly viable option.

As national President of WIFE (Women Involved in Farm Economics), Joyce Spicher is up to date on such topics as 52-car unit train economics, captive rail shipping, Interstate Commerce Commission rulings and farm inheritance tax laws. Like many Triangle wives, she is a full-time partner in family farming. With off-farm employment opportunities limited in her area and throughout much of the Triangle region, full participation by farm family members is a prerequisite for economic survival.

Within this dominantly agricultural world, Great Falls reigns as the classic regional hub

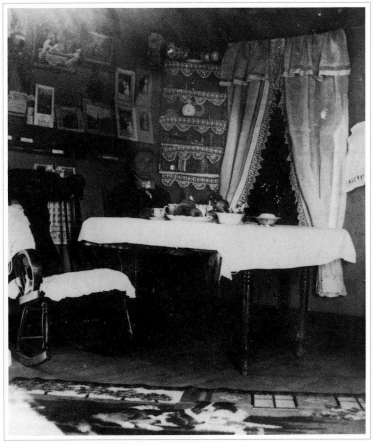

Above: *A one-room homestead "shack" in the Joplin area about 1913, this sported furnishings of a certain level of prosperity.*
Left: *November of 1916 at Big Sandy saw this cluster of grain wagons at the elevators.*
Top left: *Great Falls of the Missouri before the dams, captured by F. Jay Haynes in 1880.*

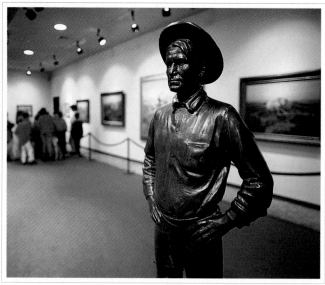

THE TRIANGLE

JOHN ALWIN

Right: Harvest-time near Great Falls.
Far right top: Charles M. Russell in bronze at the museum of his work and life in Great Falls.
Bottom: Chester's business district.

KEN FLETCHER

Above: Giant Springs near the Missouri River in Great Falls.
Left top: In Choteau.
Left: Black Eagle Dam along the Missouri near Great Falls.

city, almost eight times the size of second-ranking Havre. Perhaps the best view of Montana's second largest city is from the access road to its international airport atop Gore Hill. Behind you, in the distance, some 60 miles to the west, rise the ramparts of the Northern Rockies, and laid out before you the verdant urbanized area of 77,000 spreads along the banks of the Sun and Missouri as it swings to the east.

Unlike many other eastern Montana towns, Great Falls was a carefully planned community from the start.

This panorama would no doubt please, but probably not surprise, Paris Gibson, the man known as the "Father of Great Falls." In the late 1870s he came west from St. Anthony, Minnesota (today's Minneapolis) to begin anew on the Montana frontier. Initially he settled in the nearby commercial and transportation center of Fort Benton, but by the next year had travelled upriver to check out the Great Falls of the Missouri he had read about in the journals of Lewis and Clark.

Paris Gibson knew well the power-generating potential of waterfalls. Back home in St. Anthony he had been a partner in the community's first successful flour mill, which used energy from St. Anthony Falls on the Mississippi. Although Gibson most certainly appreciated the beauty of the thundering series of Missouri cascades, it was more their economic potential than their scenic value which lured him.

He quickly became well established in the livestock industry, knew the land, and must have sensed the agricultural potential of the Triangle region. In the summer of 1882 Gibson returned to the Missouri and selected a site for a newly planned town at the junction of the Sun and Missouri—strategically situated to tap what surely would become a rich agricultural hinterland once a railroad linked this fertile prairie to the outside world.

Back in the Twin Cities, Gibson had been a pillar of the business and civic community and had made the acquaintance of railroad entrepreneur James J. Hill. In 1879 Hill initiated plans for a transcontinental railroad, the St. Paul, Minneapolis & Manitoba, that was projected to traverse northern Montana. Gibson contacted Hill about plans for a town near Black Eagle Falls and with little difficulty convinced the railroad magnate to join in the venture, although Hill rejected the suggestion that the new community be called "Hillton" in his honor.

With the arrival of Hill's railroad still years away, Gibson set about acquiring the necessary land for the townsite and platting what would become today's north-south and east-west grid of streets and avenues. Unlike many other eastern Montana towns, Great Falls was a carefully planned community from the start. Gibson, who had training in landscape architecture, had very definite ideas on how a city should be laid out. One aspect of the urban landscape high on his list was wide streets, maybe because he had witnessed the new town of St. Paul, Minnesota, grow up around its central section of congested narrow avenues. Great Falls was going to be different.

On October 15, 1887, Hill's St. Paul, Minneapolis & Manitoba crew built into Great Falls, having laid parallel ribbons of steel from the Dakota border to that point in fewer than six months. Gibson and other eager citizens didn't wait for its arrival before establishing some of the essentials for their prospective boom town. In 1884 Gibson built the community's first flour mill, named after that St. Anthony's mill he had started two decades earlier. The first schoolhouse was completed in 1885, and the same year the venerable *Great Falls Tribune* began publishing.

The 1890 census showed Great Falls with a population of almost 4,000, where only ten years earlier the site of the town had but one resident living in a small log cabin on the west side of the Missouri. That year saw the completion of the first dam at Black Eagle Falls. Readily available and relatively cheap power became the magnet that attracted additional milling operations. Other flour mills were built and soon Great Falls had two large metal smelting/refining mills.

By the 1890s the world was going electrical and Montana's mines at Butte accounted for more than half the United States' copper production and fully a quarter of the world's total. Some ore was treated at Butte, but large quantities also were shipped to Great Falls for processing. The "Electric City" was flush with growth, prosperity and confidence (as well as pollution), and launched a brief campaign in 1892 for designation as Montana's capital.

The rally for capital city status was unsuccessful, but growth and prosperity continued at a galloping pace. By the turn of the 20th century Great Falls exceeded Helena in size and—with a population of almost 15,000—was the state's second-largest community, surpassed only by Butte. Its closest rival in eastern Montana was Billings, which had less than a fourth as many residents.

Modern Great Falls has changed. Since early in its youth, manufacturing, and specifically primary metals refining, had held a firm footing in the local economic base. That is no longer the case. In 1973 the Anaconda Company closed its zinc plant and seven years later announced the permanent shutdown of its Great Falls copper refinery and wire mill. Combined direct job losses totaled 1,500 and the city was left without a primary metal industry for the first time in 80 years.

While the manufacturing aspect of the city's economic base contracted, its role as regional trade and service center for a 12- to 15-county area increased. For thousands of residents on farms in the Triangle area and in communities like Malta, Havre, Lewistown, Conrad and Browning, Great Falls is the nearest metropolitan center. When they need specialized medical services, want to attend a Kenny Rogers concert, have to make a major airline connection, or simply feel like an all-out shopping spree, they naturally head for Great Falls. Its service role is obvious in employment statistics, which show more than 26,000 people in the metro area employed in the services and retail trade sectors, thirteen times the number in manufacturing. Labor income growth in health-related employment has been especially strong.

Malmstrom Air Force Base is the Great Falls area's largest employer. Today the sprawling 4,137-acre base provides jobs for 4,290 military personnel and 541 civilian employees. According to Sgt. Allan Niggebrugge at the base, Malmstrom's total economic impact on the community totaled $232 million in fiscal 1991.

Malmstrom's role has changed since its beginning as the Great Falls Army Air Base in 1942 when it served as a transit base for lend-lease war materials shipped via the

Saline Seep

Before whites moved onto the plains of eastern Montana, nature's vegetative cover had adjusted nicely to the natural environment. Below ground, a dense network of roots reached deep to tap what was periodically sparse soil moisture. Any bare area produced by natural causes was quickly revegetated.

The natural grassland cover is now largely gone from major dryland farming areas in eastern Montana, replaced by cultivated strips of grain and fallow. Now some of the precipitation that falls percolates into the soil and instead of being intercepted by an intricate root network of natural grasses and shrubs, it merely accumulates below the shallow and sparse overlying root zone. Areas with crop cover use some of this moisture, but fallow areas have no intercepting roots to draw up the water. In areas underlain by an impermeable shale layer (common in eastern Montana), water accumulates underground, perched above the impenetrable shale zone where it absorbs water-soluble salts. Eventually, just like a sponge, soil and subsoil reach a saturation point and water begins to move downslope along the upper surface of the shale layer.

The trouble comes when the salt-charged underground waters reach the surface. These discharge areas are saline seeps.

The relationship between summer fallow and saline seep is well documented, but still there has not been a rush to abandon the traditional strip-cropping field. Like the rest of us, farmers are creatures of habit and find it hard to abandon what has been routine for

them and for their fathers. The problem is made especially difficult to deal with since recharge areas, where the precipitation soaks into the ground, may be on fallow fields belonging to one farmer, but it's the guy next door who ends up with the saline seep.

There appears to be a number of partial solutions to saline seep in eastern Montana. The best solution is one that eliminates the problem before it appears. Less widespread use of summer fallow and greater consideration of a more flexible cropping system seem to have potential. Saline seep experts have suggested that instead of just assuming a fallow period at a regular interval for each parcel of land, grain farmers should not decide until soil moisture conditions are actually tested. Some areas may be able to support more of a continuous cropping.

A less geometric pattern that takes hydrogeologic factors into account and keeps potential recharge areas continuously covered with vegetation might also help stem the formation of new saline seeps. These new approaches to grain farming are now being tested by some innovative eastern Montana farmers.

At the earliest signs of a seep farmers can sometimes arrest its further development with appropriate action. Artificial underground drainage and land grading in the recharge area can help. Sowing deep-rooted plants in a recharge area tends to "pump" up excess water. Four-year-old alfalfa can put down 18-foot-deep roots and has proven to be an especially good "pump."

Alaska polar route to the Soviet Union. The base came under control of the Strategic Air Command in 1954 when it was assigned a jet fighter wing. That year fighter pilot Colonel Einar Axel Malmstrom was killed in an aircraft accident near Great Falls and the base was renamed in his honor.

MINUTEMAN MISSILES

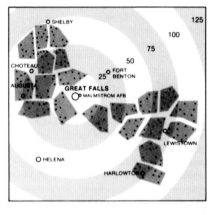

A new chapter began in 1961, when the 341st Strategic Missile Wing was activated and the base became the first Minuteman ICBM wing in the country. Malmstrom was to become the nerve center for an awesome array of underground Minuteman missiles that totaled 150 by 1963. Today 200 Minuteman IIs and IIIs are scattered in clusters of 10 missiles per launch control center (LCC) over 23,000 square miles of central Montana stretching from Harlowton and east of Lewistown to Choteau and Shelby. Each Minuteman is housed in a steel and concrete silo about 80 feet deep, called a launch facility (LF). Each contains the actual launching tube and missile mounted on a spring shock-absorber system. The launch tube is covered by a 108-ton sliding top. LCCs are buried capsules of reinforced concrete and steel 60 to 90 feet underground. An eight-ton blast door seals the top of the access shaft to the quarters for the two-person missile combat crew. With the end of the Cold War now history, one can only speculate on potential targets for this deadly arsenal.

Both LFs and LCCs are common landscape elements in central and north-central Montana where they often rise in the middle of farmers' fields. Always housed behind locked gates, chain link fences and barbed wire, these installations have the highest security. Radar-like surveillance systems, alarms on locks, and seismic sensors immediately warn security police of an attempted unauthorized entry.

Malmstrom also is home to the 43rd Air Refueling Wing with its contingent of huge KC-135R "Stratotankers." The downsizing of America's military in the decade of the 1990s is expected to actually result in growth at Malmstrom Air Force Base.

If non-Great Falls residents know anything about the city, chances are it is linked to the famed western artist Charles M. Russell. In fact, Travel Montana promotes the entire north-central section of the state as Charlie Russell Country, one of six Big Sky tourist regions. A native of St. Louis, Russell came to the Montana territory in 1880, just prior to his 16th birthday. For two years he subsisted as a hunter and trapper before becoming a cowboy, a job he worked at for a decade first in the Judith Basin Country and later in the Chinook area. In the 1890s he left cowboying with the intention of becoming a full time artist. He moved to Great Falls in 1897 and lived in several places before building his now famous residence and next-door studio on 13th Street North. This was home until his death in 1926. He is buried at Highland Cemetery in town, but his legend in Great Falls and beyond is larger than life. The C.M. Russell Museum complex is one of the state's prime historical/cultural attractions. His home, rustic log cabin studio and museum with three galleries exhibiting the world's largest collection of his original art, are a distinctly Montana shrine.

Even to the casual observer, it is obvious that Great Falls has a maturity that is absent in other eastern Montana urban centers. It has been a large town since the turn of the century, a claim that no other Great Plains Montana community can make. This maturity is evident in its urban landscape with its block upon block of early twentieth century homes on streets flanked by grand rows of elm and ash. Since the late 1980s, Dutch elm disease has claimed about a quarter of the 25,000 stately street trees, but enough remain to make the cityscape a Montana original. Downtown, substantial brick and stone architecture are testimony to Great Falls' historical depth. Economic setbacks in the decades of the 1970s and 1980s cost population both in the city of Great Falls and in the metro area. Some residents are perfectly happy with the somewhat reduced size of their community, while others would like to see it set new growth records. The prospects of increased north-south linkage and trade with Canada along an evolving Rocky Mountain Trade Corridor may hold special promise for the Electric City.

Hay-harvest geometry.

Montana's Hutterites

You can see them shopping in Great Falls and Billings, Lewistown, Choteau, and other communities, men dressed in black coats, trousers, and hats, and women in long, brightly colored dresses and head scarves. They are Montana's Hutterites and they are becoming an increasingly more important element in the state's agricultural scene.

The first Hutterites arrived in Montana in 1911, but the group can trace its beginnings to the 16th century and sections of present-day Austria and Czechoslovakia, where the sect was organized during the Protestant Reformation. Like other Anabaptists, which include the Mennonites and Old Order Amish, they rejected infant baptism and membership in a state religion, and were devout pacifists. These beliefs and the insistence on communal ownership and colony life set them even more apart from non-Hutterites. From their founding in 1528 until the late 1780s, when they settled in Russia at the invitation of Empress Catherine II, they were repeatedly on the move, searching for a home where they could live free from persecution.

Hutterites again realized it was time to move on in the 1870s when their special educational privileges and exemption from military service were about to be withdrawn. This time they chose the United States for a new home and some 800 Hutterites migrated to South Dakota between 1874 and 1877. About half these new Americans abandoned the communal lifestyle and took up their own homesteads,

but the rest organized themselves into three colonies. To this date all Hutterites in North America can trace their lineage back to one of these three colonies, each one of which became the starting point for one of three, somewhat different, Hutterite groups—*Dariusleut, Lehrerleut,* and *Schmiedeleut.* Each has its own distinctive discipline and style of dress; members marry within their particular group.

The Hutterites prospered in South Dakota and added Spring Creek Colony outside Lewistown, Montana, in 1911. Then as so often had happened before, persecution forced them to seek out a new home. This time it was war fever during World War I that whipped up opposition against these German-speaking people. In 1918, the Spring Creek Colony closed and its people moved north to Canada, joining all but one American colony in a migration to north of the border.

By the Depression years of the late 1920s and early 1930s, local groups in Montana and the Dakotas sent representatives to Canada to entice Hutterites back to the States. These efficient agriculturalists were able to remain more economically viable than most farmers during these hard times and, all of a sudden, communities realized what an economic asset it would be to have a colony or two in their vicinity. A few were convinced to return, but colonies remained few and far between until the mid-1940s when Alberta began passing legislation limiting the sale of land to Hutterites and setting limits on the size and spacing of colonies. Between 1945 and 1948, Canadian Hutterites established eight colonies in eastern Montana. By

1970 there were 22 colonies and in 1990 this figure had grown to 40.

For Hutterites, the colony, or *Bruderhof*, is the center of their universe. They view their colony as akin to Noah's Ark and believe that they must reside within it if they are going to receive eternal life. This is their pure and holy cosmos, and the only place they can maintain what Hutterites see as God's order.

Orderliness permeates all aspects of life in the colony. Most Montana colonies are built on a similar, centuries-old plan. Each building has its proper location and relationship with other structures.

Centrally located is the kitchen–dining hall complex. Like all buildings it always is of plain and functional style. It is the closest thing there is to a nerve center in the colony. Each day, first school children and then adults assemble there for meals. As with most other activities, ringing of bells announces meal times. Women eat on one side of the dining hall and men on the other, each in the proper seat ranked according to age. Homemade tables are long with benches for seats, floors are spotless and thickly varnished, and walls are without pictures or other adornments.

During the school year children meet for German school for at least an hour both before and after English school, half a day on Saturdays, all public school vacation days, and whenever the English teacher is sick. At these times students practice reading and writing German, and reciting Hutterite hymns and biblical passages. At age 14, children begin eating meals with adults in the dining hall, where they take the seat with the lowest position. After finishing the eighth grade or upon reaching age 18, children discontinue their schooling and begin working as adults.

Toward evening adults and school-age children use the school house for daily church services. The congregation seats itself according to sex and age, with each person knowing his or her place.

Additional buildings typically associated with this central cluster of structures include small outhouses behind each apartment unit, communal shower and laundry facilities, a food-storage building, and a shoe-making and repair shop. Most other associated buildings reflect the types of farming on the colony. In Montana this is a commercial, diversified farming that commonly includes cash grain, hogs, eggs and poultry, fresh vegetables, lambs and wool, cattle, and dairy products.

One key function of the *Bruderhof* is to keep members as removed as possible from the outside world. Although they are generally shyly congenial with outsiders and hospitable to guests of the colony, Hutterites view the outside world as a place where sin and temptation can too easily endanger the orderliness of their way of

life. Since an average Montana colony controls something like 12,000 acres, physical isolation from neighbors is pretty much assured on a daily basis. Radio and

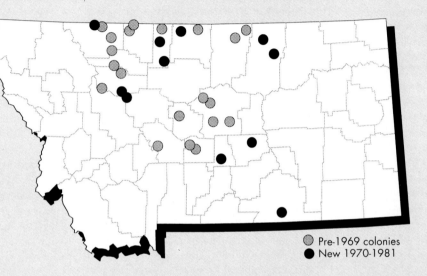

⬤ Pre-1969 colonies
⬤ New 1970-1981

television are forbidden on the colony, although there is usually one telephone.

Despite the fact that they shun many aspects of the modern 20th century and continue to make their own clothing, staple foods, soaps and furniture, and couldn't tell you who the stars are on television, Hutterites incorporate the latest advances in agriculture. Massive four-wheel-drive tractors, specialized field equipment and reliance on the best fertilizers, herbicides and insecticides make them some of Montana's most productive farmers.

The Hutterites have to be good farmers since this is their only source of the income necessary for perpetuation of the group,

With an extremely high population growth rate, which means a doubling of population about every 18 years (more than four times the national rate), Hutterites have to be able to finance new colonies on a regular basis. Once a colony's population begins to exceed 120 or 130, it is time to divide, half going to a new "daughter" colony and the rest remaining in the "parent" colony. Spacing between parent and daughter colonies varies from hundreds of miles to just a few. The capital outlay necessary to acquire the thousands of agricultural acres and to build and equip a new daughter colony is staggering, and must be borne by the individual parent colony. Once again, the new colony becomes its own discrete economic unit.

The Hutterites are an industrious people who do what they do extremely well. They have managed to maintain their noncon-formist lifestyle intact for centuries. And for centuries, widespread misconceptions have surrounded this patient group. As member Peter Hofer said, "It's nothing new to be misunderstood."

HI-LINE

Beyond the Triangle, east from Havre, lies another distinctive slice of northern Montana, part of a vernacular region identified by most Montanans as the Hi-Line, or High-Line. The name probably can be traced to the Great Northern Railway and the subsequent string of communities and tributary areas that developed along that line in the 1880s and 1890s. Given a location high to the north within Montana and linear in shape, the name seems only logical. Today U.S. Highway 2, as well as the Burlington Northern Railroad and the Missouri-Milk rivers, are the threads that tie this region together.

Away from U.S. Highway 2, towns are small and distantly spaced and paved roads are the exception.

As with most vernacular regions, the limits of the Hi-Line are imprecise. The Canadian border affords a tidy northern limit and the Missouri River demarks most of a southern boundary, but eastern and western borders are less clear. Geographer Ruth Hale, who mapped perceptual regions throughout the American Great Plains, identified a linear Hi-Line extending eastward from around Cut Bank to the vicinity of Poplar and Scobey. Her research, and common usage by Montanans, show that the northern section of the Triangle and a portion of the Hi-Line are overlapping regions from Havre west, where some residents claim allegiance to both regions.

Selection of the Havre area as the approximate breaking point between our Triangle and Hi-Line is based in large part on changing land use. East of town, the proportion of farms in cropland drops off and the percentage of farmland devoted to range increases dramatically. Here, beyond the irrigated Milk River Valley, in the western section of our Hi-Line, emphasis in most areas is on livestock rather than wheat and other grain crops. Grain fields become more scattered and ranch size increases, not uncommonly totaling tens of thousands of acres. The resultant thinner population shows up on a state highway map. Away from U.S. Highway 2, towns are small and distantly spaced and paved roads are the exception. Only in the far eastern part of the Hi-Line, in the three grain-growing counties in the state's far northeast corner, is population more dispersed.

In the western two thirds of the Hi-Line between Havre and Wolf Point, fully 90 percent of the 40,000 residents live within the Highway 2 and Missouri-Milk rivers sutland corridor. The area contains the Hi-Line's four largest "metropoles," Havre (pop. 10,201), Glasgow (pop. 3,572), Wolf Point (2,880) and Malta (pop. 2,340). This narrow, several-mile-wide stringer of settlement and irrigated agriculture constitutes one of the state's major irrigated farming districts. Large sections were developed as part of the massive, federal Milk River Project in the early years of this century. In 1911 the first water flowed into what has now expanded to about 140,000 irrigated acres along the main stem of the Milk between Havre and Glasgow.

Size wise, Havre is unchallenged along the 207 highway miles between that community and Wolf Point. Its urban prowess is reflected in the fact that it has the only McDonald's restaurant in the Hi-Line region. Regional identity here is a bit schizophrenic. Identification with the Hi-Line probably is dominant, but residents also feel they are a part of the Triangle. Using their local Triangle Telephone Directory, residents can find listings for Triangle Ford and Triangle Communications, as well as Hi-Line Glass and the Hi-Line Motel.

Havre was founded in 1891, and named after Le Havre, France, the birthplace of the two men who homesteaded the land on which the town developed. James Hill's St. Paul, Minneapolis & Manitoba Railroad (later the Great Northern) had passed through the site of the future town four years earlier as it swung to the south toward Great Falls. It wasn't until another line of the newly reorganized Great Northern struck out westward toward the Pacific from the site that there was sufficient impetus for town development at this strategic railroad junction. From its beginning, the railroad has been the major local employer, although loss of nearly one in four high-paying railroad jobs in 1992 reduced that importance.

Havre's role as a regional trade center expanded after the turn of the century with the influx of farmers, both in the irrigated Milk River Valley and the nearby dryland areas. In 1912 Hill County was formed and Havre soon was designated county seat. The next year the state acquired 2,000 acres at the former Fort Assinniboine military post ten miles out of town, with the intention of establishing an agricultural and educational center. The Agricultural Experiment Station began operating there in 1915, but it was decided that the site was too far from town for a school. In lieu of that location, the state chose Havre and established Northern Montana College in 1913, although it wasn't until 16 years later

JOHN ALWIN

A new day begins at Malta's grain elevators.

MONTANA HISTORICAL SOCIETY PHOTOS

Above: *Cowboy camp on the North Fork of the Milk River, 1894. Dan Dutro photo*
Left: *A crew of working cowhands near Big Sandy, in the 1890s.*
Top: *Except for smoking a pipe, this unidentified hand posed well as the mythical gun-shooting, hard-drinking hand on a trip to town.*

that the two-year, vocationally oriented college started up in Havre High School. The present campus was opened in 1932, and 22 years later was designated a four-year college. Programs have expanded, and students—most from the Triangle and Hi-Line—now have a wide range of academic options.

Outside the dominantly Milk River Valley sutland is a distinctly non-urban yonland to both the north and south. Between the Milk and the Missouri River/Fort Peck Lake, eastern Montana is a surprisingly diverse natural landscape that includes the Bears Paw Mountains, Little Rockies and the less well known Larb Hills south of Malta and Saco. Two of the Hi-Line's three Indian reservations, Rocky Boys and Fort Belknap, are within this huge, sparsely settled tract. Both on and off the reservations, cattle ranching dominates in these rugged and remote lands.

Perhaps no section of eastern Montana is more classic yonland than the southern sections of Phillips and Valley counties north of Fort Peck Lake. Marsha Barnard has spent her entire life on a ranch in the Sun Prairie district, 49 miles south of Malta and 10 miles north of Fort Peck Lake. Three miles out of Malta the pavement ends and 46 miles of "dirt roads with gravel" constitute her link with the outside world. "We're kind of isolated," admitted Marsha.

Her closest neighbors are one mile away to the south, two miles distant on the east and three miles away to the north. But, as she explains, she lives in a more populated valley area. Outside this population "cluster" it is not uncommon for ranches to be 15 miles apart, and along one section of the road to Malta, travelers do not come within sight of a single ranch for one 25-mile stretch.

The local Sun Prairie School closed in the 1980s, making the closest country school in the Regina community about 20 miles distant. In this yonland area it is common for mothers to move to larger sutland towns with their school-aged children and live in a purchased or rented home during the school year. Weekend trips back home and summers on the ranch keep families in touch with dad.

North of the Milk River sutland, yonland also dominates, although dryland grain farming is more common than in the southern portions. This section is home to several Hutterite colonies. Turner Colony near the Canadian border is typical of, although smaller than, many Montana colonies. Like other Hutterite colonies, theirs is a diversified enterprise. They operate on about 9,000 acres, 6,000 in crops and 3,000 pasture on which they run 140 head of beef cattle. Income is supplemented with sale of Turner Colony brand eggs in nearby Hi-Line outlets and by hog raising.

In the conventional sense, only the southern section of Roosevelt County along Highway 2 might be considered part of the Hi-Line. For our purposes, the northern portion of that county and Daniels and Sheridan counties also are included in our regionalization. Those three counties and an adjacent section of eastern Valley County stand out as the only extensive area of cash grain farming in Montana's eastern half. Continental glaciation, which subdued the physical landscape, and a mantle of fertile soil help make this productive spring wheat and barley country.

There are many similarities with the larger Triangle region. The better suited agricultural land is able to support a denser population, and track-side grain elevators have been an integral element in the local landscape for a century. But as in the Triangle, rail abandonment and freight rates are hot topics. In 1991 the Burlington Northern abandoned the westernmost 49 miles of its Bainville-Opheim branch line west of Scobey, leaving traditional grain collection centers of Opheim, Glentana, Richland and Four Buttes without rail service for the first time since the 1920s. Many growers have been forced to truck grain for distances of 50 miles and greater over less-than-adequate roads to the Burlington Northern mainline adjacent to Highway 2. Despite assurances by the railroad, few growers would be surprised if the railroad eventually abandoned the remaining 98-mile Bainville-Scobey branch.

Many growers have been forced to truck grain for distances of 50 miles and greater over less-than-adequate roads to the Burlington Northern mainline adjacent to Highway 2.

JOHN REDDY

THE HI-LINE

In the Bears Paws.

Clockwise from left:
*Hutterite girls in Chinook.
At the Bears Paw Battlefield Monument.
A type of Montana welcome in Phillips County.
Elk herd on the alert, C.M. Russell National Wildlife Refuge.
Aerial view of a tidy Hutterite colony.*

INDEX

Italic type indicates illustrations